A Mixture of Feeling_

Recipes to manage your emotions

By

Heidi C Tyler

Disclaimer & Terms of Use Agreement

This book contains content of real-life examples, that have generated a wide spectrum of emotions and could be a trigger for some readers. It contains the author's personal experiences in relation to sexual assault/rape, physical abuse, self-harm, attempted suicide/suicidal thoughts, death/dying, pregnancy/childbirth, caesarean section, mental illness/personality disorders, alcoholism, cancer, multiple sclerosis and auto immune condition.

This book reflects the author's recollections of experiences over time. It is intended to highlight how our lives are affected by events which in turn create emotions. Non-family names and characteristics have been changed, some events have been compressed, and some dialogue has been recreated from recollection.

The author would like to thank the real-life members of the family portrayed in this book. The author recognises that their memories of the events described in this book are different than their own. This book is not intended to cause them any painful recollection of memories nor resulting negative emotions. The author and publisher regret any unintentional harm resulting from the publishing and marketing of *A Mixture of Feelings*.

The content of this book is for informational purposes only and is not intended to diagnose, treat, cure or prevent any physical or emotional condition. You understand that this book is not intended as a substitute for consultation with a licensed practitioner. Please consult with your own physician or healthcare specialist regarding the suggestions and recommendation made in this book.

The companies quoted in this book are there because they have had a significant positive impact on the authors emotional life. The associated wording reflects the authors own personal view and should be considered simply as a personal review of their service. Links to their websites are included, should the reader wish to investigate further.

The publisher and author make no guarantees concerning the level of success you may experience by following the advice and strategies contained in this book, and you accept the risk that results will differ for each individual.

The emotions and recipes shared by others from around the world show their own personal results, which may not apply to readers, and are not intended to represent or guarantee that you will achieve the same or similar results. The companies they have quoted are because they had a positive impact on their emotional lives.

The use of this book implies your acceptance of this disclaimer.

Foreword

I am eternally grateful to have experienced so much during my life up to now. As a child, I had no idea that the pain and anguish I felt at school would serve me well. I had no idea that I would learn so much after I had left school. School is a one size fits all, and I didn't seem to fit that well. I had no idea that being made to feel different and struggling inside, while I was at school, could be overcome and really wouldn't matter anymore. I had no idea that I could decide for myself what values and beliefs hold true for me, so that I can live my own life, with the freedom to choose. I had no idea that the pain, suffering and incredible challenges my family encountered would allow me to be strong enough to help them, myself, and indeed others.

As an adult (so far) I had no idea that I could learn so much, in a matter of a few months, which would change my whole being, so that I am now on a fast forward to fulfil my life vision. I had no idea that the loved ones I've lost would fill me with so much help and support long beyond their parting. I had no idea that I could change the person I am, simply by changing the way I catch thoughts, own or manage them and then make them work for me. I had no idea that I really could live a 12-category smart life. I had no idea that I could share my learning so that it can help you.

As children and adults, we don't have to accept things the way they are. We don't have to keep accepting our negative thoughts as 'that's the way life is', or 'I can't help it, it's my illness', or 'I don't have a choice', or the many other reasons we repeatedly tell ourselves.

We can strive for the very best, for ourselves and others in our lives. We all have the ability to learn (from the best), change who we are, change how we feel, and be the best person we can possibly become. We all have the capability to understand and change the very thoughts that are holding us back.

Let's be who we want to be, feel how we want to feel and aim for the 'Life Vision' we want. Managing emotions is a massive step to take. It certainly was for me, but it's essential for your personal well-being. It allows you to live the life you want, to have freedom to feel how you want to feel and to achieve whatever personal success and happiness means for you.

I truly hope that when you've read this book and put things into practice, you too will take a massive step forward in your life. I was believed in. I believed in myself. I believe in you. Now it's time to believe in yourself.

Table of Contents

PART 1: MY JOURNEY

Age – 18 months

I have no recollection of being this age. I don't think many do. What I do know is I must have been a bit adventurous. I apparently climbed out of my cot, in the five minutes between my mum going out and the neighbour coming in!

I assume I walked to the living room. I was definitely walking then. In the living room, there was a wooden sideboard which had a ledge. At the back of the ledge were glass sliding doors, behind which were glasses and ornaments and at one end there was a pull-down door which was a cupboard for keeping bottles of alcohol!

I climbed onto the ledge of the sideboard. I apparently slipped and hit the wooden floorboards with my head.

I expect I cried a lot, but can't say that with any degree of confidence or fact.

I did suffer a fractured skull.

Age: 3-4

My mum used to put me to bed, in my own bedroom. In my bedroom, the first piece of furniture was my dressing table. It had three drawers and a lovely big mirror. Then there was my single wardrobe that stood next to the bay window. The round knobs on the doors had embroidered fabric inside with plastic over the top. They were matched with much smaller ones on the dressing table.

My bed was on the other side of the room, behind the door. I had a very small table next to my bed. At the end of my bed were a few toys and my dolls. On my bed was my black and white fluffy cat nightdress case. I loved that cat and it went to bed with me every night.

Then the sickness started. I would be sick and then have to get out of bed to get my mum. Except I couldn't always get out of bed. I was too scared of the creatures under my bed. If I got out, they might grab my ankles. I would call my mum, but my voice wasn't loud enough. I would try and call louder, but still she didn't hear me. I would be brave and get out of bed quickly. Oh, but then if I opened the door the creatures in the loft my open the hatch and grab me. Oh, what was I going to do, I had to get my mum, because I've been sick? It's all in my hair, and on my bed. Oh no, it's on my cat too. Now the tears are flowing. I must get my mum. I will get my mum. Somehow, I got enough courage and got to my mum as quick as I could.

'Mum, I've been sick'.

'Never mind Heidi,' Mum said. 'Let's get you cleaned up'.

'I've been sick on my cat', I told her.

Once we were all cleaned up, and Mum had scrubbed the sheet, she used to put a towel on top of my pillow so I could go back to bed. Mum always got into bed with me and would stroke my hair until I had fallen back to sleep. Then she went back to bed.

The next night, and the next night, and the next night. In fact, many nights I was sick, up to my being 5. Sometimes I was sick in my sleep and didn't even wake up. I think that used to scare Mum. She started putting me to bed on my side, with my cat cuddled up in my arms.

I used to have bad dreams too. It was always the same face. A man's face, getting closer and closer. It was a horrible face. It was a face I didn't know and it made me frightened.

No-one quite knew what was wrong. Doctors told my parents it was most likely my kidneys and there was nothing much they could do!

A friend of my dad suggested he take me to see their chiropractor. My first visit cost him 13 shillings and 6 pence. That was such a lot of money. I couldn't imagine how many years of pocket money that would be. A lifetime!

I saw the Chiropractor a lot to start with as he had a lot of manipulation to do, but had to make sure it was done gradually. My spine had a bit of an S shape although I looked OK from the outside. My sickness got better and my dad was so pleased with the result, my whole family started seeing the Chiropractor, 4 times a year to keep us in good health.

I know my mum was happy. She didn't have to be woken up with my being sick, or have to scrub the bed, or wash sheets, or wash my cat.

Oh, my poor cat. She had to be washed so often. She wasn't fluffy anymore. Her fur was matted and horrible, but I still loved her. So, my mum kept doing her best but one day she said 'I simply cannot wash the cat anymore, she must go now'. 'That is the hardest thing I think I will ever have to deal with in my life', I thought. I loved my cat. How was I ever going to manage without her! It made me very sad.

Age: 5-6

My mum helped me get ready for school. I'm wearing my new grey pleated knee length skirt, white button up blouse, grey cardigan, ankle socks and black shoes. My blonde hair is brushed into a bob haircut with a straight fringe cut just above my eyebrows. Mum told me how important it was that the skirt came to just on the knee. The teachers would know if it didn't and the child would be sent home. It was also important that my hair was brushed!

I had a bowl of cereal and full cream milk for breakfast. Mum put a tea towel round my neck to make sure I didn't mark my new clean uniform!

'Right' said Mum, 'let's get going. We must always be at school on time'. That was another important thing to remember.

We walked to school, going past our neighbour's houses and looking in all the gardens to see if we thought they were pretty or not. We always did this when we went out. It helped make walking more fun. Three roads later, we arrived at the school. It was huge. A brick building with a massive field at the front and three weeping willow trees which cascaded down and trailed along the grass. They looked so pretty. I wanted to go and touch them, but Mum said no. I'd never seen trees like that before. They looked so magical.

My brother is 18 months older than me, so was already going to the same school. He told me that every child's name gets called out and we would then have to stand in line with the adult who was going to be our teacher.

Mine was a lady, and her name was Miss P. I followed Miss P to our classroom, which was down the end of a very long corridor.

Oh no, how would I ever remember how to get to this room. I didn't count the doors on the way. Nobody had told me about this. I'm getting nervous now. Do I recognise any faces? No, nobody I know. I heard another couple of children whispering to each other. 'NO TALKING', shouted the teacher. 'Anyone caught talking will be disciplined'. I didn't have any idea what the discipline would be, but the sound of the teacher's voice was enough to keep everyone quiet.

When we entered the classroom, we were all told to sit behind a wooden desk. After the teacher had checked our names, she gave us all a small chalk board and some white chalk which we were to keep in our wooden desks. The desk had a lift up lid so we could keep everything inside. The desk seemed to be too high for many of us.

Miss P told us to copy the letters she wrote on the board by picking up the chalk and following the shapes she formed, a step at a time.

I tried so hard to write on the little chalk board we were all given. Every time I picked up the chalk and went to copy Miss P, the chalk would break between my fingers. It got smaller and smaller. I tried different ways to get the letters written. At last I got it right. Now I had to catch up. I knew I was behind the children next to me.

WOOSH

Something flew passed my head.

Then there was this crashing sound.

I didn't understand. I didn't talk. I was scared. There was total silence in the class. Not a single cough. You couldn't even hear anyone breathing. I could feel myself trembling.

Miss P came striding up the classroom and recovered the item she had thrown. I recognised it. It was what she used to clean the chalk board. It was heavy and made from wood and rubber. Wow, was I glad it missed me! I couldn't imagine what the child behind me had done to upset Miss P!

CRACK

Why did Miss P do that? She'd just cracked the rubber across the back of my knuckles, AND with the wooden side! The pain was beyond anything I have ever felt before. I desperately want to cry but somehow, I knew I mustn't. I was terrified. My trembling had turned into shaking. I just couldn't seem to stop. My mind is going crazy.

Am I lagging behind the others? Haven't I copied the letters correctly? I'm trying really hard. Oh, the pain. What am I going to do? The tears started rolling down my cheeks. I'm trying so hard not to make a sound. What's happening to me? I'm starting to feel sick. I want to go home.

The rest of the day was like torture. Every time I knew Miss P wasn't watching, I would write the letters with my left hand. As soon as I saw her turn round, I picked up the chalk with my right hand, but then I broke the chalk!

I went home at the end of the day. 'How was your first day Heidi?', asked Mum. 'OK, I said'. 'Writing with chalk is difficult sometimes'. 'you'll get the hang of it.' said Mum.

I told my family NOTHING. I couldn't disappoint them. I didn't want them to know how bad I'd been. Tomorrow I would try harder.

Tomorrow came and was the same as my first day. So was the next day and the next. By Friday it got tougher. I got told to stand up and follow Miss P to the Headmistress office. Miss K.

Perhaps she was taking me to see Miss K because I've broken so much chalk, or because I'm crying too much. She'd hit me with the rubber every day, so I must have done something seriously wrong. Thoughts just kept whirring round and round and round in my head. If I've been naughty my parents are going to be so angry.

Out came Miss K. She had a really stern look on her face. 'You've been a very naughty child. Miss P has told me you are repeatedly breaking the chalk, which costs a lot of money. There seems to be something wrong with you child'.

Something wrong with me. Mum and Dad have never told me there was something wrong with me.

'AND she tells me, she has repeatedly seen you picking the chalk up and writing with your LEFT HAND. Is that right?'.

'Yes, Miss K', I said.

'You will NOT write with your left hand. You will write with your right hand. I am going to give you the cane as a reminder to not be naughty.

WHACK.

Five whacks across the back of my knees.

The pain was so intense.

I really didn't understand why this was happening to me.

Mum had never ever mentioned my being left-handed was a problem. Mum seemed proud of the fact that my grandad wrote with his left hand. Grandad was clever and my being left-handed meant I would be clever like him.

What was I going to do? I was terrified of telling my parents. I decided I wouldn't tell either of them about it. I didn't want them to know that I had been so bad at school. That the teacher and Headmistress were having to discipline me so harshly.

Oh, now I remember. Grandad is ambidextrous. He could write with both hands. I'm not clever like Grandad.

Mum used to take my brother and I to religious meetings twice a week. Dad never came as he didn't believe in God like Mum did.

We had to be very quiet and listen to what was being said. I didn't understand lots of words. Mum told us the things it was important for us to remember. God knew everything and could see everything we did, at all times. God would know if we were bad and bad people wouldn't live forever on a peaceful earth after Armageddon. The devil, Satan, would try and make people bad and get them on his side.

Was I already bad and not be allowed to live forever on earth? I wonder how long forever is. Was the face in my dreams Satan? The face frightened me so much.

Age: 7-10

All through Primary and Junior School, I wasn't any good at sports. I struggled with running and long jump. Trying to get over hurdles was downright impossible. I tried ball games, but again I was simply no good. I tried shot putt and javelin but couldn't throw them very far. The teachers would shout at me to try harder, to run faster, to put in more effort. I was giving everything every bit of energy I had! I didn't know how to give it more than that.

In the playground I would always hold things for people rather than join in. I was the same height and size as many others in my class, but I didn't have the energy that others seemed to have.

It became easy for others at school to make fun of me. I was an easy target, just as I had been for the teachers and Headmistress.

Our Primary and Junior School was in the same place, but had separate buildings. The Junior School had an upstairs with extra classrooms. As I progressed into Junior School, I realised I was having trouble coming down the stone stairs. As I started the walk down, my knees would start to buckle and give way. I had to hold onto the rail to keep myself steady. Some of the children thought that was funny and would try and scare me. I got into the habit of waiting until everyone else was making their way down stairs so I could join on the end. That way I knew I would be safe. Over time, my knees seemed to improve and eventually I forgot I'd even had a problem.

I had a new problem to worry about. I was learning things in class, but when I needed to, I struggled to remember what I'd learnt. Was my mind drifting away and missing what the teacher had said? Why was I having so much trouble remembering things?

My school reports were dreadful, but why was no-one helping me. School Report extracts;

- ❖ Rather slow Loses concentration

- ❖ Handwriting is untidy

- ❖ Would like her to make a special effort

- ❖ Lacks concentration

- ❖ Has a tendency to 'dream' sometimes, rather than get on with the work in hand!

- Has found elements of the course difficult

- Is rather talkative at times

- Has the ability to do very much better than she is at present achieving.

- Must make a greater effort.

- Present standard is disappointing.

- She must try harder.

- Needs to keep her mind on her work.

- Does not appear to concentrate as hard as she might.

- Must improve her concentration.

- Could produce higher standard if she chattered less.

- Not worked with any real effort.

- Her ability is only fair.

- The amount and standard of work are most unsatisfactory.

- Must settle down and not allow herself to be distracted.

- Must try and concentrate

- Not tried hard enough

- Ability has remained limited

- Must try and concentrate harder to improve.

Age: 11

I moved to Middle School and had my brand-new uniform and my long blonde hair. That sounds lovely, but it wasn't. I was chubby, and not slim like most other children. I didn't eat sweets. Only when our Great Aunt visited which was every few months.

There didn't seem to be any of the children I'd been to Primary and Junior school with going to this school. Perhaps that wasn't such a bad thing. Hopefully I'd be able to make new friends.

Right from the very start of my going to this school, Mum had been very clear that I wasn't to go into the morning assembly, on religious grounds! I fully understood, and was very strong and forthright telling the Head and teachers that I could not join in. I felt proud of our beliefs and knew how important it was to stay true to them. Mum and others had said so.

What I very quickly realised was I was the only one excluded. Other children ridiculed me for being strange. I got taunted relentlessly. Children made up their own stories of why I couldn't go into assembly; I smelt, I had deformities, I was stupid, I was too fat, I was the devil's child, I had blood that was a different colour.

Every single taunt cut me like a knife.

I was suffering with repeated migraine headaches and on really bad days had to go to the medical room where they closed the blinds and left me in a dark room. I'd experience flashing lights and be really sensitive to any light. On some occasions I'd be sick as the headache was so bad.

My learning took its toll. I struggled to concentrate, my mind wandering off when I should have been listening. I couldn't remember things in my lessons. Mathematics and French was like torture.

I lacked any friendships at school. Many days I walked home and would be prodded and poked in the back by 2-3 girls from the school. Calling me all sorts of names. Telling me I was thick and stupid. Telling me I was fat and ugly.

At school I got into a fight with a girl on a mound of coal next to a coal bunker. She threw bits of coal at me and I threw pieces back. Then she grabbed me by the hair, which was down to my shoulder blades. As she grabbed a chunk, she pulled hard and then the look on her face was one of complete horror.

In her hands was the full chunk of hair she had pulled, ROOTS included. She was terrified. She could only imagine the pain she must have caused me. She was already sobbing and shouting how sorry she was and pleading with me not to hurt her.

I touched my head and could feel the bald patch. It felt huge. What I didn't understand was the fact that I hadn't even felt it. I didn't tell her that. I screamed and screamed, and my anger grew until I just blew. I picked up coal and just kept throwing it at her. Piece after piece. More and more and more. She had cuts on her neck and face. I should have cared. I'd been brought up that way, but I didn't. I should have stopped, but I didn't. Not at that moment.

We both ended up in the Heads office and got reprimanded for our actions. We got detention.

I was so lucky. I didn't get told off at home when I showed my mum and dad the bald patch on my head.

My mum noticed that a bit more hair came out when it was brushed, so she took me to the doctors to find out what was wrong.

Alopecia! We were told it was nothing to worry about. Mum was handed a prescription for ointment she would need to put on the bald patch, and surrounding area, every day and my hair should grow back. Hopefully it wouldn't reoccur, but if it did, we were to go back!

My hair did grow back. As each week went by it got easier and easier to hide the place where it had been. After a few weeks, the bald patch had gone.

The rest of my time at Middle School, from a bullying perspective got better. Children seemed to keep me at a distance, and some even spoke with me. The fight seemed to have changed things. What I really wanted was to have some friends, like everyone else seemed to have. That didn't happen. I really wanted someone to notice me and be my friend. I felt so incredibly lonely.

It wasn't the end of my health issues though. I started getting chronic pain in my feet and as the day went on it got almost unbearable to walk. I ended up walking on tip toes just so I didn't have to put the full foot to the ground. One foot was worse than the other. Off to the doctors we went and then to a local hospital for tests. They X-rayed my feet. The results found nothing conclusive and they decided I'd probably got stress cracks in the bones! On the worse of my two feet, they put what looked like wads of cotton wool dressing under the foot arch and bandaged it up. My mum had to cut up a shoe as nothing would fit. I had to limp all the way home. We did laugh as it looked incredibly funny. After a few days, the pain disappeared as if nothing had ever happened.

Age: 12

We lived just around the corner from a lovely common which was broken up into several areas. One area had a field, tennis courts and a playground. Next to that was an area with a pond which had ducks, moor hens and two swans and another large field which had a wooden building. In the summer it was open and sold ice creams and soft drinks. Behind the building was a fox's den which was contained inside a wire fence to stop children getting in.

Across the edge of the middle field were the woods. My mum and dad had often taken my brother and I up to the woods to take an early evening walk. We used to take torches so we could see any branches along the way.

After school, I told my mum I was going out to play and would walk up to the top field and woods. Sometimes I would just walk around, or walk down to my wooden house (that's what I called it), sit down by the pond or go in the playground if there wasn't anyone there that I recognised.

On one particular day, I had walked across a main road to the edge of the woods and a man was standing there. He said he needed my help and that it was really important. He kept telling me that I was a very grown up young lady and that he knew I was clever and would understand how to help him. He kept talking to me as we walked into the woods. I felt very grown up and special. He seemed really nice and kind. I really hoped I could help him like he needed me to!

He stood next to a tree, and took his penis out of his trousers. That shocked me, as I had been told by my mum that I shouldn't look at a man's penis. That was bad.

The man kept telling me how clever and special I was and that he needed me to hold his penis and help him try and move it backwards and forwards. He took my hand and put my fingers round his penis. It felt very warm and soft. As he moved my hand up and down it seemed to get harder. I didn't understand why that was happening. I didn't know anything about a man's penis, other than I shouldn't look at it as that was bad!

After a few minutes, the man made some strange noises and white stuff came out and went over the leaves on the bush and ground. He thanked me and told me I had been very very clever and that I had helped him so much. I was a special friend, but I was not to tell anyone about our friendship.

I had no idea what had just happened but I knew I couldn't say anything to my mum as I had looked and that was bad!

I didn't go to the woods anymore after that.

As I got older, I saw the man in his car on several occasions. He knew I recognised him. I knew what he had done and that it was BAD.I knew I wasn't very very clever. I knew I wasn't special.

I felt disgusted with myself for what had happened. I so wish I had been very clever, and special.

Age: 13

I have no idea how my day started. I'm pretty sure I'd gone to school as normal. It was my last year at Middle School and I'd be finishing soon. What I do remember was standing in the dining room with my brother. There was a hatchway between the dining room and the kitchen.

My dad was standing in the kitchen with our family doctor. My mum was shouting and swearing at the doctor and our dad. My mum didn't swear! She would wash your mouth out with soapy water if she heard a hint of swearing. This didn't make any sense. This wasn't my mum. What was happening.

She came running into the dining room. She looked so scared. She tripped and fell, banging her head on the corner of a cabinet. The doctor told my brother and I to stay where we were. We were not to touch our mum.

Why couldn't we help our mum? She'd hurt herself. We could see blood on her face. We were both frightened by what was happening. We didn't know what to do.

The next thing we knew, there were two more people in the room. They had white coats. They took hold of our mum, who was crying and screaming. I just couldn't comprehend what was happening. My dad was talking to the Doctor.

Our mum was taken out of the house, into an ambulance. Dad told us that Mum wasn't well, she wasn't her normal self, she was very confused and that she would get medication in the hospital. We were going to the hospital straight away and would be able to see Mum.

Dad drove us to the hospital, which took around 30 minutes. It seemed like an eternity. None of us spoke. I felt so anxious and scared. What was happening to my mum?

When we got to the hospital, I saw that it was a mental hospital. I'd never been to one of these places before. Dad found out where we needed to go and we followed him along several corridors. We walked through a day room which had many patients sitting in chairs. Some looked a bit scary as they had hospital gowns on. One man didn't have all of his body covered! Everything in the hospital seemed very grey and scary. It felt so dark and gloomy.

We got to a waiting room and Dad went off to talk to one of the hospital doctors. Dad came back and said that Mum wasn't well enough for us to see her and that we were going to leave. As we left the waiting room, I saw my mum being pushed into a room. The door had a small barred window in it. We were told Mum was being put into a padded room for her own safety. Her face was so frightened. The image of my mum being put in a room, like a scared wild animal was the last image I saw for a few weeks! It haunted me when I went to bed at night.

Dad sent me to stay with the daughter (Caroline), husband and children of a friend of his. I had not met them before, or if I had I certainly didn't remember. They had an outdoor swimming pool, which was amazing. I spent most of the day in the pool with their children. My brother came and joined us after a few days.

One day I had blood in my underwear, but had no idea what to do. I spoke to Caroline and she said I had probably started my first period and gave me some tampons to try and gave me some brief instructions. I had no idea but tried to do as she had said but couldn't. I was shaking. I was getting hot and bothered. I didn't understand why I couldn't do what she'd said. I told her I was having trouble and she took me to a local store and bought me some pads. That was my introduction to 'womanhood'.

My brother and I stayed with them for 2-3 weeks and then returned home. We helped our dad do chores at home after school and at weekends. Dad used the boiler to do the washing. Boiling the white sheets in with some colours proved to be an error but didn't get talked about.

I would sometimes go to the local shops to pick up shopping. As the days went by, I found it so hard to get all the things on the list with the money I had been given. I hated having to ask for more money each week. I felt like I was a failure. I had no idea about prices of food items going up so quickly, or that some foods were selling out because people were buying more than normal.

We were so pleased when Dad said we could go with him to see Mum. Dad told us she was still heavily sedated with medication, but at least we could sit and talk to her. Mum didn't say very much, and we were often interrupted by another patient who kept asking, 'are you all together'? Yes, we would say, again and again.

As the weeks went by, Mum seemed to be getting brighter and she became more talkative. The lady asking us, 'are you all together' turned from being annoying for Mum, to being humorous. Without realising it, we were seeing our mums' own measure of improvement.

After a couple more weeks, Mum was at last able to come home. It was good to be back to normal!

Nothing was ever said about what had happened or why. All we knew at that time was that mum had a nervous breakdown.

I started at High School. It was all a bit of a rush getting my new uniform but we somehow managed it.

Autumn came, we spent many an evening playing board games as a family. Listening to Dad's music in the background. It helped Mum a lot. It helped all of us. One evening I had a chronic searing pain in the left side of my rib cage. The pain was incredible and I would sit frozen for several minutes at a time. Mum and I had a look to see what was causing the pain. There was a small patch of spots. Then we found another patch just under my left breast. She took me to the doctor the next morning.

The doctor examined me and told us I had SHINGLES. He said it was very unusual to see this in someone of my age! I was given ointment to put on them which had to be repeated regularly until all the spots had shrivelled and gone.

Not a very good start for my first year at High School!

Age: 14

Even though I was at High School, I still hadn't made any real friends. I would hang around with different groups of girls, but didn't seem to fit in with any group in particular. I had no skill with pottery, but did at least enjoy playing around with the clay.

I found Math's increasingly hard. My English teacher seemed to hate me for some reason, even though I loved writing stories and reading. I had a good use of words and my spelling was always of a high standard! I enjoyed art, although had absolutely no talent whatsoever.

The one lesson I excelled at was Typewriting. My level of accuracy and speed were good. Shorthand – No. Biology, Science, French – No, No and No.

Oh, and I was still hopeless at sport. I would try and run or jump or throw, but I always ended up in so much pain. My muscles felt like they were burning and yet I hadn't done very much. Even when we spent a term going swimming, I'd swim a short way and have to stop because my muscles would burn. The teachers never believed me and said it was because I wasn't trying hard enough and would not be allowed to sit out of the lesson!

I had made friends with a girl through our religious organisation. She had a brother who was a bit weird but OK. Their parents were both blind and had a Labrador guide dog each. They were so lovely; the parents and the dogs. I used to help her save milk bottle tops which were collected to help buy guide dogs for the blind. I spent a lot of time at their house.

Her brother had tattoos on his arms. He'd done them himself. I thought that was so cool. One day he said he wanted to have his ear pierced and said I could do it for him. He gave me a dart (yes, a real dart, for a dart board), told me to put it into the flame of his lighter, wait for it to cool down and then I could push it through his earlobe, which his sister was going to freeze with ice cubes. It all seemed quite crazy, but we did it. He didn't wince or show any flicker of pain. That was so cool.

He was a smoker and introduced me to smoking. My first puff on a cigarette made me cough so badly and I felt dizzy and light headed. He told me I had to keep trying and it would get easier and better. I tried again and this time I felt really sick. He laughed and so did his sister. Every time I went to their house I would try again, until I got really good at it. I learnt how to make smoke rings and thought I was so grown up.

I even got so grown up I started smoking as I walked down their road, until one day a car pulled up at my side and one of Mum's religious friends got out of the car and told me to get in. He was going to take me home to my parents to tell them what I was doing. I told him I could do what I liked and that it was none of his business.

Despite saying all of that, I was terrified of what was going to happen. I got myself home. My dad smoked, so I wasn't sure what he would say. I knew my mum would be angry and disappointed in me if she knew.

Nothing was said to my parents. I decided I would stop smoking, or at least that's what I thought. What I didn't know until I tried was that stopping was hard. I kept wanting another cigarette and would use my school dinner money to buy them, or cadge them off my friend's brother when I went to their house at the weekend.

I made friends with another girl who lived on the same estate, and would spend time at her house too. Her dad smoked so she would get cigarettes for us. Her mum was permanently in bed with some illness. I used to go upstairs sometimes and talk to her. Both her parents were quite old, so I thought that was why she was bedridden.

They had a caravan outside the front of their house and one day we decided to tell my parents and hers that we were staying at each other's houses. We went out to have some fun and we're going to sleep in the caravan. The trouble was the key to the door didn't work and we couldn't get in. We had to creep into her house and I slept on the floor in her bedroom. That wasn't my idea of enjoying myself and we fell out of touch after that.

My mum wasn't happy with my choice of friends and certainly didn't want me associating with my friend's brother, as he wasn't in our religious group. That put an end to my friendships. Now I was back to having no-one.

I hated school. I hated my life. I wanted someone to notice me.

I started cutting my left arm. My brother caught me one day and asked me what I was doing. I said I was making a tattoo. He told me not to as putting ink in it was dangerous. That wasn't my plan, but I said I wouldn't.

I don't know what led to my cutting my face, but I did and told my parents I had been cut by a group of girls. My dad called the police and they asked me a lot of questions. After they had gone, my dad put me in the car and drove around to see if we could find them. We couldn't, but then I knew we wouldn't. Nothing more came of it. Nothing was said.

I just wanted someone to notice me. To help me.

Later that year, I woke up on a Sunday morning to find I couldn't feel my legs from the hip down. I kept calling out and eventually my mum and dad came upstairs. My mum called for an ambulance and I remember my dad had to carry me to the bathroom as I needed a wee. I got taken to hospital and by the time I got there my legs were starting to return to normal but I was kept in for two nights. My period started on the 2nd day and the numbing of my legs was put down to that. I was discharged from hospital.

It gave me something to talk about at school for a few days, but after that school life went back to how it had always been. No friends and hopeless at all subjects, except 1. I did seem to have a bit of skill for typing.

I stopped going to the religious meetings, much to Mum's disappointment!

Age 15

My lessons at High School didn't improve. If anything, they deteriorated. Several teachers had left, so we had new teachers for our final year. I was only put down for a few CSE exams as I wasn't good enough to do O levels. My English teacher hadn't changed. Her dislike of me had moved to new heights. Every piece of English writing she drew lines through and told me to do it again. I couldn't take this anymore, what was the point of being there.

I stopped going. I bunked off school. Every morning. I would leave home as if going to school. Then I'd get a bus and stay on it until it reached the end of its journey. I often ended up at Crystal Palace. Then I'd get the bus all the way back again. I'd waste time wandering around and then get home at normal time. This carried on for 6 weeks.

Then one day I was walking to home and saw my dad's car out the front. 'Dad's home early. Dad's never gone early. I wonder why'. When I got in, I found out why alright.

The 'school board man', as he was called, had visited my mum to tell her I hadn't been to school for 6 weeks and wanted to know why. That's why my dad was home. He was furious. I was terrified. Even my brother was terrified and he'd done nothing wrong!

'You'd better have one hell of an amazing explanation'. 'Well, I'm waiting', said Dad. Then he said, 'Why can't you be like your brother'. My brother was so clever and doing really well at school.

I mustered up enough courage and told him how I worked hard on all my English work. How EVERY piece of work had red lines through it telling me to do it again. What was the point of me going to school? I was stupid, couldn't do what was being asked of me and I didn't want to go back. Dad asked to see my school work and went through it with a fine toothcomb. I waited for him to say something. I felt sick and wanted the ground to swallow me up. Tears were building and building until I thought I was going to burst.

'You will be going back', said Dad. 'Right now, with me to see the Headmaster. I've read several pieces of work and they look fine to me'.

WHAT? My dad thinks my work looks fine. That didn't make any sense. I was terrified of going to the school with him. What if the Headmaster said he was wrong or didn't agree? What if the teacher was there? I never wanted to see her ever again.

Into my dad's car we got and he drove us to the school. My dad's anger was different to anything I'd seen before. We had to wait outside the Headmaster's office for a short while and neither of us spoke. I didn't know what to think, let alone know what to say.

We went into the Office and I stayed very quiet. My dad was far from quiet. He threw my work onto the table and said in a raised voice, 'I want an explanation on why my daughters work has been persistently crossed out by her teacher, NOW!'.

Whoa, I wasn't prepared for his being so forceful, and to a Headmaster. The Headmaster sat down and started reading the pages in my workbook. He read several while we sat in silence. Then he said, 'I agree with your Mr. L, I also don't understand why this work has been crossed through. I will ask Miss W to come into the office so she can explain. We waited and then she arrived. Oh, how I hated her. The Headteacher asked her for a full explanation of why I had to rewrite every piece of work in my English book.

Miss W said, 'I simply know that Heidi is capable of so much more and thought it would benefit her by getting her to go further with her work'.

My dad turned to me and said, 'Was that explained to you every time you submitted your work'? 'No, it wasn't', I said.

The Head told Miss W that from now on, she would NOT cross out any of my work, that he considered my work to be of a good standard, and that any re-writing would be with explicit agreement with my parents, notified in writing.

YAY. Miss W left the Headmasters office visibly angered, but I didn't care. She got what she deserved. That was the greatest day of my life.

I went to school every day after that. Not because I enjoyed it, or felt there was much point, but at least I knew my English was OK and that I was still doing OK with typing.

Trouble was I started getting trouble with my knees giving way. It was terrifying going up or down stairs. I never knew if they would be OK or not. Mum made me an appointment and we saw the Doctor who referred me to the main hospital. They gave me a series of checks and x-rays. The x-rays showed nothing of any concern. They suggested there was some form of weakness but no known cause. They wrapped each of my legs with a layer of cotton wool padding, bandaged over the top, then another layer of cotton wool padding followed by another layer of bandages. They taped around the top of each leg to keep the padding in place. They were meant to stop me bending the legs and after a couple of weeks the expectation was, they would feel better.

We left the hospital and could see our bus was coming. We didn't want to miss it, so we started to run, or in my case waddle. By the time we got on the bus, the padding and bandages on both legs had worked their way down to below each knee. I don't think I had laughed so much for a long time.

We did our best to re-do the layers when we got home, but in a short period of time it had all concertinaed down below the knees again. We gave up. We didn't go back to the hospital. I got on with my problem knees and after a few days the problem disappeared!

Age 16

I got through to the end of school having done just 5 exams. 3 of them were CSE's; English, Math's and Art. I wasn't even good enough to do GCSE's. They were for children far cleverer than me! I also did 2 RSA exams; typing and shorthand. I had to go to each subject class at specified times to sit down and wait to be told the exam result and collect my certificate. Everyone would know how badly I had done. Oh, how I wanted to leave now. I didn't want to go through this torture.

I went to Art. My result was a Grade E.

I went to Math's. My result was a Grade D.

I sat in my English class waiting for Miss W to hand out the exam results. As she read out each person's name, she gave their result. Then it got to my name. 'Heidi L, you have an exam result of'. There seemed to be a particularly long pause which she hadn't done with the others before me. I prepared myself, convinced I was going to hear the word 'fail'. Then she spluttered my result which I didn't catch at all. I asked her to repeat what she'd said as I didn't hear it. Then she said, 'you've passed, and you have a Grade A. I could hardly believe my ears. I stood straight up, walked to the front and got my certificate. I looked her straight in the eyes and told her she could rot in hell. Then I walked out. I was shaking from the words I'd said, but I didn't care. I would never have to see that witch ever again.

Finally, I went to the typing & shorthand class. I got on OK with the teacher, especially with typing. She called out the Shorthand results first. My result wasn't good at all, but then I knew that. I had never been able to grasp the squiggles. They made no sense and I couldn't ever remember them.

Then came the typing results. Lots were read out and then came mine. Heidi L, you have passed with Merit. Me! Get a Merit! Oh, I was lost for words. Two good results from school. English and Typing.

I left school on 14th May, 1976. I already knew from my dad that I needed to go to the job agency as soon as I'd left school and that I needed to get a job. The job advice I got from school was just one recommendation; Copy Typist. I wasn't qualified or bright enough to do anything else.

The very next day I went to the agency and was given a job for 3 days which started the next day. Once I'd finished that, the agency told me they'd found me a job as a Copy Typist. I went for the interview and they gave me the job. My career had started. My dad took 33%

of my take home pay for Housekeeping. What was left covered my travel to work and some money to spend.

My mum had another breakdown and was taken to the same mental hospital she'd been in before. We went to see her regularly and she wasn't in hospital too long this time. They put her on medication to stabilise her. It meant she was a bit slow to do things, but that was better than being so poorly.

Dad decided we were going on a holiday together, to Canada. Mum's sister and family lived there. Dad thought it would be a good way for Mum to get better, by being with her sister.

I still went to see my friend and her brother and had got to meet a friend of theirs who lived nearby called Tina. Tina and I used to walk around quite a lot over the weekend, just to see what was going on in and around the estate they all lived on.

One day in July, she saw a couple of guys in a pub car park and said, 'Go and ask the blonde one out for me, cos I fancy him'. So, I did. They came over and Tina made arrangements to see Steve the next evening. Steve said, 'Bring your friend and I'll bring mine'. That was it. We met them the next evening and that was the start of my very first relationship. I didn't have the nerve to tell my parents. I just had no idea what they would say. My mum wouldn't approve as he wasn't one of her religious group. My dad! I had no idea. I was too afraid of what he'd say. So, I chose to say nothing. If I was going out with Josh, I simply said I was meeting Tina. A lot of the time that was true, because we all met up together, but sometimes it wasn't.

In the September it was time to go to Canada with Mum, Dad and my brother. My mum's sister and husband lived near Toronto. Their 3 children and respective families lived in Canada too. I had been so excited to be going, but now I didn't want to. I didn't want to leave my boyfriend. What if he found someone else while I was away? I asked him for something he owned that I could take with me. He gave me a silver St Christopher on a chain, which I wore all the time.

While we were in Canada, I told my Aunt all about Josh and how much I loved him. My Aunt was the loveliest person. She asked me lots of questions about him. She was genuinely interested and understood my resistance in telling Mum and Dad. Then one day we were all out sightseeing and my Aunt said out loud, 'Heidi, you'll have to invite Josh round for dinner one day, when you all get back'. I wanted the ground to swallow me up. 'Whose Josh, said my mum. 'Oh, he's Heidi's new boyfriend, and a lovely young man, from what I've heard so far, said my Aunt. My dad said, 'I'll look forward to meeting him when we get home'. Nothing more was said throughout the rest of the holiday. I had no idea whether my dad wanting to meet him was good or bad. It worried me for the rest of the holiday and flight home. My dad was a hard man. Not one you could talk to.

Oh, before I forget. During the holiday, my young cousin and I were diving in a lake. We were all staying at a log cabin for a couple of days. During one of the dives, the chain round my neck came off and went to the bottom of the lake. It wasn't deep. We could stand up easily. Trying to find it was impossible though. The bottom was silt and sand and the more we searched, the more the silt and sand stirred up so you couldn't see anything. I couldn't stop thinking about it for the rest of the holiday. It made me feel sick with worry.

Now I had two things to worry about when I got home.

Age 17

'd not been 17 very long. My friend Tina and Steve weren't together anymore which made things a bit more complicated. I wanted to spend time with Josh but he wanted to go out with Steve.

One evening, Steve rang Josh and said he wanted to go to a bar in Balham and arranged to come and pick us up in his car. I had a very strange feeling about it all and really didn't want to go, but Josh did. In the end I relented and agreed to go with them both. The downside of that decision was that Steve had come to collect us in his 2-seater sports car which had only a parcel shelf in the back.

'You'll be alright', said Steve as I climbed in the back. Once Josh got in, his seat was sitting firmly on my feet. The car had a soft top roof and my head was just touching it at the back. It was soft enough. It was a chilly evening, but otherwise the weather seemed reasonable.

We went to the bar and enjoyed the evening. There was live music which was pretty good. We left the bar and all got back into Steve's car for the drive home.

That's the last I remember!

My parents got a call in the early hours to say I was in hospital and had been in a car accident. They had to come to the hospital, in Tooting, to see me. I had no idea they were there. They came again later in the day, but again I didn't know. I was conscious apparently but, oblivious to everything going on around me. My mum later told me that I had asked to have the bed rest put down as I wanted to sleep. She had gone and asked the Nurse in charge, who had said no. I had to sit upright as I had a chest infection. I'll spare you the language I apparently used at that point.

On the third day, my mum and dad arrived. This time Dad had a camera and was taking photos of me. My dad told me I'd been in a terrible car accident. Steve's car had gone around a tight bend, mounted the pavement at an angle where the rear end of the car had struck a Royal Mail red letter box which had split into 3 parts and was strewn down the road. 2 individuals, being Josh and myself, were thrown through the soft top of the car (closed at the time). I had landed in a privet hedge in a front garden and Josh had landed head first onto the pavement. When the police and ambulance arrived, they thought there were just two people; Steve, who got out of the car unharmed, and Josh who was unconscious on the pavement. Fortunately for me, one of the ambulance crew hear a sound and realised there was a 3rd person; ME!

There was a gradual flow of tears running down my face, which got stronger and stronger. 'I need to go and see Josh NOW. Is he alright? What injuries does he have?' I had so many questions each one being asked while I sobbed my heart out. I kept saying 'I knew we shouldn't have gone out'. My mum and dad didn't have any answers for me but promised they would find out and arrange for me to go and see Josh.

My injuries consisted of severe bruising in many places, cuts, abrasions, stitches in my forehead (near the hairline), swollen legs and a fractured skull.

Dad did ask about Josh's condition and was told he was in a critical condition. The only visitors he was allowed was his mum and dad.

It was my 9th day in hospital before Mum and Dad were able to take me to the ward that Josh was in. They took me in a wheelchair as I still wasn't strong enough to walk and the hospital wanted me to be careful as I was still in recovery.

As Dad pushed me into Josh's ward, I could see his Mum sitting at the side of his bed. I asked Josh how he was. 'OK. I've got a lot of damage to my face', he said. Josh had bandages around his head and across one entire eye. The conversation was really slow. It seemed I had to initiate each sentence or question. Josh asked me how I was. Very polite! I said I was gradually getting better. My mum and dad said we shouldn't tire Josh anymore and took me back to my ward. Josh apparently asked his mum who I was after I'd left.

I left the hospital at the end of the 2nd week. Everything felt very strange. I noticed I had a funny lump on my right thigh, but it was the last things I cared about. Josh was far more important to me. I rang the hospital to see how he was doing.

The Nurse said Josh was doing fine. She told me he was so funny and kept making all the nurses laugh. I asked why. She said, 'he says his name is Napoleon and he lives on Coronation Street'. 'WHAT?', I said. I was so distressed. I was thinking the worst. What if he was never the same again!

I rang again the next day. A different nurse explained that Josh's brain was still in a very confused state which was not uncommon with such a severe head injury. The bandage across his eye was because he'd had emergency surgery when we were first admitted. He had glass fragments embedded in his face, including around the eye and down the nose. Fortunately, none had penetrated the eyeball, but he would need reconstructive surgery at a later date.

I remember seeing Steve one day at the hospital, but when my dad saw him, he told him to leave and never come near me again. My solicitor would be dealing with the damage I had been caused. I had no idea I even had a solicitor!

My dad explained that the solicitor would be filing for physical damages caused by the accident, which had been caused by Steve. There had been no other cars involved and, for his car to have caused so much damage he must have been speeding round the bend. The damage was of course to the car itself but also the red pillar box which was split into 3 sections and its contents (letters) strewn across the pavement. Then there was the brick wall at the front of a house. That was completely destroyed. The garden had a privet hedge which I had completely crushed by landing in it. Lucky me!

Josh got released from the hospital after 4 weeks. He still had stitches around the eye and down his nose, but otherwise was considered to be well enough to go home, where he would likely recover quicker. I couldn't wait to go and see him.

Josh's family were his mum, dad and 5 brothers and sisters. When I got there, they wanted to hear everything I could remember from the accident. The only thing I could remember was getting into the car to come home and reminding Josh that his seat was on my feet. Josh didn't even remember that. His mum asked me what the weather was like. I told her it was a bit chilly but otherwise a reasonable evening. 'Had it rained?', she asked. No, I don't think so, I said.

The family gave me snippets of information on what they'd found out so far. Steve's dad was a policeman working at the station in charge of the area where the accident occurred. Steve had been around a couple of times, but Josh didn't want to see him again as he wasn't going to take responsibility for what had happened. Josh's parents had also instructed a solicitor to seek compensation for his injuries, which were significant.

Weeks and months passed, with neither Josh or I remembering anything more. My bruises and cuts had disappeared, I had a scar in my hairline, my skull had mended well. I still had a lump on my right thigh, which turned out to be a misplaced muscle, caused by the car hitting the pillar box and the car panel that indented into the car impacted my backside which caused a dimple in my behind and a protruding muscle in my thigh.

Josh's injuries took much, much longer. Josh had plastic surgery in a private London hospital, paid for by the insurance company. I remember travelling up to see him and took a book by Les Dawson (Comedian) that I'd bought for him. I read the book on the underground train and kept laughing out loud. I read a couple of pages of the book to him and he started to laugh, but quickly told me to stop or he'd damage the stitches. Being able to laugh felt good after so much trauma.

I got paid compensation to the sum of £400 as none of my injuries had been life threatening and I was left with no long-term damage, except my misplaced muscle which they said could be kept covered!

Josh's took an eternity it seemed. All of the plastic surgery had to be fully healed as the insurance company wanted to determine what Josh's facial condition was like at the best possible stage! Josh wasn't the same person he had been before the accident. He was far quieter and slower that he'd been before. His solicitor claimed that there had been some brain damage, which whilst not life threatening was impacting his life. Josh was going to have lifelong scarring too. None of this changed how I felt about Josh. How could it. I loved him.

Eventually his solicitors advised him to accept an offer they considered to be fair. We thought it would be a great deposit on a house.

Age 18

I was working for a local company as an advertising secretary. Dad had called me to say Mum was in hospital as she wasn't very well. On this particular day I was having a bit of a chat with the receptionist, Annie, and she was showing me how the switchboard worked. It was nearly lunchtime, so it wasn't very busy in the office.

While I was with Annie, she said; 'why don't you ring the hospital from the switchboard. That way you'll get to have a go at making a call'.

If anyone is vaguely interested it was a PMBX-4 switchboard with cords. I sat at the switchboard and put a cord into one of the empty sockets for an external line and dialled the hospital telephone number for the main switchboard. I asked to be put through to the ward number my dad had given me.

After a few rings, a nurse answered the phone. 'I'm ringing to find out how my mum is, her name is Margaret'.

The nurse asked me to hold and then came back and said, 'she's as well as can be expected under the circumstances.'

'What circumstances', I asked.

'For someone who has attempted suicide', she said.

'Thank you, I'll be in to see her later when I've finished work, I said.

I ended the call, stood up and could feel myself falling.

The next thing I remember is an awful smell which brought me round. A work colleague had a heart condition called 'angina', and happened to have smelling salts in her bag. That was the smell!

Everyone around me asked what had been said and I told them My mum had attempted suicide. I really had no idea what else to say. Then the tears started flowing until I quickly reached a point where my whole body was shaking and I was sobbing. I was so distraught. This was my mum. I kept asking myself, 'why didn't she want to be with us anymore?'

The whole office was amazing. A hot cup of sweet tea was put in my hand. I had several offers of a lift to the hospital. The big boss came out and told me to go now. There was no need to stay and I wasn't to come in the next day, but asked me to keep them informed. One of the Managers drove me to the hospital which wasn't too far.

The hospital was all white. It is quite a landmark. I walked into the main building and found my way to the ward. I immediately asked a nurse where I could find my mum.

'Down the corridor and 2nd door on the right', she said.

I walked down and looked into the room. All I could see was an enormous lady laying in the bed on her side. That wasn't my mum. My mum was much smaller. Perhaps I'd misheard or misunderstood.

I walked back up the corridor to the nurse who'd given me directions and asked her to confirm the room as that wasn't my mum.

The nurse walked down the corridor with me and into the room. She said 'Margaret, your daughter is here to see you'. I walked closer to the bed and looked, then realised it was my mum. It was almost too much to take in. What had happened? What had she done that had made her body so big? What can I do?

Mum didn't say or do anything. She didn't acknowledge that I was there. She looked like a frightened child.

I remember crying all the way home, just like I'm crying now remembering how she was. When I got home, I told Dad that I'd been to see Mum but she hadn't responded in any way. I told him I'd found out at work that she'd attempted suicide and asked why he hadn't told me.

'I didn't know what to say or how to say it', said Dad.

I asked him what had happened. 'Mum had swallowed over 100 paracetamols, but had gone straight over the road to a neighbour we all knew well and was thankfully was a nurse. Fortunately, for my mum, she was home. Mum told her what she'd done, and that she didn't want to kill herself. Our neighbour called immediately for an ambulance, then took my mum to her bathroom and put her fingers down my Mum's throat to make her sick. This got rid of some of the paracetamol in her system while they waited for the ambulance.

Once at the hospital, they had pumped Mum's stomach which is what caused the extreme bloating of her body.

Every thought imaginable ran through my head for hours. I couldn't get the look of my mum's face out of my mind.

Why hadn't I noticed something was wrong?

What could I have done to prevent it?

Why hadn't Dad told me that Mum wasn't well before it had happened?

Did my brother know?

Mum went from the hospital to the psychiatric hospital. We visited and after a few weeks she came home. Over time everything got back to normal! Whatever normal is!

Mum was coping well at home, doing all the things she did before.

We all got back to getting on with our lives. How quickly life moves on!

Josh and I went out occasionally, with his sister Joyce and her boyfriend Kenneth, to play pool somewhere locally. One particular evening we'd gone in Kenneth's car. As we were driving home, we went under a railway bridge. I was looking out the window and wondered why the bricks of bridge, at the side of the road, were glowing an orange/red colour. I couldn't see any lights shining and thought it particularly odd. The car was going up a small hill as I started to tell Josh about the glow on the brick. All of a sudden Joyce said, 'Kenneth look. The paint on the bonnet is melting'. 'I can see it is', said Kenneth, just as the car ground to a halt.

Joyce and Kenneth jumped out of the car and ran up the road. Josh and I tried to do the same but couldn't. The back doors of the car didn't open. At the same time the car was filling up with smoke. Josh and I were both screaming and banging on the windows. We were both starting to choke and trying to open windows. Kenneth had run back to the car and opened the door from the outside. Josh and I couldn't get out fast enough. Within minutes of us getting out, a fire engine had arrived. Apparently, some people who lived in a house next to the bridge had seen the fire underneath the car and rang 999.

The firemen sprayed foam all over the car, and underneath. After about 15-20 minutes, the firemen checked the car. They looked under the bonnet and under the car. The fire had been travelling along the electrics which appeared to be in very poor condition.

We had a very lucky escape Josh and I were told. That's when I broke down into tears and started shaking. I'd got through the emergency on pure adrenalin. Now that was fading fast and the enormity of what had happened hit me. We weren't too far from my house, so Josh walked me home. Josh didn't look too good himself, but he was kind like that.

All we could both smell was smoke. I didn't say a word to my mum, or my dad. Mum hadn't been well and Dad would have been furious with Josh, when it wasn't even his fault.

They say bad things come in threes. Let's hope not!

Age 19

I was nearly 19 and my boyfriend announced he'd been contacted by a former girlfriend who wanted to go back out with him. He told me he wanted to go and see her. My response was a resounding 'No, I don't want you to'. 'Well I'm going anyway, whether you like it or not,' he said.

I was simply devastated and terrified he would want to go back to her, whoever she was.

A few days went by. Days of utter pain and turmoil for me. We'd been together over 3 years. Didn't that mean anything?

Was she pretty? Was she slim? Wasn't I good enough? Over and over and over in my head I prayed he wouldn't want to go back out with her. The day after he'd been to see her, we met up and I asked him what he wanted to do.

'I'm going back with her', he said.

My world had just fallen apart. I cried and cried and cried. He tried to console me, but I didn't want him near me, until he'd gone that is.

Then I wanted him back, just for a little longer, so I could delay the agony.

I couldn't live without him. He was everything to me. I wasn't good enough.

There wasn't a night that went by where I didn't cry myself to sleep. My mum kept giving me hugs, telling me there was someone else out there for me. That I could meet a nicer boy if I went back into the religious group.

I used to walk past his house twice a day going to work and back. There was a bus that was closer to my home which I could have caught, that didn't mean walking past his house, but I wanted to catch a glimpse of him if I could.

Three painstaking months went by and I saw him outside his house working on his motorbike. I said hi, and asked him how he was. 'Fine', he said. I asked if he was still seeing the other girl, and he said 'no', he wasn't. I asked him if he wanted to go back out with me and to my delight he said 'Yes'.

Over the coming days he told me all about the 3 months, how crazy the girl was and how fortunate he was to have got out of the relationship.

I forgave him for everything and we went back to being a couple.

We got engaged soon after and started talking about buying a house.

Josh convinced me to leave my secretarial job and get a job with the GPO/Post Office.

I applied, took a test and started working with them a month after my 19th birthday and my pay went from £19 per week to £36 per week. WOW. Things were looking up.

Josh and I went for a day out in his car. It was a really lovely place with a beautiful lake. We'd been there a few times and it was lovely to go again. On the drive back we got caught up in a traffic jam. I had a bit of a mild headache so had reclined my seat so I could lay back a bit. We were sitting stationery as nothing was moving. I vaguely remember Josh telling me something about work when there was an almighty crash and our car catapulted forward into the car in front. Josh got out to see what had happened. We had ended up in a 6 -car pile-up. We were 2nd from the front. Luckily Josh and I were OK. The car wasn't. Now I know bad things come in threes!

Age 20

Dad had told my brother and I that he wanted to talk to us. My brother was living in London, so travelled down. We had absolutely no idea what was coming. We stood in the kitchen and waited to hear whatever it was, thinking it was to do with Mum in some way.

'Your mum and I are getting a divorce and we will be selling the house. Out of the house sale I will purchase a flat for your mum and you Heidi. Whatever monies are left, I will retain for my own life going forward. It won't be enough for me to buy anywhere, so I will be living with a lady who I have been seeing for some time'. Her name is Joy.

We were dumbfounded. Speechless. Shocked. This was too much to take in.

Then we had to sit in the front room, with Mum sitting on the sofa next to us. Dad repeated what he'd already told us.

I looked at Mum and she was shaking. Tears were welling up in her eyes. I held her hand. What else could I do.

Dad assured me that he would be around until the move had taken place, and that Mum and I were settled in. My brother was at University, so he didn't seem to come into the equation!

Over the following few weeks we went to see properties and found one in the same road as my boyfriend. It was nice enough. Dad already had a buyer for our house, so put in an offer which was accepted.

Dad told me he was sick and tired of Mum's continued breakdowns and her religion. He'd had enough, so that's why he was leaving! There was no room for discussion.

Mum was worried on so many levels. How she was going to manage a property on her own. How she would manage financially as she didn't have a job. How she would get a job when she hadn't worked for so many years. Who would give her a job with her medical history?

I told her she had me, and that I would do everything I could to help her. I'd increase the money each month, that currently went to Dad for housekeeping. 'We'd manage', I told her.

I had no idea what running your own home meant or whether we would manage, but I was dammed if I'd say that.

It was only a couple of weeks from Dad putting the offer in on the flat and Mum had another breakdown. The sale of our house and flat purchase was stopped.

Mum went onto strong medication and over the coming weeks improved.

Dad put the house back up for sale, got a buyer and back round we went looking for a suitable flat. We visited an upstairs maisonette and Dad persuaded us this would be OK for us. It had one double bedroom, one small single, a small living room, small bathroom and a tiny kitchen which had enough room for less than 2 people.

There was a bit of garden that belonged to the property and that was at the bottom end accessed by a path that ran between the maisonettes next door.

So, the offer went in and then we had to start thinking of what furniture to take and not take. I didn't have much in the way of personal possessions or clothes. Neither did Mum, so that wasn't a problem. There was kitchen equipment, which we reduced down to the bare minimum as the kitchen we would have was so tiny. It had polystyrene tiles on the ceiling, asbestos guttering, wooden windows and a single gas fire in the sitting room. There was no central heating. All of this meant nothing to Mum and I at the time.

We did, as a family, have an amazing number of photos and photographic slides which were from our birth to the current day.

Dad seemed to get angrier and angrier as the weeks went by. He was frustrated by how long the sale & purchase was taking.

Then, without warning, he declared he was going to destroy all the photos and slides. Mum screamed at him and said he couldn't do that. She desperately grabbed what she could from the cupboard in the hall, stuffing photo's, a couple of photo books a small number of slides into a carrier bag.

I have no idea where he took them, if he burnt them all or why. He never said. I never asked. It hadn't occurred to me that my entire life's memories had just gone in a moment of rage. There were too many other pressing things to worry about right now, like my mum.

The day came to move to the maisonette. I gave my mum all the strength I had. Making sure she was alright was my primary concern.

That night, my dad slept in the small room and I slept in the double bed with Mum. That was ideal for her as it gave her comfort when she needed it. I kept telling her everything would be OK and we would manage.

The next morning my dad announced he was going and wouldn't be staying after all. He said if I needed anything, I was to ring him. His girlfriend wasn't happy about him staying, so that was it. Gone! Mum and I on our own.

In just a couple of days we started encountering problems with the bathroom. The toilet seemed to be leaking from the tank up on the wall. The handbasin's hot tap wouldn't turn on or off very well as it was so stiff.

Fortunately, my boyfriend Josh was extremely good at many things and he did a temporary fix on both. Mum and I scraped money together and bought a new toilet, with a low-level cistern and a new handbasin and taps. The bath was OK, so we kept it as it was. Josh plumbed in the new toilet and hand basin and helped me put some tiles around the bath. We'd bought an off cut of carpet and fitted it. It made the bathroom look a lot nicer.

We'd only been in the maisonette for 9 weeks, and Mum had another nervous breakdown. I'd not managed this on my own before. I didn't know what I needed to know or do. I rang Dad and asked him to come and help me. 'No'. you need to do this without me. My girlfriend won't like me coming back or getting involved', he said.

I didn't give a stuff for what his girlfriend would or wouldn't like. This was my mum and she needed help.

My dad hung up, and I was on my own.

I rang the doctor's surgery and told them Mum had had another breakdown and I didn't know what to do. They said the GP would be round as soon as possible to see her. The GP arrived later that day and gave her an injection. He prescribed tablets and told me she needed to take one every day.

Every day I made sure she took her tablet, and over the following couple of months she got better and better.

It wasn't too long before Mum was in a reasonable state of health. Mum knew she needed to get a job and went to the job agency to see what, if anything, she could do. She got a job in the local CO-OP department store. It was a great start for her. I kept giving her pep talks about doing well and she would get better at the job over time.

Things were looking up again!

Age 21

My brother had been at University in London and living with his girlfriend, who was Danish. Being clever with languages, he was learning some Danish. When it came to the end of their degrees, she was moving back to Denmark and naturally my brother wanted to go too.

My brother asked me if there was any way that Josh and I could move them in a van or something. We thought that would be a really fun idea and Josh bought a transit van using some of the money he had received as compensation.

We drove to London the night before and loaded all their personal effects and some small pieces of furniture. One piece of furniture were two cinema seats joined together and bolted to a thick board. We wedged that in behind the passenger seats so we had enough seats for all 4 people. With all the boxes and cases surrounding them, it looked like they were part of the van design.

Josh drove us to Harwich where we drove onto the DFDS ship heading for Esbjerg, Denmark. We had a lot of fun on the ship and slept in bunks with nothing more than a curtain to shut out the noise. I don't think any of us slept particularly well and then Josh had the long drive to the house where my brother and his girlfriend were going to live for a short while. Josh and I had a great time in Denmark and then had the return journey with an empty van.

When we got back Josh sold the van but unfortunately lost £1000 on the sale price. My dad said he would cover the cost as and when he had the money!

It wasn't long after that when my dad fell off a chair in the kitchen of his girlfriend's house. He'd started limping immediately and it deteriorated so quickly that he couldn't work. In no time at all he was walking with a stick.

I had no idea how Dad was going to be able to pay Josh the £1000. I certainly didn't earn enough to be able to find it. My brother had only just moved and didn't have a job, so no money there either.

Age 22 - 23

I suppose it didn't come as any surprise really, but Mum had a series of breakdowns. I rang my dad asking for help, but that hit a brick wall. Dad said it wasn't his responsibility anymore and that he had moved on!

WHAT. How was I ever going to move on! Mum needed help. It wasn't her fault. I was so angry I stopped talking to my dad and was quite determined to never talk to him again. I had been left to handle Mum's breakdowns. I cried myself to sleep every night. Why me? What have I done wrong? How will I ever be able to leave and have my own life? At least I've got Josh!

Or did I? I started to realise that something had changed and I had a suspicion there was somebody else. Josh's behaviour and the way he spoke to me was argumentative. A few days went by and as we were climbing the stairs to my mum's flat, when I asked him outright. 'Are you seeing somebody else?'. 'Yes', he said. I was speechless. Devastated. Angry. Hurt. Confused. Tired. Desperate. Yes, desperate. I couldn't bear the thought of losing Josh. I needed him in my life. I needed someone in my life. I pleaded with him to stay with me. I sobbed and sobbed and sobbed. Josh had decided he wanted to move on from our relationship, so that was that.

Yet again, I deliberately walked past his house every day in the hope I would catch a glimpse of him. After a couple of months, I did catch a glimpse, but not just of Josh. His new girlfriend was standing outside his house with him and spotted me walking on the other side of the road. She made some remark to Josh, who didn't look my way. Her look was just what I didn't need. I felt like dirt on the floor. I felt ugly. I felt fat. I felt like I wanted to die. My life was a wreck. I was a wreck. I had no friends. No true friend I could talk to, or bare my soul to.

My mum could see how desperate I was and ironically became the shoulder for me to cry on. She kept telling me that I needed to join a local group or something like that so I could start meeting people my age.

It took me a few weeks but I did join a local Endeavour Club and worked in the 'tuck' shop. I met another local girl and we met up on a couple of occasions.

Perhaps life was going to get better. Maybe I could make a life for myself without Josh and forget all about him.

Or not. Josh started ringing me regularly. Hassling me for the money he was owed. I didn't have any money. My dad was ill and he didn't have any money. Besides which, I didn't care about my dad anymore. I didn't care that Josh was owed money. I told him he could go to hell as far as I was concerned. I wanted it all to stop.

Every night I kept thinking that I didn't want to carry on like this anymore. I didn't want a life like this. I'd be better off dead. I wanted a way to make it all stop BUT I couldn't leave my mum. She needed me. My mum wouldn't cope on her own.

So, my life continued. I became a Union Representative at work. I attended the annual conference and made some friends. I also decided to join the Labour Party and met more people. I joined a friendship group in my local area and we went out regularly as a crowd. We spent a lot of time in our local pub. I'd go to bed really late every night and was surprised I managed to get to work each day!

I also joined a 'Jane Fonda' workout group that one of my work colleagues ran in a local telephone exchange.

My fitness started to improve, as did my physical appearance. My bank balance struggled most months due to the amount of drink I consumed every night!

I was 23. I could do what I liked. So, I did.

I stayed up for 63 hours solid at the union conference.

I got intimate with one of the delegates from up North. It didn't come to anything.

I almost had sex with one of the Labour Party crowd except he passed out before we got that far. I had a dead weight body on top of me, so had to push and pull my way out, get dressed and walk home.

I was thrashing about with no clear sense of any direction to my life. I drifted from day to day and night to night. Giving an outward appearance of being OK but on the inside, I was desperately unhappy. Convinced I was going to be like this for the rest of my life.

Thank goodness I didn't go to Mum's religious group meetings anymore. I certainly didn't believe in God and definitely didn't want to live forever!

Age 24-25

Mum was at last becoming more settled and her medication was working well. We had turned a corner; except she had now been told she was diabetic. The nurse had told her everything she bought needed to be less than 4g of sugar per 100g.

I did the weekly shop for both of us. I don't think I've ever looked at so many labels to find things that were OK for her! Why on earth do savoury foods have sugar in them? It was much harder than I had ever realised. Mum was good though, she cooked many meals from scratch but she did have a sweet tooth, so that was hard.

I was still going to the pub regularly. So much so, I was getting on really well with the owners. Through a chance conversation they said they had a job for someone to work in the kitchen doing washing up and generally keeping it clean and tidy. I thought it could be ideal for Mum and arranged for her to go and see them. It was. Mum got the job and she loved it. In fact, they loved her.

I got friendly with one of the bar staff called Matt, who was living there with his girlfriend. We flirted a lot, which made me feel better about myself. After a few weeks his girlfriend wasn't behind the bar anymore. I asked him about her and he said he'd ended the relationship because he wanted to go out with me. Wow I thought. Someone is interested in me. We started seeing each other on his occasional night off. He made me laugh and was a perfect charmer!

I had been talking to Dad on and off for a short while. My anger had subsided and as Mum kept reminding me, he was my dad. Dad's health had declined. I went to see Dad a couple of times, by train. It was such an amazingly long journey and Dad picked me up at the station in North London. I met his girlfriend, her daughter and baby. I resented it. Seeing my dad making a fuss of the baby when it wasn't his Granddaughter. I kept my feelings to myself, like I'd always done.

Matt didn't drive and he wanted to go and see his family for a few days. I had a car, so I drove him to see his family - in Wales.

After a few months, Matt left his job working behind the bar. He'd got into a bit of a scrape with someone drinking at the bar, so had been let go. Matt was good at getting jobs, and was quick to secure a train guard job. He found a rented room in a house only 15-minute drive from where I lived, so it was easy for us to carry on seeing each other. I stayed over most nights because I didn't want to be without him.

Then, a short while later, the guy that owned and lived in the house said he didn't want me staying over any more as I wasn't paying rent. I didn't use anything in the house. I had all my showers at home, so didn't see what the issue was. He didn't see it that way!

I found it really tough not being able to stay over and got more and more miserable as the weeks went by with me driving home each evening.

Months went by, and then the landlord said he wanted Matt to move out. He was going back to having his house to himself and may even sell it.

My dad's health deteriorated quickly. At last he had a diagnosis, but the news wasn't good at all. He had Multiple Sclerosis. I was devastated for him. His girlfriend ended the relationship as she couldn't deal with it. Luckily Dad was moved into a flat by the council. Walking was only achieved by using a Zimmer frame. At least he could still drive the car which he'd had specially adapted.

Age 26

I looked for somewhere for Matt to live and found a flat which we could both move into. The rent was quite high, but with both our income, it was just about affordable. I talked to my mum at length and she was OK with me moving out.

She wasn't entirely happy, as she didn't want me 'living' with Matt. I wasn't moving too far and she would still see me a few times a week and I would still pick up shopping for her.

At last I felt like my life was moving forward and I had a happy future.

Matt and I moved into the flat.

I was doing well at work and was starting to think about what my next role could be. I was constantly keeping my eyes open for something more stretching to develop my knowledge and skills. I also wanted to find something that would give me a promotion so I could earn more and not be quite so strapped for money.

Part of my job was spending time in a concession store talking to customers. An elderly man came in to pay his bill. I took it and started writing on the counterfoil, to then hear his words, 'Weren't you cured at birth?'. It left me speechless and completely ungrounded. It resurrected the trauma that was deep in my being. I looked at my boss and said, 'I need to you to take over. I need to take a break'. Maggie was a wonderful person to work with and she didn't challenge what I'd said. She knew me well enough to know that my taking time out was needed and important. Later I told her what had happened. Margaret was speechless and wished she'd known so she could have told the man to leave!

Matt and I were at last on our own and were getting married in the Summer.

I'd worked everything out. We could get married at the local register office and have a small reception in our flat, with just immediate family and a friend on each side to be witnesses. Matt's dad would make the wedding cake, as he was a chef. I would make my own wedding outfit to save money. I'd even make my own bouquet and could do the small amount of catering myself.

I told Dad about the wedding and asked him to come with me in the wedding car and walk me into the Register Office. Dad said yes. I was delighted.

I was so excited.

Age 27

We got married at the end of June. Everything went to plan. Matt's dad made our wedding cake. We had immediate family and a couple of friends as witnesses. I'd made my own satin skirt, top and jacket, along with my flower bouquet.

Our honeymoon was a few weeks later and we took my dad with us to Devon. Dad was in a wheelchair now, but was still able to drive his car. We went in two cars, so we could be independent as and when we wanted to.

On our second night there, Matt and my dad had a blazing row. It became very clear that my dad didn't like Matt and had no intention of getting on with him. That was really distressing. I'd only been married a few weeks. I could only hope it would get better with time!

As the weeks went by, I found myself doing more and more. Matt was working nights and I was regularly taking him a hot dinner to work! I did all the washing and ironing, along with going to work every day. I'd often get a call late at night to go and pick him up from work.

We had a couple of blazing rows, which I suppose most newlyweds have. During one of these, I was sitting on the floor going through some paperwork. He came flying across the room and forced my head to the floor. The anger in his face was something I'd never seen before. I was frightened, but I somehow remained strong. I told him if he ever did it again, I wouldn't be responsible for my actions. I made sure Matt got the message.

Matt came home one day and said he'd been sacked as he'd got into a fight with someone on the train. I was extremely worried, but true to form, Matt got himself another job as a Postman. After a few weeks we even had an evening with the boss and his wife. They seemed very nice.

Money was very tight living in the flat and our 12-month contract came to an end. The rent was going higher and we simply couldn't afford it. Good old Mum agreed we could both move into the flat with her. She would have my old room so Matt and I could have the double room.

At work I'd heard of a potential role that interested me and it would be a promotion. It was to become a trainer for a new computer system. It was the biggest computer programme in the UK at that time. It had been running in a couple of districts for 9 months, and was having a phased national rollout. I had no experience, hadn't seen it or used it, but for some reason I didn't doubt I could do the job.

It was nearly Xmas and at last the job was advertised. I immediately applied and was interviewed by the Senior Manager. She was quite clear with me that she had reservations about my suitability for the promotion, but was going to give me the opportunity. I was going to have to prove myself.

I had some immediate training early in the new year and then went to have 6 weeks extensive training in Newbury. I drove to Newbury early on a Monday morning and drove home again on the Friday evening. I rang home every evening. Matt worked varying hours, so sometimes he was there when I rang and other times I spoke to Mum. After about 4 weeks, I consistently didn't get to speak to Matt as he was always out. I quizzed Mum and she said she didn't know where he was or what he was doing. I felt very uneasy. As soon as I got home on the Friday evening and Matt wasn't home, I started going through pockets and drawers in our bedroom. I found a couple of receipts. One was for a hotel! I felt anxious, nervous and uneasy. I could feel my whole body starting to shake. I had an intense feeling of being nauseous. I didn't want to think. I didn't know what to think. I wanted to shut down. I needed to keep my control. I kept myself calm and decided I would see how things went over the coming week, convincing myself that I was mistaken.

Off I went on the Monday, and as usual rang home every evening. Matt was never there when I rang and Mum felt sure Matt was not always coming home at night. It got to Friday and once again I was searching through pockets and drawers. I found another hotel receipt!

The penny dropped with an almighty clunk. Matt was having an affair. I even knew who it was with. How could I have been so stupid and blind. We'd had an evening with the boss and his wife. Matt had been very flirty which we'd all thought was funny at the time.

I drove straight round to his boss' house. There on the front gate was a 'For Sale' sign. I knocked and his boss opened the door. He looked dreadful. I asked him if my husband was having an affair with his wife. He was shocked and apologised as he 'thought I knew'. If he'd realised I didn't know, he would have contacted me and told me the news.

I thanked him and apologised to him. Why, I don't know. I was sorry it had happened to him.

I drove straight home and burst into tears. My mum was a tower of strength. I got on the phone and rang my best friend. She came straight round. We found Matt's suitcase, dragged all of his clothes and stuff out of the cupboards and crammed it all in. The case was so tight I had to jump up and down on it so she could get it to stay closed.

I put the case at the bottom of Mum's outdoor staircase. My girlfriend went home and told me to ring her as soon as I'd heard from Matt.

It was about another hour when I heard someone running up the stairs. I opened the door and there was Matt.

His words were; 'I don't know what he's told you, but it's all wrong. I did have an affair, but she doesn't mean anything to me. It was because you were away. We can make it work'.

Whether I believed him or not, he'd stepped over my line of what I would or wouldn't accept. I told him to leave and pointed to his case at the bottom of the stairs. My mum came and stood right behind me and said, 'Get off my land, you are not wanted here anymore'. Whoa Mum, you were awesome. I felt so strong at the moment in time. Until I got back indoors that is. Then I crumpled, cried and felt like an absolute failure.

They say both parties go through the same stages and they are often referred to as the 5 stages of grief. They include denial, anger, bargaining, depression, and acceptance.

I went through them all, and yet I'd done nothing wrong.

✳ ✳ ✳

1. Denial: My denial stage started at the point I had my first gut feeling. I kept denying what was happening even as I found the evidence in his pockets. I still kept trying to convince myself it wasn't happening, even after having seen Matt's boss and heard it from him. I kept trying to tell myself it was all one big mistake.

✳✳✳

2. Anger: I got angry. Very angry. I tried hard to let my anger go as my girlfriend and I packed his bag and threw it down the stairs. That didn't work. My anger turned into almost hatred. I've never hated anyone. I'd always kept that for if I ever came across the most despicable human on earth. I hated Matt, for what he'd done, what he was putting me through, for the humiliation I felt, for the waste of my time having been with him. I saw nothing of any value. My memories of anything we'd done together were drowned out by my new thoughts of hatred. I dissected every event during our short time of being married. I started blaming myself. It was all my fault. If I'd not been so intent on getting promoted and earning more money, I wouldn't have been away from home and Matt wouldn't have had an affair. We'd still be together. It was all my fault. I wasn't worth being with. I hated myself.

✳ ✳ ✳

3. Bargaining: Matt tried to convince me that it still all meant nothing and that he really wanted to be with me. With his usual charm I gradually started to convince myself that maybe this is what he really wanted. He'd moved into a rented flat not far from me, and I went down there on a couple of occasions to have a chat. He professed his love, his wanting to come back and that we could make it all work. I was getting hooked but said I needed more time. Too much had happened. The flattery carried on and we ended up in a loving passionate embrace.

✳ ✳ ✳

4. Depression: The realisation came that all the flattery was nothing more than sweet talk. Matt only wanted to come back so he didn't have to pay rent on a flat while he waited for 'their' house to be sold. Once that was over, they would be moving to a new home together. How could I have been so stupid. Why did I get treated like this? What was I doing to deserve all this? I was overwhelmed with feelings of guilt, anger, hatred and self-loathing. My mum was a tower of strength and so supportive. I don't know what I would have done if she hadn't been there for me. No that's not true. I do know what I would have done.

✳ ✳ ✳

5. Acceptance: As the weeks went by, my being consumed with guilt, anger and hatred started to deplete. My feelings about myself didn't. I did meet up with him after a couple of months. We talked, we laughed and we even briefly got on. Matt said he thought we could get back together. I realised then that his affair had ended. I was briefly flattered, but knew deep down in my heart it was time to move forward on my own.

✳ ✳ ✳

As always, I threw myself into my work. I was doing incredibly well as a computer system trainer. I even surprised myself some days. It all seemed to be perfectly logical and I could answer any question that arose. I even started to see things that needed to be improved in the future.

Being on my own was tough, and I spent a lot of evenings round at my best friend's house. She used to go to a night club with her sister and some mates, and they regularly went to the local football club. I went with them and had a lot of fun. I ended up seeing one of the guys in their crowd for 6 weeks. He was separated from his wife and our relationship was what each of us needed. Toward the end of the 6th week, we were having a rather passionate embrace in his car (which we'd been doing regularly) and I got a searing pain in my lower back. When he dropped me at home, he had to help me get out of the car. The pain was unbearable. The following day, which was fortunately a Saturday, I got an emergency appointment to see a chiropractor who said I had damaged 2 discs in my spine. He gave me a strict regime of laying down and walking for two days if I was to have any chance of working on the Monday, which he thought was doubtful. I found out the guy I'd been seeing had decided to go back to his wife! That was the end of that.

Oh no, here I go again. There really is something wrong with me. No-one wants to stay with me. I'm not special. I'm not worth anything. I'm never ever going to be happy or find someone special.

I did everything the Chiropractor told me to do, and got a friend to drive me to work on the Monday morning. I had borrowed a walking stick and spent the next week continuing with training people, often laying on the floor to relieve the pressure and pain.

When it came to work, I was strong, but my personal life just felt like it was getting harder. Harder and lonelier. Yes, I was lonely. AGAIN.

My girlfriend could see how unhappy I was and even after a couple of weeks, I was still walking around with a walking stick. She decided to cheer me up and gave a friend of hers a ring so he could take the two of us out for a drink. I sure needed a drink.

She picked me up in her car and took us to a local pub. Not long after we arrived, Paul came in and she introduced him. I recognised his face and was sure I'd met him when my girlfriend and I had gone to a pub near where we both worked. I couldn't remember. It didn't matter.

Paul asked me lots of questions about what I did for a living. I told him I was a Computer System trainer and was training over 150 people on multiple modules. I told him all about it being the largest computer billing system anywhere at that point in time. Paul was captivated and asked me more and more questions. We'd been talking non-stop for over 40 minutes when our friend chipped in and said we needed more drinks. We'd both been so distracted, she'd had been totally left out of the conversation. We didn't stay much longer as my pain was increasing at a rapid rate and I really couldn't drink very much as I was still on lots of painkillers. I realised I didn't know all that much about Paul, other than he was divorced, had two sons who lived with him, his mum who also lived with him and his dog.

Our friend told me Paul would drive me home. Mm, was she trying to match make!

Paul did take me home and said he'd like to take me out again so we could talk more about my job. I realised all I knew about him was that he was a service engineer and had a great company car. I hadn't asked him any questions. I didn't have the confidence to do that. He'd only come for a drink because she had asked him. He wouldn't be interested in me. No-one was.

Paul said he would love to see me again! WHAT? I was so taken aback. Why would he want to do that? Paul suggested we go to the pictures on Saturday night and that he would bring his two boys with him. His boys were age 13 & 15.

I had no idea how I was going to handle this. What would I say to them? How should I act?

I said YES.

We met up at the cinema. His two boys, were very well behaved and very polite. They looked really lovely. We saw Jungle Book, which happened to be a Disney film I really loved. Paul and I sat next to each other and the boys sat on the other side of Paul.

After the film had started, Paul went to hold my hand, but because it was dark, he ended up touching my leg. We both saw the funny side of it and we held hands through the whole film. I had no idea what to think. I didn't want to think. I must not think. Thinking means you are letting yourself become enamoured and that gets you HURT.

Paul gave me a gentle kiss goodnight. That was on 11th August, 1988

We met again the following week. Paul joined me at the local football club, with his two boys. I thought it would be a good idea for Paul to meet the crowd I drank with. We spent the evening there and Paul noticing a woman was giving me daggering looks. She was the wife of the guy I'd been seeing for 6 weeks. Yes, he was there too. Then there was another guy apparently drooling over me. I didn't believe that for a second. No-one drools over me. Paul said he didn't particularly like any of the crowd. The boys didn't look comfortable either. The atmosphere had changed somehow. I didn't feel comfortable either, so we left.

Paul took me for a meal a few nights later. I dressed up as he'd said we were going to an Italian restaurant in Wimbledon Village. How posh. I couldn't quite believe that Paul was wanting to see me again, or why.

We carried on seeing each other and I got to meet his mum and 'Pepi dog'. I became a regular at his house on a Saturday and again on a Sunday for lunch. Paul and his boys loved playing computer games and I often used to drive home really late because we'd become addicted to a game called 'Lemmings', working as a team to overcome all the challenges.

I didn't know, but Paul had talked with his boys and asked them if it was OK for me to stay the night. They were fine, Paul told me. I couldn't quite comprehend the situation. Paul explained that his boys came first and he didn't want them to be unhappy with any situation. Now I understood.

My regular visit on a Saturday, became every weekend stay. I had completely fallen in love, with Paul, his family and 'Pepi dog'.

Paul made it very clear to me that he would never get married again and that he didn't want any more children. He had his two boys, his mum and a dog. I made it clear that if he loved me, he'd have to marry me. Paul made it clear that if we were still together after 2 years, he would marry me, and no children. I was in love. I agreed!

New Years' eve was fast approaching, and the football club were having a special evening. My girlfriend and several of her family were going, so Paul and I agreed to go too. A lot of drink was being bought by everyone, and I consumed every drink I was given. It came to the time for Paul and I to leave and I stood up to go. My girlfriend's brother put his hand out to shake mine and say goodnight. As he withdrew his handshake, I kept going and felt backwards, crashing into all the chairs behind me. I was completely drunk and hadn't realised it until that point. Paul helped to get me back up and I told him I'd drunk a lot to see out the old bad year and see in a new good one. Paul hadn't been drinking as he was driving. Paul got me to my feet and held onto me as he walked me to his car. Paul said, 'I really don't need this. I have two beautiful boys and the last thing I want them to see is a drunk or hungover girlfriend!'.

Paul drove us to his house and helped me up the stairs. Paul had to help me undress and get into bed. I didn't wake for hours and when I did, I felt incredibly groggy. I was still having trouble keeping myself steady. The last thing I wanted was anything to eat, but it was nearly Sunday lunchtime and Paul's mum had cooked dinner.

I took my time getting downstairs and sat with them all at the table. Paul explained to his family that I had drunk more than I should, that I wasn't feeling too well and it wouldn't happen again. Nothing more was said. I ate some dinner and gradually improved as the day went by.

Age 28-29

Paul and I seemed to be getting on really well and our weekends were always together. We seemed to be getting closer and closer and I felt very much at home with his family. I wasn't entirely sure his mum liked me, as she regularly talked about his former wife and telling me how good she was, all the things they'd done and all the places they'd been to. I found that hard to deal with and it often made me feel inadequate. I told Paul what was happening, and he told me to ignore it. It was just his mum had known her since she was 15.

I tried very hard to understand, but knew I was often consumed by jealousy. I worked really hard not to let it show.

Paul regularly got phone calls from his former wife asking him to go around to her house to fix things. She had a partner and they'd been together for some time. Paul was always willing to help. I hated it. I struggled with it. I didn't know how to cope with it. I was being jealous of a relationship that was purely platonic, was historic and something I'd never had. I didn't understand it and couldn't cope with it.

Paul and I had arranged a holiday together in Gran Canaria. We had an amazing time and while we were there, Paul bought a ring, got down on one knee and proposed to me. It was so beautiful. The sun, the sea, the romance. I was swept away. I said YES, of course.

Our life carried on in the same way. My living with my mum and staying with Paul and his family at weekends.

I met many of Paul's friends. Paul had been the lead of a motorbike gang. The number of friends seemed endless. We met up with one of them every week for a drink, went for dinner with another, and his partner, from time to time and went to parties where the whole crowd would meet up. I gradually became one of the gang. My best friend was also one of their group, as she'd been a later member of their gang.

I went to see my dad every couple of weeks, driving the long journey from south to north London. My dad's health was getting worse, he was having to have more medication and sleeping tablets for night.

I got a call in the early hours of one morning from my dad. He'd been burgled while he was asleep. He was very distressed. I drove straight to North London at 3:30am. When I got there the police had already been and left. He'd had his Hi-Fi stolen, wallet, cash, watch and some of his music collection. They'd apparently broken in through the window of Dad's bedroom. That was very concerning as that meant he was at risk. The window was repaired by the Council and we claimed on Dad's insurance. I found replacements for his Hi-Fi and some of the music. I was feeling extremely stressed, just thinking about what had happened, and what could have happened.

Just 6 weeks later, he was burgled again. Dad rang me first and once again I drove the journey to North London. The police were there when I arrived. They were baffled about how the burglars had got in as the window wasn't broken and was still closed. One of the policemen was leaning against the bedroom window as we were talking. All of sudden, the window slid and opened at the end.

We couldn't believe it. The window that was meant to be fixed, actually slid across and opened. That's how they'd got in. It turned out that the windows had never been fitted properly in the first place. On checking, several flats had the same problem.

Even though the problem got solved once and for all, my dad was in very low spirits. He hated the flat, he hated the area and he felt extremely vulnerable with having been burgled twice in such a short time, and while he was asleep in his bed! I had to find a solution. I felt like I had the weight of the world on my shoulders.

I spoke to the housing dept, as did Dad, and we insisted he be moved to a warden assisted property. To our delight, Dad was offered a single storey ground floor flat which had an on-site warden who would check on him at least once a day.

One of Paul's best friends was an ex-marine and he was more than happy to help move my dad. Between us all, we moved Dad from one flat to the other. My dad had his mouth wide open as he watched Paul's friend lift an electric reclining armchair off the floor, onto his shoulder, out the door and into the van we'd hired. The move was effortless. Dad was so grateful. It was hard to leave him and come home. I had no idea if he would be OK. The warden reassured me that she would keep checking in on him while he got settled.

I became firmer with Paul about his being at the beck and call of his former wife. Paul didn't see it like that, but did agree to put more distance between them. Paul could see how upset I was getting, although didn't fully understand why I got so upset over it.

I had given Paul an insight into some of my past, but only some. There was so much he didn't know. Maybe he'd get an insight over time.

With being so in love, and spending so much time at work, with Paul and his family, I wasn't taking any notice of how my mum was getting on.

Mum had another minor breakdown. I'd missed the signs of this one coming! I'd become complacent.

I managed to get her to see the GP straight away and between us we got her back onto her medication.

Paul and I were considering buying a house the next year and get married. How was I going to do that AND care for Mum?

We started looking at houses to see what we liked and didn't like. Paul put his house on the market. His mum and boys were all OK with moving, which was great. I was excited and nervous all at the same time. Paul's house sold really quickly, so the race was on to find a house we liked.

We both saw the Estate Agent details for a particular home and knew straight away that it was the house we both wanted, without even going to see it. We did see it of course, and by the time we'd been round all the rooms and garden, we knew an offer would be going in. We could afford it and for me, it was just two roads away from the house I'd lived in for most of my life. It was strange really. I had so many bad memories, but none were associated with the house I'd lived in. That was a safe place in my mind and carried a lot of nostalgia.

Our offer was accepted, and it was full steam ahead. We expected to move in before my 30th birthday.

The move day arrived and Paul told me to go and collect the keys from the estate agent so I could be the first person to set foot in the house. Paul knew how important that was for me, even though I'd never said anything. I was so incredibly happy to be moving into my own home, nervous about living with Paul's family and worried about how my mum would manage without me. We didn't live far, so I could be with her in minutes if I was needed.

Opening the front door felt so amazing. Not long after, Paul arrived with his mum, his boys and last but not least, 'Pepi dog'.

I made sure Mum came to have dinner with us every Saturday and did her washing for her too. Mum and Paul got on really well and that made my new life even happier.

Our wedding plans got underway at full steam ahead. We were to be married just 3 months after moving into our house together.

Age 30

The Register Office was organised and my girlfriend and I spent most evenings making my wedding dress. It was more complicated than we'd realised as I wanted the top part from one pattern and the bottom part from another. I don't know exactly how much wine we consumed while we were making it, although I do know we were drinking between 2 & 3 litres every night. I was also making her dress as my chief/only bridesmaid. My dress got made and it was beautiful. We went to the wire on time and it left me with just one evening to make her entire dress. I have no idea how I managed it, but I did and she looked amazing.

Our wedding reception was being held in our own garden and several friends spent time getting it all set up. I was staying with my mum the day before and my brother was over from Denmark. On the morning of our wedding, I went to the hairdressers. My brother came with me and was taking photos of me from just about every angle imaginable. Other ladies who were having their hair done kept looking to see who I was. The closest I'd ever get to feeling like someone special.

We got home, and my best friend had delivered strawberries and champagne for us to have before we left for the register office. My dad arrived and looked lovely in his suit. His walking had deteriorated and he had to be helped into the wedding car, with his wheelchair in the boot. Photos of us together in the Rolls Royce showed a lot of strain on both our faces. I knew my strain was just sheer nerves. I never knew what thoughts were going through my dad's mind. I just never had the confidence to ask!

Our wedding went beautifully. My mum looked lovely. Paul's mum looked lovely. The boys were both in suits and looked so grown up. All of our guests were amazing.

Just as we had our last photos taken getting into the car to drive home, the sky had turned black and torrential rain came down.

Everyone got to our house as fast as they could. We all ran through the house to bring as much as we could in from the garden.

The sun came out a couple of hours later, just as Paul lit the BBQ.

The rest of the day was beautiful and I was so happy.

We had a week in Yorkshire for our honeymoon and then came home to get on with the rest of our lives.

My mum continued coming every Saturday. I was so delighted she was managing on her own. Everything was going so well.

Age 31

My mum used to get a bus to our house, or on a good day she would walk. I used to drive Mum home with her clean washing. Paul would drive Mum home from time to time.

On one Saturday, Paul got back and said 'when I was taking your Mum home, she said she was delighted as she'd been told she didn't need her medication any more'.

Alarm bells.

Action stations.

I had a total feeling of DREAD but my entire body was being driven by adrenalin.

I grabbed the car keys, ran out of the house and drove like a 'bat out of hell' to my Mum's.

I sat with her for hours trying to find the mental door to get me in and convince her to take the medication. She ignored me and sang! Not a tune that anyone would recognise. I called two of her closest friends who came around. They tried too. Mum ignored us all and carried on singing the same tune. Then she was talking to herself, although none of us could work out what she was saying. The situation was going downhill fast.

'PLEEEEAAAASE MUM. You need to take these. They keep the chemicals in your brain more stable. '

We all pleaded with her.

Then all of a sudden, after several hours, the mental door must have opened. Mum decided to take them!

There was an immense sigh of relief from all of us.

Mum getting back onto a better track only took 2-3 days. The medication she was on worked so much quicker than ones she'd had in the past.

When she was better, she said, 'you never stop trying to fix things do you'.

'No' I said, I will always find a way to fix things if I can'.

I meant it. I saw it as being my responsibility. My job!

Paul and I went together to see my dad and sometimes Mum came with us. Mum said she wanted to help, if she could. She'd known Dad a long time and was over the divorce now. Mum was an amazingly selfless person.

Age 32 -33

My mum's health was really stable which meant I was under no pressure and could relax into my married life. My work was incredibly strong. I had taken over managing a team in Croydon. A great team and we worked really well together.

I asked my boss if I could bring my stepson in on work experience which would also give us an extra pair of hands. It was agreed and he came to work for me for 6 weeks in the Summer Holidays.

My stepson came to work for me again the following summer, working well with the team. It fitted in well with his going to college, especially as he was learning IT.

Work was going so well and life was going so well. At last my life had become peaceful and calm.

Age 34-35

Dad had rung to say he was in incredible pain. I told Dad to call 999 and I'd drive to North London in the meantime. When I got to his flat, his Warden told me he'd been taken to the main hospital. I drove straight there and found Dad still in the A&E.

I could see Dad was visibly in excruciating pain and ended up having to have a blazing row with the Doctor. My temper was off the scale. Even my dad was taken aback. The Doctor insisted it was the MS that was the problem. I insisted he had a bladder infection and if they didn't do something quick, he would deteriorate even more. I actually said, 'If you don't do something now, I won't be responsible for what I do next, and you will be on the end of it'. I also told him he wasn't fit to call himself a Doctor and spotting a urinary tract infection, caused by having a catheter was pretty basic for any Doctor. He immediately agreed to admit Dad into the hospital and put him on antibiotics. In a couple of days, Dad was back to feeling himself again and was taken back to his flat.

A few days later, I was running my hands up through my hair at the back of my head. I could feel under the skin in lots of places. It felt awful. I went straight to my local chemist and said I needed his help. He felt my head and explained that the skin had scaled which is typically caused by severe stress. I bought some special shampoo which he said might help, but more importantly I needed to de-stress my life. If only!

My eldest stepson had moved out of the house as he wanted a room to himself, and his mum had offered him that option. He was moving into the world of work and wanted to be more self-sufficient. My younger stepson benefited as it now meant he had the bedroom to himself.

I was nearing 35 and becoming broody. It surprised me. I'd been 100% OK with not having children. Paul and I had got married on that agreement. I was finding it harder and harder to deal with. What was I going to do? We'd agree no more children! I had to talk to Paul. Ignoring it didn't feel like an immediate option.

We discussed it and Paul said he needed to think it through. A short while later, we talked again and Paul said yes to having a baby of our own. WOW. How amazing was that.

We started trying for a baby.

My dad's health was deteriorating at a rapid pace and my visits were having to become more frequent. Dad needed to move to a nursing home as his daily care was so much more demanding. I told Dad I needed to move him nearer to me in South London. Dad agreed and I got straight into finding nursing homes that could manage his needs, and were within the budgetary limit his council in North London would cover. That was a challenge, but eventually I found a brand-new nursing home that was within the price range. Dad wasn't well enough to visit the home before the move. He trusted my judgement.

We moved him into the home. The staff were lovely and he had a cosy room with his bed, hi-fi and TV, with room for his wheelchair. He had an on-suite shower room. It meant I could go and see him several times a week and my best friend came with me on occasions, and other times it was Paul and I. We wanted to visit often, as he was missing the neighbours and warden he'd had before and who were good friends.

Our trying for a baby continued, with nothing happening. I told Dad we were trying and he was over the moon for us.

Over the next few months my dad's health deteriorated and he was permanently bedbound. He was very poorly for about 3 weeks but then got a lot better, so we were all delighted.

Paul and I were decorating our hall at the time and we were scaping wallpaper off the walls. We had two telephone sockets in the hall, one of which was an old business line which was now dead. I unplugged the telephone and covered the socket while I scraped paper off with water. Later that evening we cleaned around the floor and bagged up all the paper we'd scraped off. I plugged the phone back into a socket. We went to bed extremely tired.

The next morning, I was in the shower, washing my hair, when Paul came in and said, 'Heidi, there are two police downstairs who want to see you'.

'Why do they want to see me, I haven't done anything wrong! They'll have to wait until I've finished my shower', I said. I stood in the bath getting the shampoo out of my hair, desperately trying to think if I'd run a red light, driven badly, got a fine that I didn't know about. I couldn't think of anything, but felt really nervous.

Paul said, 'Sweetheart, you need to come now. Your dad passed away last night'.

I got really angry. My dad hadn't passed away. He was doing really great and his health had improved. I threw back a response. 'No-one rang me last night. They would have rung me from the home if there'd been anything wrong'.

'They must have the wrong person'.

I could see by Paul's demeanour that it wasn't a mistake. Paul put me into my bath robe and I went downstairs.

The two police officers apologised for disturbing with me such distressing news, but there had been no other way of contacting me. They told me dad had a heart attack at around 8pm the evening before. The care home had tried ringing me but there was no answer. I was so distressed. The tears were falling down my face and just kept coming. I could feel my body shaking. I should have been with my dad. It was my job to be there.

It was shortly after they'd left, that I went and checked the phone. There was no dial tone. Then I realised I had plugged the phone back into the dead socket before I went to bed. I went over and over and over in my head, trying to work out why I had done it. I worked for BT (telephone company), for heaven's sake. I always plug phones back in and then pick up the receiver to check it's working, but I hadn't done it this time. WHY?

Paul worked incredibly hard to console me. He kept telling me it wasn't my fault. These things happen. Maybe it was meant to be that way. None of it helped me.

Even after I'd taken a couple of weeks off work to arrange the funeral, I still struggled to come to terms with it. The funeral didn't go according to plan. My dad was an atheist and we'd made that quite clear to the funeral director. There was to be no religious ceremony. We were just going to play a few of my dad's favourite record tracks. My brother had created the play list. We sat in the crematorium and the man at the front started a religious theme service. I was mortified and wanted it to stop. Paul told me to stay in my seat and not do anything about it. Eventually he stopped and we got to play the music which is all we'd wanted for the service. Listening to the music reduced me to incredible sobbing tears. The songs were a fraction of the music I used to wake up to when I was a little girl. They were from records my dad had played on his record player, which he treated like the most expensive and prized item in the world. Music had always been his passion. He'd played records at a local club, which is where Mum had met him so long ago. Mum was at the funeral and it brought tears to her eyes too.

I went back to work but ended up in tears most days, over trivial things. The thought that I'd let my dad down by not being there just wouldn't leave me.

It was nearly Christmas and I realised my period hadn't come on time. I didn't dare hope, but took a pregnancy test to work with me. During my lunch break I did the test and fell to the floor when I saw it said POSITIVE.

I was beside myself with excitement and rang Paul at his work. I said, 'I've got something I need to tell you. 'I'm pregnant'. The only words I heard were, 'I'll ring you back'.

WHAT! Ring me back! I'd just told Paul the most exciting news and all he said was 'I'll ring you back'! I felt so confused. We'd agreed to try for a baby. Had he changed his mind?

It was only about 4 minutes later when my phone rang and Paul said, 'That's fantastic news. I just needed to get my head round it'.

That evening we told the family. What that meant in reality was that Paul's mum would need to move out otherwise there would be no room for a baby! She took it surprisingly well and said she should probably have moved out years ago and found her own life. A gracious comment from the lady that had given up everything to help Paul and his boys. A realisation hit me. I'd conceived less than 2 months after my dad had passed away. He would never see or know his first Grandchild. The tears flowed and I struggled to come to terms with that. That brought back the memory, with a thundering crash, that I hadn't been with Dad when he died. My emotions yo-yoed from being ecstatic & happy to incredibly sad.

Age 36

My pregnancy was going OK. I did everything I was told to do and didn't miss a single appointment. We had our first scan at 13 weeks. I was naturally concerned because it was just before my 36th birthday. I knew I was at higher risk being that bit older. The scan went fine and everything was OK. Phew that was a relief.

I was 5 months pregnant when my best friend and I were due to swim the BT Swimathon. I could only swim 2-4 lengths in one go, because my arm muscles just couldn't cope with anything more than that. She was insulin dependent so had to be careful, but could swim for England. We spoke with the organisers and they let us split the swimming so I could do 4 lots of swimming. In the end I had managed 10 lengths and my friend did the other 30. I felt a real sense of achievement and told my baby she had done well. I didn't know what sex my baby was, but felt sure it was a girl.

A month later we flew to Denmark to see my brother. We had a lovely time and I'd even tried running for a bus, which was hilarious.

I had planned to work through to 36 weeks and then take maternity leave. Paul and I had made the decision from the outset that I would go back to work and he would become a house Dad. It made perfect sense, plus I was the higher wage earner. We'd worked out our finances and were sure we could manage.

My visits to the Midwife were every two weeks. Every visit confirmed everything was going well. The Midwife wanted me to increase my visits to weekly now I was getting closer, but she agreed I could skip the week that clashed with my last day at work.

My last day at work was lovely and the team had given me some beautiful gifts, for our much-awaited baby. The following week was spent getting things ready at home. Our baby would be coming into our bedroom for a few weeks, in a basket next to the bed. Paul's mum was still living with us. I felt absolutely fine.

On the Friday I took the bus to go and see the Midwife. She did all the normal checks and said, 'your test is showing you have protein in your urine. I'm sure It's nothing, but I'd like you to go the hospital now to get checked out'. I left her and walked straight to the bus stop. I decided not to ring Paul. I'd wait until I'd got there and knew what was going to happen next. She'd said it was probably nothing, so I'd most likely be home before him anyway.

I got to the hospital and was directed to the maternity unit. Once I got there, they told me to lay on a bed and have a monitor attached to listen to the baby. I laid there for SOOOOO long.

I'd been there over 3 hours, when a doctor came to see me. He pushed my belly from side to side and then said, 'your baby is very sleepy and doesn't seem to want to wake up. I want an ultrasound done to see what's happening'.

I have no idea why, but I felt incredibly calm. I rang Paul and said, 'Darling, I'm at the hospital. They want me to have an ultrasound as our baby is being very sleepy'. Paul agreed to come straight to the hospital. He arrived just as I was going in for the Ultrasound. All the time the scan was being done we were talking about what we were going to do at home that evening and what we'd have for dinner. The lady doing the scan stayed very quiet until the scan was finished. Then she said, 'I've heard you laughing and joking about what you're going to do when you get home, but I'm afraid that won't be happening. You need to be admitted as an emergency. Your baby needs to be born, NOW'.

Paul and I just didn't know what to say or what to think. We got taken to another room where the doctor told us that they would try and trigger contractions by giving me some medicine. I was there with my legs in stirrups for less than 15 minutes and could feel some mild contractions. The doctor came back in and said 'This isn't happening fast enough. We are going to take you to the surgical room. You are going to have to have an emergency caesarean section.

My whole body started shaking violently. Paul went with me but he was taken through to get scrubbed up, while I was given an injection into the back of my hand. The violent shaking didn't stop for a second. I was moved to sit on the edge of a bed in the surgical room. There were so many people. Paul came in and was told to hold me very tight so they could give me a spinal block. Paul held me with my head locked in a hold under his arm which was so tight because I couldn't stop the violent shaking. Paul was terrified he was hurting me, but if he didn't, they would struggle with the injection and he didn't want them to slip!

The spinal block was done and after just a few minutes I was moved to the surgical couch. I had the surgeon in front of me, an anaesthetist behind me, Paul at my side with a man wearing what looked like a nightclub bouncer suit on! How odd. There were several other people around. They were all wearing surgical outfits.

I kept being asked if I could feel a bag of ice on my skin. They told me when it reached the stage of me saying no, they would begin the caesarean. It didn't take more than a couple of minutes for me to stop feeling anything. The anaesthetist had a really funny hat with flowers on it. We kept laughing and cracking jokes. The surgeon told me I was on good form. I knew things were happening. You can feel it, but there's no pain. How weird is that.

I asked them who the guy was that was standing behind Paul in the very nice suit. The surgeon said, 'Oh, he's just there to make sure your husband behaves himself and doesn't try and attack anyone in the room'. 'Why would anyone want to attack any of you', I asked.

One of the team said, 'because some people think we are hurting their partners or don't like us touching them, so lash out. He's your husband's very own bouncer'.

Paul and I thought that was brilliant. We'd got our very own bouncer. Then the surgeon said, 'This is like rummaging around in a lady's handbag'. I could feel my belly being moved left and right. All of a sudden, he said, 'we've got a baby'. 'Turn the baby around so we can see what it is', said the anaesthetist.

My baby was turned around and the anaesthetist said, 'it's a girl. You've got a beautiful baby girl'. They lifted her up and laid her on my shoulder. I looked straight into her eyes, which were wide open, and said, 'oh my goodness, you look like my dad'. It was such a tremendous moment. Then she was whisked away and wrapped her up. Samantha was taken out of the room, with Paul following rapidly behind them.

While I was being stitched up, the surgeon told me that she was being taken straight to the specialist neo-natal unit. Paul had gone with her and would stay with her until she had been placed in a cot. They would ensure he was with her to check and make sure she got all her documentation and wrist band put on correctly. I was still very giggly and making some jokes. I didn't have a worry in my head and besides Paul was with her, so everything was great.

I didn't get to see Samantha again that day. I was taken back to the maternity unit and put into a room. The room was infested with insects. I insisted they move me to another room. I was put into a multi bed room which had two ladies who hadn't given birth yet. I had difficulty getting to sleep. My baby had been delivered, but I didn't have her with me. I quietly cried myself to sleep.

The next day Paul came into the Maternity Unit with a wheelchair. He was allowed to wheel me into the lift and take me to the neo-natal unit. Paul told me that Samantha was a small baby, just like he and his eldest son had been. Samantha weighted 4 pound and six ounces. When we got to her little plastic cot, I couldn't really see how small she really was. Samantha apparently had a baby vest on, then a baby grow (sleepsuit), then bubble wrap (yes, I said bubble wrap) and then 3 blankets. She had a woolly hat and gloves on too.

Samantha's body temperature was incredibly low. Samantha was incredibly cold when she was delivered and her blood sugar reading was less than 2. The bubble wrap was to help bring her body temperature up. Every 4 hours she had a foot prick to test her blood sugar and the drip was to give her vital fluids to try and raise the sugar levels quickly. Neither of us were allowed to pick her up. They wanted to conserve every bit of energy Samantha had. I so desperately wanted to pick her up and give her a hug. I wanted her to know her mummy was there. That she was safe. That she was loved and wanted so very much. My heart ached with longing to hold my baby girl. I had to keep all of my emotions inside of me. I wanted to cry and scream. I felt helpless and so distressed.

Paul took me back to the Maternity Ward and wasn't allowed to stay very long. The visiting hours for the Maternity Unit were very different to the times we were allowed to go to the Neo Natal unit. I found this even harder than the day before. I'd seen my beautiful daughter, couldn't hold and cuddle her and now didn't have my husband with me either. There were mum's all around in the ward with their babies by their sides. I had nothing. The tears were welling up and I had no-one to talk to. I felt completely alone. I laid on the bed and cried to sleep again.

The next day I decided I was going to walk from the hospital to the shops. In a normal state of health, it would take 10 minutes to walk there. I'd been told there was a baby clothes shop which had early birth baby clothes which Samantha desperately needed. All the baby clothes Samantha was wearing were twice her size and I wanted her to have her own clothes that fitted.

I knew I wasn't meant to walk very far as it was still very early after having had major surgery, but I went anyway. I took the walk very very slowly. The walk took me 35 minutes, but I got there. I found a couple of baby grows (sleepsuits) for 4-5lb babies as well as some all-in-one body vests. I bought them all and then started the walk back. I realised quite quickly that I'd overdone it. My body was starting to feel bruised inside where the surgeon had made the cuts. I kept stopping and crouching over to try and give myself a rest. I had to repeat this more and more often. As soon as I got into the main hospital building, I found a seat and sat there. After 20 minutes, I got up and walked down the corridor to the lift, got in the lift and out into the maternity ward. I went straight to bed, laid on my side and pulled me knees up toward my chest. I drifted off to sleep, only to be woken by one of the nurses who asked me if I was OK. My face colour was concerning her. I told her what I'd done and unsurprisingly she read me the riot act. I'd been totally stupid and irresponsible. I couldn't disagree. I was left to rest, sleep and recover. Later in the day the nurse came back in and asked to see the clothes I'd bought. She agreed they were lovely and gave me an encouraging smile.

The neo natal unit had told me to express milk and then I'd be able to give it to her through the intravenous drip. The nurses in the maternity ward gave me the necessary kit to do so. I tried and tried but nothing. One of the nurses, who told me she was very busy said I just needed to relax. I tried throughout the day but all I managed was a 1 fluid ounce. The neo natal team were so lovely. They told me every ounce was precious and showed me how to give it to Samantha using a syringe. I repeated this every day. I felt totally inadequate. I couldn't feed my baby. What was wrong with me?

It was Day 4 when Paul and I were at last allowed to pick Samantha up and cuddle her. At last her blood sugar was rising, although only just above 2.5 so still had a way to go. Her body temperature was considerably improved and I was allowed to change her into the clothes I bought. Now she was our little girl. Little being the key word. Laying her down my arm, the top of her head was at my elbow and the bottom of her feet were touching my fingers. My hand was at a 90-degree angle from the wrist. Samantha was smaller than a baby Annabelle doll!

Family and friends were allowed to come and see her now, and were allowed to hold her for a minute or two. What fascinated the nurses and all of us was that Samantha had her eyes open a lot of the time and seemed to be watching what people were doing. We all knew she couldn't, because babies don't see that far at this stage, but the nurses said, your daughter is very knowing'. Like any new mum, that was so lovely to hear.

Samantha wasn't being discharged with me as her blood sugar was too low. I almost couldn't bare leaving the hospital. I wanted to stay, but I couldn't. They wouldn't let me. Paul took me early every morning to the hospital so I could spend the day with Samantha. I was still trying desperately to express milk, but still didn't get more than 1 ounce at a time. Some days even less. I did notice I had some small lumps under my armpits, but I was totally focussed on Samantha. Every day went I went home, her blood sugar had risen throughout the day, but every morning when I arrived it had dropped through the night. A total yo-yo of emotions; being overjoyed to overwhelmed. We'd be back to square one. It was day 12 when we at last got the result everyone wanted. A blood sugar level of 4.0

Day 13 remained stable and I was told I could stay in the special bedroom within the neo natal unit, with Samantha at my side. Providing I managed OK with her through the night, I'd be allowed to take her home the next day. Everything went well and Paul came to get Samantha and I so we could at last all go home together. The nurses had swaddled Samantha in one of the blankets she'd been bought. It made it so easy to put her straight into the car seat and keep her comfortable and safe.

At last we were at home. Now family life could start. I couldn't be happier.

Happier until I went back to work when she was only 14 weeks old. The first day was so incredibly hard and heart wrenching. I wanted to stay at home but I had to go back to work. I knew she was in safe hands with her dad. I knew the only way I'd manage was to switch my brain off and not think about them. I would ring Paul each day at lunchtime so he could give me updates. Once I'd put the phone down, I switched my brain off again. As the days and weeks went by, I got better and better at doing it. Paul and Samantha were doing great and I got to do the last feed, bath-time and bedtime once I got home. I spent my entire weekend with them both. This was a really important ritual and one I would never stop doing.

Samantha was 7 months old and Paul knew something wasn't right. It didn't matter how much formula milk he gave her, or at what time, she'd projectile vomit soon after. Paul took her to the GP straightaway and they referred her straight to the children's unit at the hospital. I got there as soon as I could. Paul had the horrendous job of holding Samantha in-front of an x-ray chart, but was only allowed to hold her head with two fingers and with her bottom propped on a ledge with her feet hanging. No parent wants to see their sick baby like that. They weren't convinced there was anything wrong with Samantha until just after the team started to walk away, along came the projectile vomit all over the floor.

Samantha was immediately admitted to the hospital. Paul and I took it in turns to sleep at the hospital so we were in the room with her. She was put on two medications which had to be measured based on her weight. Every day she had to be weighed and a recalculation done by the doctor. After a week, we were told we could take her home, but she would need to continue with the medication. We were also given a monitor to put on her, inside the cot, which would be triggered if she was sick and stopped breathing. That was a terrifying thought and stressed us both. The doctor gave us a sheet which had the two medications written down and the calculation we had to do, based on her weight each day. They gave us the two bottles of medication and syringes to draw the medicine out.

Each night we would hook Samantha up to the monitor. In reality we would both have known if she'd been sick in her sleep. Neither of us slept very much and when we did, we'd be awake again at the sound of a pin drop.

Every morning we would weigh Samantha and I multiplied her weight by the amount shown on the sheet of paper. I was surprise by how much one of them looked like as it seemed to be more than the hospital had been giving her. On the second day I mentioned it to Paul. We agreed I would have a chat with a pharmacist. I took the sheet to our local pharmacist and explained my concern. He looked at the sheet and instantly recognised why I was concerned. Whoever had written it in the hospital had put a decimal point in the wrong place! I was so angry and stressed. He went straight to his book to see what the side effects would be for an overdose. The side effects were extreme drowsiness. Samantha wasn't drowsy at all. She woke every four hours, exactly as she had done in the hospital. The pharmacist told me not to worry, just correct the dose for each day going forward, which we did. When we went back to the hospital for her check-up, I got extremely angry and said a few words, which I think Samantha shouldn't have heard at such a young age! What was most important was Samantha was now OK and could come off the medication entirely. We didn't need the monitor anymore. We could restart being a family!

It also meant we had to start thinking about the room we had at the house. We had 3 bedrooms; 1 for Paul and I, 1 for his son and a small room for his mum. Samantha was in with us, but the time would soon arrive where she would need her own room.

Paul and his mum were in regular contact with the council to see if they could provide her with a flat, taking account of her age. The reality was they could only consider doing anything if she was being evicted from her home with us. Paul knew he had to say the words, but found it hard. The day came and he told the council he was evicting his mum. His mum knew it was only words that he had to say. They would remain a strong bond as always. In no time at all, the council notified us that they had a 1 bedroom flat on the first floor of a 2-story block which was warden assisted. We all went to see it and it looked fine. It had been freshly decorated and was within walking distance of many shops. There were also good bus services into a couple of local towns and we were only 30 minutes away by car.

The move was easy, as there wasn't much in the way of furniture. We took her out shopping to buy the extra furniture she needed and to make the flat into a home. If she found it hard, she never said. That wasn't her style at all.

Paul took Samantha to see her each week and over time she had bought toys and puzzles which she kept in a very large cupboard.

Paul had found himself a part time job for a couple of hours, 3 days a week, with the company he had previously worked for. It wasn't far from his mum, so it became a regular trip to drop Samantha off to play, do puzzles and colouring with her Nan. That was great for all of them. It made the transition much easier.

My mum was still spending time with us on a Saturday. Samantha would play with my mum's cuddly toys when we picked her up or dropped her off.

Our life was going well now.

Age 37 – 41

The next five years saw my work getting more and more involved with complexity. My working week got longer and I sometimes had to ring Paul from the train to hear the words 'are you only just getting on the train again!'.

I would get in the door flustered, spend time with Samantha playing in the bath, reading books and telling her bedtime stories. Then I'd have my dinner which Paul had kept warm for me.

It didn't enter my head that I worked such long hours, or even needed to do some extra work at home in the evening. I loved being recognised for doing great work. I loved feeling part of a team that were making significant progress for the business, including launching new products and services. I loved that I'd worked my way up to being an Executive Assistant to the Vice President of our business unit. It made me feel like I'd achieved something. I felt justified with my reasoning for working late. My dad used to work late doing his paperwork. He'd worked incredibly hard and so did I!

Paul brought Sammy to see me a couple of times. On one occasion they were outside my work building. By chance I picked up the call but couldn't go down to see them as I was about to go into a meeting. Both Paul and Samantha were so disappointed. I didn't consciously think about it as I had a job to do. I was the wage earner, so my job had to come first!

My weekends were solely about spending time with Samantha. Going into the local town and meeting up with a friend and their little girl. I loved every minute of it.

Paul and I did reap the reward of my hard work. I got recognised by the organisation and it included a trip to Brussels with an evening meal, cabaret and overnight stay. Paul and I hired our outfits for the evening. We arranged for Samantha to spend the night with Paul's ex-wife and family. Sammy knew them all and it would put her in a family environment. We knew that neither of our mum's would be able to look after Samantha for a night. It wouldn't have been fair on either of them. My mum would have been too stressed and Paul's mum was already in her late 70's.

Paul and I couldn't believe how posh the hotel was. We could see all the way down to the bottom of the grand staircase from our bedroom window. No-one could see us. That was amazing. We'd never seen anything like it before. We enjoyed getting dressed up and looked and felt fantastic at the event. I felt it was a way of saying thank you to Paul for being the house Dad. I just don't think I actually said it.

My brother was in distress and I knew he was struggling mentally. One of his closest and dearest friends had passed away, having contracted AIDS a while before. I'd never known Torben, but knew how heart wrenching it was for my brother, and Torben's family of course. The grief, the disbelief of losing his best friend. My brother needed someone to talk to, to go through his grief with him, his own mental turmoil, and that person was me. He couldn't talk to our Mum about it as he knew she wouldn't be comfortable talking about someone who had been gay. Her religious beliefs wouldn't allow for that. Talking to me just didn't feel enough somehow and I worried about him deeply.

I was too busy to notice I wasn't feeling so great. I kept feeling incredibly hot and flushed. I was overweight so put it down to that. Then when I was just 41, my periods stopped. A visit to the GP made me realise I may well have started menopause. I hadn't appreciated this could happen so early.

I was travelling a lot and on one particular day, I'd left home at 05:00 in the morning to be at a meeting which was due to start at 09:00. The drive was going to take me over 3.5 hours and I liked to have a bit of time to spare. I was over half way there when I got a call message. I pulled over when I got the chance in case it was from my boss who I would be meeting up with. It wasn't. It was from Paul's mum, telling me that Paul had fallen and crashed into the wall. He was feeling extremely poorly and she'd got an immediate appointment with the doctor. I rang my boss to explain and we agreed I'd turn around and drive home immediately.

Paul was O.K but the GP arranged for immediate blood tests to see what was going on. The results were back in a matter of days and he got a call to go and see her. The diagnosis took my breath away. I was so overwhelmed with panic. My husband was clinically an alcoholic. The man who I loved and trusted to care for our young daughter, every day! How could this be happening.

Paul assured me that he wasn't an alcoholic, he just enjoyed a glass of wine in the evening while he was making dinner. When we talked it through, Paul realised he was having a bottle of wine most nights. He even recalled that one evening he'd put our daughter's hat, coat and boots on to walk down to the off-licence to buy a bottle of wine, because there wasn't one in the house. Paul restricted his intake to a couple of bottles a week after that and in a matter of weeks his blood tests showed he was back to normal.

My work was continuing with ever increasing pressure and the company was going through a lot of change. I'd moved into a different team which was delivering a highly complex system. My role meant I was interfacing with and meeting with teams up and down the country. My work base was in the middle of London. My knowledge and skills were being stretched. I had so much to learn. Courses to go on and get qualified in. I was finding some of that hard. My memory didn't work well trying to recall specific phrases or words. I'd never been good at that. On one particular qualification I got through the foundation stage, but needed to get to the next level. Nope. My brain was not going to play ball. I did learn a lot of new standards and worked hard to apply the knowledge I'd gained. I was keeping my head above water. The hours I worked were incredibly long. Many a week I worked 70+ hours but remained tough on not working weekends.

Then one evening my mum rang me at home. I couldn't make head nor tail of what she was saying. I was concerned enough that I jumped in the car and drove straight to her flat. When I got there, she was sitting on her dining room chair and she tried to talk to me. What came out of her mouth was utter rubbish. She knew it was happening and could hear the babble she was talking, which clearly wasn't what she was thinking or trying to say. I could feel the stress and pressure rising in my body.

I rang her GP surgery immediately and they told me a GP would be round to see her as soon as possible. We sat together for nearly an hour, not being able to have much in the way of conversation. It was more about me telling her things or asking questions which she could simply nod or shake her head. The doctor arrived and sat down to talk to Mum. He recognised immediately what was happening. Mum was having a transient stroke. We were told not to worry. It would pass through very soon and her speech would come back to normal. He told me to ring back if I had any concerns, but was assured Mum would be fine and back to normal that evening. Within 40 minutes of his leaving, Mum's speech was back to normal. Mum felt and looked fine, so I drove home, leaving her with strict instructions to ring me if she needed me for any reason. I let out a sign of relief as I drove home.

Paul hadn't been feeling well for a while, and I was naturally worried that he'd taken his eye off the ball with his drinking. It didn't look or feel like the same thing. He was run down and had constant fatigue. A full set of blood tests revealed that his body was fighting an unknown virus. The doctor told him there was nothing they could give him to help it and that it could take anywhere between a week and a hundred years for his body to fight it off! That's not what you want to hear from a medical professional. Paul did what he always does. He kept on going, as best he could, making sure he was looking after our daughter and making sure she was OK. The virus went on for months. You hear of stories where viruses attack the body and win! We were both determined he would beat it. He had to. I couldn't manage without him. Thank goodness for his mum, she was invaluable.

My boss could see how much I was struggling. I was overwhelmed. I'd got so many things to worry about. I couldn't cope with it all. My mind was trying to shut down. It was arranged by our Human Resources team for me to see a private counsellor, paid for by the company. I had a one-hour session each week for 12 weeks. Over that time, we went through every single thing that was worrying and overwhelming me. We broke it down into distinct items. Then we worked through which items were in my control, which weren't. If they were in my control, what priority would I give each one and what actions did I need to take. On all the ones that weren't in my control, could I or did I need to influence any of them. If not, it was time to let them go. If yes, then what action would I take and why. What the 12 weeks did, was made me see my own overwhelm as a complex project. Like the ones I was used to working on. Breaking the complex project down into smaller deliverables, then working on them. I was hugely appreciative to my boss and HR team. It was the help I needed and at a time I needed it.

Age 42

Just a handful of weeks later, Mum had a stroke. This time she went into hospital. They helped her to recover and she did quite well. Mum was weak on one side of her body. The hospital did point out that it could be the first with others to follow. They highlighted that with Mum living in an upstairs maisonette with outside concrete stairs, it was extremely dangerous for her.

I knew what I needed to do, but that meant having an incredibly hard conversation with Paul and Samantha. I plucked up the courage. I said, 'We need to sell our house, Mum's maisonette and buy a property with an annexe or somewhere for Mum to live. It needs to have accommodation for her downstairs. She's at risk of falling down her stone staircase. Oh, and I know the council won't house her as she has her own flat. I won't put her into a nursing home either'. It was a relief to have said it all, but I knew I was asking the world of my husband and daughter.

Neither Paul or Samantha wanted to move. They loved our house. I didn't give myself the luxury of stopping to think about whether I loved the house or not. I just knew what I needed to do. My mum needed my help.

Paul explored every alternative with me, but realised there was only one answer that I was ever going to be happy with. He agreed. We'd sell the house and Mum's flat.

Along with the demanding job I was doing, I managed the sale of Mum's flat and Paul worked on the sale of our house. Eventually Mum's flat got a buyer and likewise so did we for the house. We spent every weekend going to see what seemed like an endless list of houses. I was so tired and stressed.

We eventually found a 4-bedroom house which had rooms downstairs on one side of the house that we could convert into an annexe. It would mean a lot of building work, and we'd have to live in it at the same time. It had an unofficial room in the loft that I could use for an office. Samantha would get to have a small bedroom and a separate play room. Paul would get the kitchen of his dreams built across the rooms at the back of the house. It was all coming together.

Mum's flat sale completed a week before our house, so we moved her in with us. All her furniture and belongings went into storage. Our entire house was packed up in boxes as we were expecting a completion date any day now. All I had for Mum to sleep on each night was a mattress on the floor surrounded by boxes! Mum, as always, took it all in good spirits and still had her sense of humour. I couldn't see anything funny anymore. There were daily issues cropping with the solicitors. I was driving around trying to physically pick up search data and deliver it to our solicitors. The man we were buying from was driving us crazy. We just had to keep going and get the move done, at whatever cost.

At last the day arrived and we were moving. It was only 8 days until Christmas. We took Mum to one of her friends' house so she could stay there for a couple of nights and not have to deal with the physical move. It would give us a chance to get a room ready for her to move into downstairs. It would be temporary while we got the annexe done.

All of our furniture, and Mums', got placed in rooms and packing boxes were piled high. We unpacked just enough for our first night in the house. We made our beds and would worry about the rest the next day.

Paul's former wife and his mum came around early the following morning. They were going to help with unpacking. Although the large kitchen and dining room were going to be converted into the annexe for Mum, but over Christmas and New Year we would use it as the kitchen for us all.

Someone opened one of the kitchen drawers and said, 'Oh my god, what on earth is growing in here'. I walked straight over and saw huge pieces of mould. I could feel myself retching. I walked straight out, grabbed my work bag and walked out of the front door. I travelled to a local office and worked there for the day. I didn't want to think about what else they'd find in the house. When I returned home, Paul gave me a run down on everything they'd found so far. It was pretty grim. I knew I couldn't bring my mum to this house for a few days, so drove to her friend's house and asked if she could stay for a bit longer. We needed time to do cleaning and making it a lot nicer than how we'd found it. It meant I'd have the weekend to get things done and not have to worry.

A couple of friends came over on the Saturday. Sammy wanted to have a bath, so we ran it for her and left her upstairs while we carried on cleaning. Paul was working through a load of wiring to see if he could find out why the power shower, which was in a separate room, wasn't working. It's so lovely having someone who can fix things.

Sammy shouted as loud as she could, 'Mum you'd better come and see this'. I ran upstairs, my friend close behind me. I couldn't believe my eyes. There were huge chunks of white stuff floating on the top of the water all around Sammy's body. I lifted some out and knew straight away what it was. The b****y family we'd bought the house from had painted the inside of the bath with GLOSS PAINT!! Why on earth would they do that. I lifted Sammy out, wrapped her in a towel and let the water out. All of the paint was lifting off.

Paul called up and said, 'I've fixed the shower. Whoever wired up the water pump didn't know what they were doing. They'd wired it up wrong. It was never going to work. It does now!'.

Great I shouted, now you can come and look at the bath. Paul couldn't believe his eyes. Paul went and got a scraper and came back up and scraped the inside of the bath. Once all the paint was off, we could see it had no enamel. It was rotten. Hey, at least we had a shower room!

That night I cried myself to sleep. What on earth had I done. I'd moved my loving husband and daughter into a dreadful house. I felt an overwhelming feeling of being a failure.

There wasn't a day that went by without our finding a new major problem. Paul had tried tracing the internet connection cables to find a mass of cabling under the floor in the cupboard under the stairs. They were running in every direction. A mass of cabling was running under the lounge floor and up the side of the chimney breast. When we checked, we realised the side of the chimney was plywood. There was no brickwork. Someone had smashed it out to run cables, covered it with wood and papered over the top so it wasn't visible. This house was becoming a nightmare. The more we looked the more the horrors kept appearing.

I had kept delaying Mum coming because I couldn't bear the thought of her having to cope with any of this. It was going to be Christmas Eve the next day. I couldn't delay it any longer. I made sure the room she would sleep in was clean, tidy and as organised as it could be. I went and got Mum. Mum knew as soon as we got in the car that I was desperately unhappy. I told her everything. I had to. I couldn't keep it all inside me head anymore. She told me not to worry. We'd come through it. So typical of my mum.

Christmas Eve arrived. I had bought our fresh turkey, vegetables and all the bits and pieces we normally have. Mum didn't celebrate Christmas, but was fine about eating with us. Mum was simply looking forward to the company. Paul's mum would be with us on Christmas Day too.

It would just be lovely to have smiling faces in the house. We'd see the rest of the family too.

I've always started cooking the turkey in the early hours of Christmas Day. I wasn't so sure about doing that with a cooker I'd not used before, so I decided to stay up later and put the oven on before I went to bed and let it cook longer and slower. As soon as we switched the cooker on, it made the most horrendous noise; 'BANG BANG BANG BANG'. I switched it off really quickly. Paul had a good look over the cooker to see if he could work out what was making the noise. It seemed to be coming from the fan at the back. As with anything that's serviceable, Paul works it out, which I was grateful he did with the cooker. Somehow, he managed to stop the banging noise and keep the cooker working. Back on it went and we just had to hope it would cook through the night. Oh, and not burn the house down in the process.

I didn't sleep particularly well that night. I was forever waking up. Listening. Sniffing. Quietly getting out of bed and creeping downstairs to check on the cooker.

Luckily the cooker kept going, the house didn't burn down and, in the morning, I got on with the rest of dinner. As lovely as our dinner was, and despite trying to be happy and positive, the joy of Christmas was gone.

I couldn't wait for the year to end. It had been dreadful.

Maybe the New Year, and our builders arriving, would bring some joy and happiness!

Our builders arrived and there was a lot of re-configuring of the house to do. I had put my desk in the middle of a room. It was the only place I could get an internet connection to be able to work from home. How crazy is that. A house that had miles of cabling for computers, but none of them worked!

The builders were knocking walls down in parts of the house. As I was working, I could see a drip of water hitting my desk. It was a very slow drip, but constant. I shouted out to anyone who was listening and asked them to stop whatever they were doing upstairs as it was causing a drip through the ceiling. Our main builder came walking in and said 'we're not working upstairs'. He saw the drip and went upstairs to try and work out where it was coming from. He opened the boiler cupboard on the landing, and found a tray underneath the water tank which was overflowing with water. The boiler had a leak and clearly the previous owner had known all about it. Why else would there be a tray underneath!! He put a large container underneath and told us to empty it each day until they were able to replace it.

My daughter came home from school, walked into the room and said, 'OH Mummy'. She came up to me and wiped her finger across my eyes and mouth. I hadn't even noticed, but all the brick dusk had been in the air and my hair, face and body were covered in a layer of it. I got up, found a mirror and realised I looked like something from a horror movie. We laughed so much. It was a much-needed moment of humour when all I wanted to do was cry. I needed to stay strong. I had so much depending on me.

The building work continued at pace and we at last had all the rooms reconfigured. Mum had her own annexe so she could be independent.

Over time we decorated the rest of the house. We encountered problems every step of the way. My budget was soon blown and the house became a money pit. None of us had any love for the house, but it was serving the purpose for us moving there.

My mum.

Age 43

Mum wasn't too well. She'd gone out to do a bit of shopping, which she always took her time with. She hadn't gone very far when she fell. A lady had come out of her house and found her. She decided to call an ambulance and Mum was taken to hospital. I received a call from the hospital to tell me mum had been admitted.

I got there as quick as I could, by which time they'd decided to take Mum off all her medication as they wanted to see what her 'baseline' was. I don't think I have ever heard of anything so absurd. Mum was diabetic, schizophrenic with high blood pressure and cholesterol. Taking her off all the medication was taking us straight into disaster I screamed, shouted, got angrier and angrier. Would they listen? NO. They were the experts and she was in a 'controlled environment'.

In less than 48 hours her blood sugar hit over 18. Our next stop was a mild stroke. How dare they play around with her health and treat her like nothing more than an animal they do tests on. I demanded she be put back on all her medication, which I was glad they agreed to. Fortunately, it was quick enough for her mental health to remain stable. Mum remained in hospital for some time while they tried to establish what had caused her fall. We eventually got a diagnosis.

Mum had Parkinsonism. With the likely cause being her schizophrenia, and her not being able to stop the essential medication, it was highly unlikely they could stop the root cause. It meant we had to be extremely vigilant and meant Mum could no longer go out on her own anywhere. I took over doing her shopping and trips out were by car by the family or her friends.

Mum didn't react to anything that happened to her. She just got on with it, not once did she complain or ask 'why me'. Me, on the other hand, kept asking 'why my mum'. She is such a kind and gentle person and doesn't deserve this.

Mum seemed stable again and there were no lasting effects from the earlier stroke.

I have no idea how I was managing everything with Mum and my job. I managed to work at home at times, and it often meant working in the evening to cover for time I spent doing things for Mum during the day.

I had started to notice I was getting some strange pains in my jaw, arms and my legs. It wasn't there all the time, but when it was, I certainly knew it. One particular day, I drove my daughter Sammy, and a friend, to Kent. We were going to see wild cats who were part of a restoration project. We were chatting as I drove until I realised my throat was so painful, I couldn't swallow properly and found talking to be a problem. I had to remain quiet the rest of the journey and just listen to them chatting away. By the time we got there, the pain had eased a lot, and in no time, I had forgotten all about it!

Age 44

Paul and I were heavily involved with Sammy's school and preparing for a Summer Fair. I had got the school supporting us doing a 'Rolf on Art' experience. It was a big deal at the time because Rolf Harris was doing a series on the BBC called 'Rolf on Art' which had captured people's artistic imagination. I had already been in touch with Rolf's Personal Assistant and got agreement for us to do 'Rolf on Art' using a picture of Rolf himself. They sent me the photo we could use.

I got the photo copier and enlarged and then cut it into exactly 36 sections. I wrote the instructions and created 36 packs to be given out to the children and adults that were going to take part. Each pack contained a 1' x 1' piece of card, instructions and the section of the photo they had to create on the card. The photo was 2"x2" so they would need to scale it up to size. Each piece was numbered so it would be easier to staple to the frame in the right place. They could use paint, tissue paper, material or whatever they wanted. It just had to replicate the content of the photo. Each child would get family and friends to sponsor their painting, raising much needed funds for the school.

Mum told me she was feeling particularly tired and I had noticed how much slower she had become. Sammy had a huge show she was performing in, with the school, at Wimbledon Theatre called 'Music for Life'. We all went to see it. Helping Mum climb the stairs and then down more stairs to our seats made me realise just how exhausted she was. We thoroughly enjoyed the show and Mum was pleased she had gone to see Sammy perform.

We made an urgent appointment for Mum to see her GP. Something had definitely changed. The GP did an immediate set of blood tests. The very next day when we got asked to go back and see him - urgently. The GP told Mum and I that she needed to go to the hospital and that an emergency appointment had been made for her to see a specialist there.

I took Mum to the hospital immediately and we went in to see the consultant together. The consultant arranged for some additional blood tests and we were told to wait for the results. We waited and after some time, were called in to see them.

There was no beating around the bush from the consultant. He said, Mrs. L, I am sorry to have to tell you, you have Myelodysplastic syndrome or MDS for short. It's a very rare blood cancer. There is no cure, but you can extend your life expectancy by having regular blood transfusions. That hit me like a steam train. I could feel the tears welling up inside me but knew I needed to stay strong. I wanted to scream.

My mum, of all people needing blood transfusions. NOOOOOOO. This couldn't be happening. Surely after having been a Jehovah's Witness for over 40 years, without ever a bad word or doing anything wrong, God couldn't be testing her like this. To the bitter end! If ever there was a day when I hated God, this was it.

I could see Mum was visibly shaken, but she calmly and clearly said, 'I will not be having any blood transfusions. That is my decision. It is against my beliefs, so I will not be swayed into doing so'. The consultant looked at me with a questioning look on his face. My response was 'I fully support my mum with the decision she has made'. The pain, grief and anger were consuming me on the inside, but my outward appearance was one of pure strength. Strength for my mum. She needed that. Now more than ever.

I asked the consultant how long Mum would have without the transfusions. Nothing could have prepared either of us for the answer. '6-8 weeks', said the consultant. Mum visibly shook in her seat. I grasped her hand and held it tight. The consultant told us we could sit in an adjoining room so we could have time to digest everything that had been said. If we then had any further questions, we could ring the buzzer and a nurse would come in to see us. I hugged Mum and we just sat and sobbed. We sobbed our hearts out. All of a sudden Mum said, 'it seems I am being tested'. I wanted to scream, but who should I scream at. Not my mum. She didn't deserve that. My whole mind was in turmoil. There was nothing for me to say or do, other than keep hugging her and hoping it would all go away.

We drove home and after I'd got her indoors and settled, we told Paul and Sammy the devastating news. Sammy cried immediately but then gave her Nan a big hug. Once Sammy had calmed down, she asked her Nan if there was anything she would like.

Mum said, 'you can draw me a picture so I can look at it every day'.

'What would you like in the picture', asked Sammy.

'A piece of cake, a cup of tea and some flowers,' said Mum.

Sammy drew the picture later that day and we stuck it to Mum's cupboard so she could see it from her chair or bed.

It was important for all of us to carry on each day doing whatever we had planned, but knowing every day was one step nearer to our last. I felt numb and so incredibly sad. I felt like I was already grieving, and Mum was still with us.

I tried to find out more about the rare cancer Mum had, and found an organisation in America. It was the only site that had any information. I sent them an email asking a load of questions. I wanted to be as prepared as possible and be able to do whatever I could to help Mum be as comfortable as I could. I was blown away when I got an email back from the President of the organisation asking me to phone her. We agreed a time and spoke on the phone the next day. She didn't hold anything back and told me that it wouldn't be pleasant. One of Mum's vital organs would fail and after that, the rest would follow in close succession. She couldn't have been lovelier, and apologised for her bluntness, but there was no easy way of talking about it. She told me to get in touch with her at any stage, even if I just needed someone to talk to who knew what was happening. My mind was reeling with everything I'd been told. I was terrified of what was going to happen. How would we cope. How would I cope. My throat muscles kept getting constricted, with the stress my body was going through.

My brother flew over to see Mum and spend some valuable time with her, but of course he had to return back to Denmark. It's where his work and life were. I know Mum found it hard to see him go. They understood each other so much and had a lovely supportive nature for each other. Mum said, 'You will look after your brother once I'm gone, won't you. He needs you as he's not strong himself'.

'Of course, I will Mum, he's my brother', I told her. Besides it was my job. Mum had worried about him all his life as she knew and understood the mental anguish he struggled with.

Mum had friends coming to see her at an increasing rate. Mum's sister and her husband came to see her. I find it hard to comprehend how 'family' turn up when someone is facing death, and yet they hadn't been bothered to come and see her when she was in better health! My mum didn't like her sister's husband. He'd made very disparaging remarks about Mum in the past, as well as about some of her friends. After they'd gone, my mum told me she didn't want him at her funeral. She didn't want him making fun of her friends.

One of my mum's dearest friends was going to conduct the Service. Mum had helped him many times in his life when he'd had mental health issues, and she could think of no-one lovelier to conduct her service. He was so moved when she asked him and he told Mum it would be his pleasure and a privilege. Mum confided in him that she was afraid of dying, but he spent a lot of time reassuring her that she would only be asleep for a short time, then she'd be part of the resurrection they were all waiting for. They chatted, prayed, laughed and cried every time he came to see her.

Mum was deteriorating so quickly and I was talking to my brother every couple of days to keep him up to speed with developments.

I was spending more and more time during the day with Mum. Her carers were doing as much as they could in the limited time they had. The doctor came to see Mum and I was told to get in touch with the local hospice as we were getting very close to the end.

Mum was really supportive of what we were doing to create a great Summer Fair at the school. It brought together the families and teachers, and raised much needed funds for things the school simply didn't have the budget to cover.

I was in turmoil as I still needed to get the Summer Fair work done but more importantly needed to be with Mum. My work colleagues and boss were being incredibly supportive. I was running purely on adrenalin. It's the only thing that kept me going.

I was sitting on the side of the bed holding Mum's hand. Her carer was sitting on a chair at the side of the bed. Mum looked at me and said, 'I feel so alone'. That tore me apart. I could barely speak. My throat muscles were so tight with the strain of it all. 'You're not alone', I said. 'You have more friends than I could ever imagine, and family, and we are all here for you every step of the way. Mum looked so small and withdrawn. I kept squeezing her hands and trying to reassure her.

I couldn't get what she'd said out of my head. It kept flashing through my mind when I was in bed at night. Then I realised what was happening. Mum was alone going to her death. No-one would be with her at the end. She'd be on her own and she was afraid. Afraid that she would fail the test that God had set her. It broke my heart. I sobbed and sobbed and sobbed. There was nothing I could do or say to make it any easier for her. Mum had to face this on her own.

The next morning the Marie Curie nurse arrived to see how Mum was and I was told that she had deteriorated too far for her to go to the hospice and we would be better caring for her at home. They would come and be with us each day until the end. I rang my brother and he made immediate arrangements to fly over the same day. My brother arrived late in the day and sat with Mum holding her hand and talking in a low calming voice. I left them to have time together.

Later that evening, Mum went into a coma. It was like she'd held on for Mike to arrive and now, knowing he was there, she felt she could let go. I was sitting with her when all of a sudden, her eyelids opened and her eyeballs rolled backward. I screamed for my brother to come. I told him what had happened and also told the Marie Curie Nurse. She said it was quite normal and nothing to worry about. We were told to go to bed and she would wake us when it was time.

We did all go to bed but I don't think any of us slept. It was early hours of the morning when I felt the Nurse touch my arm and say 'Its time'. I got straight out of bed, went and got my brother and we both went and sat with Mum. We were both holding her hands and telling her we loved her so much. In a matter of minutes, Mum had passed away. It all happened as it should be for someone who was so gentle and kind in life. A beautiful, peaceful and calm death, with no pain or trauma and with her two loving children holding her hands.

The nurse told us we should go back to bed and she would prepare Mum before she left. I didn't really know or understand what that meant, but did as I was told. She told me to contact Mum's GP in the morning, so he could issue a death certificate. Once we had that, we could arrange for Mum's body to be collected. Paul was awake when I got back into bed and I told him Mum had died. We agreed we would keep Sammy home from school if she wanted to.

I found it hard to sleep, but did drift off for about 3 hours. When I went downstairs, I opened the door into Mum's room. There she was laying so peacefully. Now I understood what the Nurse had meant. She had changed Mum into the clothes she had wanted to be cremated in. She'd brushed her hair, put on a light touch of make-up. All round the bed she's sprinkled rose petals and there was a beautiful smell of Mum's perfume in her clothes, bed and around the room.

Paul got Sammy up at her normal time and he brought her down to me so I could break the news. I told her that Nanny had died. Sammy cried a lot. It was a lot to take in and I told her she should stay at home with me so we could help each other with the grief we felt. I don't know why, but I asked her if she wanted to go and see Nanny. To my amazement she said yes, so we walked into Mum's room together. I sat on the chair at the side of the bed and Sammy sat on my lap. I explained that Nanny's body was there but Nanny had gone. Sammy saw how peaceful Nanny looked and it seemed to help her. Sammy gave her Nanny a goodbye kiss on the cheek, as did I.

I rang the GP surgery the minute they were open, to be told the GP wouldn't be able to come and do the death certificate until later in the day. It was due to be an extremely hot day, so far from ideal. The spray of perfume in the room was going to be a great help!

I had to keep myself busy, so Sammy and I got on with building the wooden frame, in the garden, for the 'Rolf on Art' experience. Paul told me not to worry. Everyone would understand that it wasn't going to happen under the circumstances. I just couldn't let that happen. Mum would have wanted me to carry on. We would get it done and it would be a success!

I had to concentrate on something, distract myself from the overwhelming desire to shout, scream, sob and lock myself away from everyone and everything.

Eventually the GP arrived and wrote the death certificate. As soon as that was done, I rang the funeral home and they collected the body just 30 minutes later. Unfortunately, through nothing more than bad timing, Sammy saw the body bag being carried out the front door.

Sammy was incredibly distraught as it suddenly made it all real. Nanny had gone and she wasn't going to see her ever again. We hugged and cried together for such a long time.

I had to speak to the funeral company and finalised the funeral arrangements which included our running the service.

The next day was Saturday. The day of the school summer fair. We loaded up the car to take everything to the school, including a toolbox. It was a much-needed distraction. A distraction from the feeling of grief that was constantly bubbling under the surface.

We had a bit of a blow when we found out that not all the pieces had been taken by children, so we had 10 pieces that had no-one to paint them. I put the frame together and decided to concentrate on all of the ones that had been done. Paul had a great idea and got some teachers and children at the summer fair to come and paint the remaining pieces. They were painting as fast as they could.

As children arrived with their piece, and their sponsorship money, I stapled them into place on the wooden frame. Then as children or teachers who were painting sections in the playground finished and dried a bit, they got stapled into place. As soon as we were about to staple the last 4 pieces, Paul called the Head Teacher over and rallied the families to come and see the finished project. We had also counted the money raised. It wasn't as high as we'd originally hoped for, but we still managed to raise over £120 which was a great contribution for the school. The final pieces were put in place and everyone could see the big picture and who they had been painting. It looked absolutely brilliant and we were all so proud of the children for doing such great work.

At the end of the fair, we drove home feeling content that we'd made a difference, but the grief reared its head so quickly. I was going home to a big house that didn't have my mum anymore. I had to do something to remind me of her. To keep her memory alive.

On the Sunday I spent all day creating a lasting memory of Mum. I found some favourite photos, including some with her friends, her family (sisters), with my dad, brother and I. I created an A4 sheet which I folded into a concertina style card, so it had a front and back cover. I wrote a message on the back which ended with 'until we meet again'. I wrote it for Mum. It's what she would have hoped for. It's what she had believed in for over 40 years. I just didn't believe what I'd written. How could I. She'd been faithful to her god for so long and he'd snatched her away in the cruellest way possible. That's not a loving god. My belief in god was finalised. I no longer believed in his existence. I didn't replace that view with anything and I didn't feel I was missing anything either, apart from my mum.

Mum was being cremated and we'd contacted as many of her friend's as we could, along with telling her two sisters. One lived in Canada, so we knew she wouldn't be able to come. I'd made sure she knew her sister's husband wasn't welcome and that the message would get passed on.

The day of the cremation, Mum was taken in the funeral car with Paul, Sammy, my brother and I in the car behind. As the two cars drove up the incredibly long drive to the crematorium, Paul told me to look out the back window of the car. There were cars following us as far as the eye could see. I'd never seen such a long procession of cars. I thought perhaps some were for a later funeral. Paul told me they were all for my mum. I was overwhelmed with grief, tears streaming down my face, but at the same time so incredibly proud of my mum. The mum that was loved by so many people. In one of the cars was my eldest stepson and his mum. It was such a touching thought that they came to support me at my mum's funeral. I will never forget their kindness.

We got out of the car and to my horror I could see Mum's sister with her husband standing in the car park. I shouted that Mum didn't want him here, but my brother held my shoulder and told me to leave it. He felt sure it would all be OK.

I had lots of prints of the memory cards I'd created. I stood in the crematorium and handed them to people as they came in. More and more people came in and we were just blown away by how many people had arrived for our mum. It was breath taking. Friends had travelled from one end of the country to the other. All to come and pay their respects for our mum. I ran out of cards and had to take email addresses so I could send them a copy.

Mum's dear friend ran the service. It was utterly beautiful. He knew Mum so well. He'd known her for so long. He made us smile, laugh and cry with the words he said. As we all went outside, we all received so many wonderful comments about what a loving and kind woman she had been. How they would treasure the card made in her memory.

Another friend of Mum's had invited everyone to their house for tea and cake. It was a lovely experience and we chatted with so many people, many of whom had known me since I was a child. My stepson came up to me just before he was leaving, to comment on what lovely people they all were, how lucky my mum had been to have such lovely friends and what a beautiful service Mum had received. That was a truly precious moment for me.

Paul, Sammy, my brother and I left the house and made our way back home. I felt stronger than I'd felt since Mum passed away, but the tears still kept flowing every time I thought of her, which was most of the time.

It was around 3 weeks after the funeral. I was lying in bed. Paul had dropped off to sleep and I was just letting thoughts run through my head. As I turned to face the door, I felt the coldest sensation run over my body, arms and shoulder. It made me shiver. I got out of bed thinking I'd left a window open, but I hadn't. Very odd. I hoped I wasn't coming down with something, like Flu!

Age 45-46

Life does go on after you've lost a loved one but it's hard to accept. They say time heals. You don't want to believe it and it doesn't seem right, but it is true. When I first went back to work after the funeral, I'd often find myself weeping because of something someone said, something I heard or something or someone I saw.

It was several weeks before I felt myself calming down and being able to get through a day without tears. I'd taken my time about sorting out the annexe and disposing of Mum's clothes and her few possessions. It wasn't difficult to execute the will and I'd done it all in no time. That didn't seem right. It all came down to sorting out a bit of money and deciding what to do with some personal possessions. I found that so hard. Was that it. I had the memory of who Mum was and what she'd done in her life. Now wasn't the time to dwell on a lot of it. I had a house to work on and a job to get back to. I had a family and bills to pay.

I went full force back into my job. My job was getting harder and I had a lot to get done and deliver. My working day got longer and longer. I spent time travelling to London a lot and further afield.

I had times when I didn't feel so good and Paul was worried that I was going to burn out. We kept talking about the house and that we didn't need it, with it being so big for just 3 of us. There were some parts of the house that needed to be finished so we worked on them every weekend.

Mum had been gone just over a year when we put the house on the market. We decided we were going to move to the country and that would help me. We decided moving to a more relaxed environment, away from the city, which would take a lot of pressure off of me!

We didn't really know where we wanted to move to. Paul wanted to carry on with his photography business, so we knew we'd have to find a home which had an out-house or room for a small studio. We thought of Somerset or Wiltshire. I found a number of properties online and arranged viewing across a couple of days. The three of us drove down early on the Saturday, saw each house I'd planned, and drove home in the evening. The next morning, we did the same. There was nothing we particularly liked. Somerset was not for us. We'd try Wiltshire next.

Again, I found properties that were potentially suitable and lined up viewings over a couple of days. The first day we saw three. They were awful and not even close to being suitable. The second day we saw what was an Antique Shop, which was part of a house. Part of the house and shop were built in 1720. We had a good look around and had a positive feeling about the place. The shop could be the photo studio. The upstairs part of the shop could be converted into our daughter's bedroom. It had an old workshop attached to the house which had no upper floor, but did have windows at an upper floor level. It had been partially converted many years before but never finished. We worked out that with a floor put in, and doorways created from the main house and shop, we could have another photo studio room downstairs and a master bedroom upstairs. We sat in the village pub and talked it all through. We asked the staff about local schools for Sammy. The information we got about the school they mentioned, and the fact that it centred on Performing Arts, was exactly what we were looking for. We decided there and then to put in an offer. The offer was accepted as we drove home to Surrey.

Moves are incredibly stressful and this was no different. There was an extra challenge of Sammy needing to start the new school in Wiltshire in the September, but the 'chain' wasn't going to be ready in time. We found a holiday chalet for Paul and Sammy to rent for a week and a different holiday chalet for a second week. If everything then went according to plan, we'd move into the house at the end of their two weeks.

It did go according to plan. I carried on working during the day, finished packing up last minute things in the evening and then on the day supervised the removal company. I packed the car with personal belongings, two dogs and a cat and then drove for just over 2 hours.

Paul had picked up the keys from the estate agent so we were able to go in together as soon as I arrived. Sammy was at school. We got the pets into the house and unpacked both our cars. The removal van was with us soon after and everything got unloaded into the rooms we specified.

I'd already got a quote for the work we needed doing and the builders were starting some monumental changes just a couple of weeks after we'd move in, including knocking doorways through 18-inch-thick stone walls. This time I didn't have to be in the vicinity of the work, so could get on with my job in relative silence.

In the garden was an apple tree. It brought back memories of an apple tree my mum and dad had in the garden of my childhood house. That seemed to make this house all the more special.

All the work was completed and we were delighted with our new home. The following spring our front garden had masses of bluebells. A favourite flower of my mum's. Was this a sign from Mum that we had got it right or was it just me trying to make a connection?

Paul got his studio up and running which brought in the funding for Sammy to go to a Musical Theatre Performing Arts group every Saturday. Sammy also joined an after-school choir. We could see she was developing well with both and were so happy with the move we'd made.

We started out with great intentions of going to local events and getting involved with the community. We enjoyed the scenery, taking our dogs for walks across multiple fields, seeing the cows along the way. I taught myself to make things (cooking) to put into the village 'Annual Autumn Show' which included fruit and vegetables people had grown, art (including photographs, paintings, drawings, sculpture) and children's contribution from the local school. Sammy and I were asked to be judges for some of the children's written work and paintings.

We spent time at the weekend learning Sammy's dance routines for the next show she was performing in, and became more and more involved with the Performing Arts group. Paul became the photographer for all the children's show photos and filmed all the shows so parents could buy the DVD. The price charged to parents was never sufficient to cover the hours of work, but we became more and more part of the team; with both teachers and parents.

I was starting to feel tired and achy, but as usual I kept going.

Age 47-49

I was experiencing pain in my joints on and off, and at times would feel extremely tired. I became a regular visitor at the GP surgery as something was clearly wrong. My diagnosis was repeatedly put down to menopause, my age and working too hard.

As the months went by, the symptoms got worse. I was finding it harder and harder to concentrate. I was extremely tired and finding it hard just to walk from one room to another. I was getting headaches, pain and tenderness over the temples, jaw pain during work calls and my vision was all over the place. I went to the opticians for an eye test, got prescribed a new pair of glasses. When I went back 4 days later to collect them, I tried them on and they were all wrong. They retested my eyes to find the prescription had changed! That kept happening, so I scrapped any idea of getting new glasses.

Paul was getting more and more requests to run photography weekends, teaching amateurs. Paul also ran glamour model weekends, for several amateur photographers. There were regular models who came. They earnt good money. Both Sammy and I got to know most of them. It wasn't something I particularly liked, but I knew Paul wanted to make a success of the studio.

What I hadn't taken the time to understand, or appreciate, was the impact this was having on Sammy. With her bedroom being above the studio, there was many a time she would hear the amateur photographers talking about the models and how they looked. Sammy was at a critical stage in her teenage years and, as I did at that age, had many issues with self-confidence and indeed body confidence. Hearing a man talk about a models' beautiful face or sexy body/shape was not what she wanted to hear. I should have realised the guys would talk that way. I got to know when the damage had already been done. When her self-esteem took a plunge.

I also didn't take time to appreciate the impact it was having on me or my marriage. Hearing your own husband flirting with models and telling them how fantastic they look didn't help my own self-esteem. I was incredibly overweight, at 240 lbs, and seeing the models made me feel wholly inadequate. I turned my back on it all. Many times, I'd said to Paul, 'You never tell me I'm sexy'. He'd say, 'You're different, I love you!'. I hated it and switched myself off from it. I had to.

I had to focus on my job. I was up early in the morning, working all day. Rushing downstairs for dinner, then rushing back up to carry on working until late into the evening. Saturdays and Sundays were spent with Sammy, going to her Musical Theatre group, going around the shops, having breakfast or lunch in a coffee shop, making dinner and then watching TV in the evening.

Paul's social life was with his models and photographers and mine was with Sammy two days a week. My social life was my work. The people I worked with, managed and knew, which was hundreds of people. Working in a global team, with so many characters is such an incredible network of people. Everyone having a professional edge, with differing skills and character traits. Managing and working with such a diverse group is something I had learnt over so many years. I didn't always get things right, but I loved every minute of it. As a team, we could deliver so much and the reward of knowing we'd achieved a great result was worth the effort, as well as the potential financial reward when it came to pay review and bonus time!

Our marriage hit an all-time low. Sammy was sitting at the dining room table and all of a sudden said, 'you talk like you two hate each other'. She was right. I did hate him. I hated him for the work he was doing, the people he was photographing, for not feeling like I was valued, for not feeling loved, for not loving or caring about myself. I hated myself for the mental and physical place I was in.

We knew we needed help and went to Marriage Guidance. We only went for 2 sessions. We found the lady that ran the sessions so incredibly boring, we actually came out laughing. We laughed so much we started to cry. A mix of tears of sadness and joy. We knew at that point that we did love each other and needed to work hard to make things better.

As my symptoms got worse, my diagnosis changed. Initially I was diagnosed with Polymyalgia Rheumatica, but later was told it could be Temporal Arteritis. I was urgently referred to the hospital where I had an operation to remove a piece of my temporal artery. A few days later I was told I didn't have Temporal Arteritis and was then referred to the Rheumatology Department.

I suppose I should have laughed when the consultant said, 'I don't know why they thought you have Temporal Arteritis. I can see immediately that you haven't'. Why the hell had I had a piece of my artery removed! He was a very abrupt man and after an incredibly brief conversation, he said he was going to refer me to a neurologist. He implied that whatever was wrong with me was most likely neurological! The implication of his words were that he clearly thought it was all in my head!

I felt so tired, exhausted and crushed. Was I imagining it all? Was I making myself ill? How could my own brain make me like this? I walked so slowly to the car, my limbs were so tired and so heavy. I got in the car and cried. I cried until I couldn't bear the pain anymore. Until my throat muscles felt like they were crushing my windpipe. What was happening to me? Me, the person who helps other people. The person who always works so hard. The capable and dependable one.

I sat in the car for nearly an hour. Eyes shut and trying desperately to focus. Focus on what I needed to do next. Drive home. It wasn't a long drive, and I knew the journey inside out. The traffic was reasonably light, so I got going and drove home very slowly. Concentrating on every car, traffic light, junction, pedestrian, zebra crossing, dog, cat, rustle in the trees. At last I got home. Home felt safe right now. I told Paul about everything that had been said and cried all over again. Paul, ever the pragmatist said, you need to go to the GP tomorrow and ask for a private referral to the neurologist. You've got work health cover, so use it. Of course, he was right, but right now I just needed to be told it would all go away and everything would be O.K!

My visit to the GP got my private referral to the Neurologist completed really quickly. I had no idea what the neurologist would say or do, but I had to remain hopeful.

My first visit was for a brain scan which was followed by a face to face discussion with the Neurologist. The Neurologist said there was nothing in the scan that gave any indications of there being something neurologically wrong, although did mention that my arteries were rather narrow!

He asked me if I would mind him giving me a physical examination as he thought he knew what the problem might be. He could have asked me to jump out the window if it meant getting an answer.

I laid on the couch and he pressed either side of my body, starting at the outside of my shoulders and working his way down to my ankles. There were so many places that he pressed where I screamed with pain. In less than 10 minutes, since laying down, he told me I had Fibromyalgia.

I was utterly speechless. A girlfriend of mine had Fibromyalgia and had done so for many years. She hadn't been able to work for years. I'd spent many an hour over the years talking about just some of her symptoms. I had even resonated with some of them, recalling things I'd experienced over the years. I'd never made a connection. She had, but didn't tell me, in the hope she was wrong.

Over the coming weeks I was prescribed Tramadol painkillers which it was recommended I take with Paracetamol as this enhanced the effects. I was allowed to take up to 8 Tramadol in 24 hours, together with up to 8 Paracetamol. In those early days I took the lot. I've heard stories of people falling asleep on just 2 Tramadol. There were times I wished they would make me fall asleep, but I had already been victim to night time insomnia over the years, and it didn't change. They did help with the pain relief though, so that was all good.

My exhaustion went unchanged. I'd get up in the morning and go straight into my home office, work all day, mostly eat meals upstairs and then collapse into bed in the evening. Paul had already taken to sleeping in our guest room, just to give me an uninterrupted night. The doctor had also prescribed me Nortryptoline, which had historically been an anti-depressant but was often used as a medication to aide sleep. I found that by taking it at 8pm, and then taking my last Tramadol and Paracetamol at 10pm, I could go to bed at 11pm and sleep through until somewhere between 4am and 6am.

My boss came to see me several times to see how he could help. There was nothing that was going to help. I had to find a way for me to cope with it and be able to work and continue to pay the mortgage and household bills. That was my responsibility. I was determined to keep going.

I was assessed for all sorts of equipment so I could work at home effectively.

I had a huge desk, a custom-made chair, large screen, voice recognition software to minimise my need to type, a special phone with cordless headset so I didn't have to hold the phone.

It took time to adapt to all of the new equipment, especially the voice recognition. I got so frustrated with it that I often resorted to typing myself. Then my hands would cramp and become so painful I'd have to stop. Even with all the new equipment, I was constantly on calls and speaking so much that my throat muscles would be in excruciating pain and I'd struggle to eat and swallow.

The medication was helping with pain to a certain level, and I was getting a few hours' sleep each night, but I was experiencing higher levels of exhaustion and fatigue.

I rarely ventured anywhere for work, but was told by my boss that he wanted me to attend a work conference which was extremely important and my input was needed. I knew I couldn't do the drive; I was given permission to arrange a taxi to take me there and for another to bring me home on the final day, the cost was over £200 each way. I thought it was mad for me to go at that expense, but I was considered important enough to attend.

The conference went well and my attendance was appreciated. My boss was incredibly caring and over the coming months gradually changed my role to become more consultative, which took a lot of physical strain away. I was hugely grateful and felt I could cope each day.

Over time I got more and more involved in a small project to create a bespoke system which could have potential benefit to the wider global organisation. I worked on this with a handful of people in the team. We struggled to get financial backing and, in the end, we closed the project.

There was a wider system requirement which the global organisation needed to capture everyone's requirements for, as it would affect many countries and their bespoke systems. A conference had been arranged for over 100+ people to attend. One of them being me! I had a wealth of knowledge which I could contribute.

I pushed myself harder than ever and managed to attend the conference. It was hugely complex and was going to need radical changes to multiple legacy systems across the globe. Some systems I knew inside out but many others I hadn't encountered before. My pace of walking was painstakingly slow. My legs were like lead as I dragged one in front of the other. I can't imagine what I looked like to others I'd never met before. I was so grateful my brain was functioning well enough for me to add value to the event. I thoroughly enjoyed meeting so many people from across the globe.

We'd had enough re-organisation and changes at work over the years I'd been with them. I knew enough and should have been more prepared than I was for what came next.

The organisation I was working with was to be disbanded. Most of the senior managers had agreed to take redundancy or had found alternative roles in the company. My boss told me it had been agreed I would be transferred to a new team. I was to manage the transition of our former organisational team who would be moving across to the same team as myself, or to another part of the company.

I managed it with my usual attention to detail and professionalism, making sure every person was managed professionally. There were 00's of people to be organisationally moved, and involved many countries around the globe. My attention to detail came at a high price. I was having to work harder and longer hours to achieve what was needed and what I'd in the past done in half the time. I'd often work through the night just to keep up.

As this piece of work came to a close, I was gradually given more and more project related work. I hadn't done project work at this level for quite some time, so had to get myself back up to speed. I was finding it hard as I was finding it hard to recall things. I had to take more and more notes, which increased my physical and mental fatigue.

Age 50-52

I still took Sammy to her Musical Theatre group every Saturday. I'd conserve energy until it was time to go, then drive the 20-25-minute journey. Then I'd sit in a side room and lay across several seats or stay in the car with the seat back and doze until Sammy was ready to return home. I was so determined to keep this routine going and wasn't going to let the Fibro stop me.

Occasionally we'd go into town early and Sammy would walk at a snail's pace with me from the car to a coffee shop so we could have brunch together before going to her group. It was lovely to spend our time together and watch the world go by.

We took a family holiday to Denmark, so we could spend some time with my brother. He'd managed to borrow a flat from his friend Thomas, so we had a base to stay. Paul and Sammy worked out every trip so I could conserve all of my energy. It was a great flat, and even had a projector and large screen so we could watch films on a big screen.

As the weeks and months went by, I became more and more entrenched as a member of a small team who were managing the global system project. I was then informed I was to be the sole Project Manager and given a delivery timescale and budget to deliver against. ALARM BELLS!!

The alarm bells were ringing at all levels; my ability to deliver a global project which many of the senior team were unsupportive of, a delivery team who didn't have the knowledge or skills to deliver, a budget that was too small and an impossible timeline.

I was flattered they thought I could manage the project, but was concerned about whether I could actually deliver it.

My working hours increased exponentially. I was working flat out from 07:00 to often 01:00 the next morning. I was on non-stop project calls with people across the globe; taking account of time differences, language barriers, knowledge barriers, interpretation issues. None of this is unusual in projects that run into £multi-million, but my health was diving to an all-time low.

I was managing calls and not being able to recall the last conversation I'd just had. I had calls where my hearing would stop me picking up certain voices due to their pitch and I'd be receiving messages from people asking why I wasn't responding to what they'd said.

My Fibro symptoms were increasing. In a book I'd read, there were a list of 60 symptoms. In the space of 6 months, I had encountered 59 of them!

I was falling apart. I was under so much strain. I was initiating calls with my boss and senior leadership team and ending up in tears. I wasn't planning to cry. It just happened and I couldn't control it. It happened to be one of the symptoms on the list. I explained it repeatedly.

I kept going, and eventually another person was put onto the team to take the lead role in getting the system delivered. They had a systems delivery background. We worked really well together. I took them through everything that had been done, that couldn't be done, that needed to be done and reasons why it hadn't. They could immediately see why I was struggling. The project couldn't be delivered at the budget or timescales required. We worked together to keep driving it forward and they took key messages back to the Head of the Global Organisation.

We met a couple of times, when I felt well enough to travel to London. They were amazed at how I was able to work with such a debilitating condition and repeatedly asked if I should be working at all. I kept asking myself the same question and repeatedly got the same answer.

I had to keep working. I paid the mortgage and the bills. I wanted to be the capable, high performing person I'd been all my working life.

So many times, Paul asked me, 'When are you going to stop trying to prove to your dad that you're good enough?'

A great question, but one I didn't have the answer for right now.

Age 53-54

enjoyed working with my new boss, but continued to struggle each and every day. I was trying to work at the same level, but finding it harder and harder to achieve. We agreed a change to the way we worked and they took more of the work from me. I felt we were being more effective with our new way of working, but the pressure to deliver to unachievable timescales never went away. I knew the stress was having an impact on me. I was more and more exhausted. There didn't seem to be anything I could do to recover from one day to the next.

All employees had regular performance reviews. I was now being told I was under performing. In all of my 35-year career in the company, I had been classed as a very good or outstanding performer. This was a devastating blow to someone who constantly excelled at work. I had to work harder, but knew I couldn't.

Sammy was doing incredibly well at her Musical Theatre group and they had been chosen to perform at Her Majesty's Theatre in London. Paul and I had made arrangements for our dogs, so we could go with them all and see their performance. Paul drove us to the meeting point, and Paul helped me onto the coach and got us seated downstairs. Sammy sat with all her friends.

When we arrived in London, Paul and I had to find things to do for a few hours until showtime. Paul walked me across the road, very slowly, to an Art Gallery. I simply didn't have enough energy to walk any further. Paul looked around the gallery and came back to find me, when he found things, he thought I might like to see. I got to view a couple of art pieces which were interesting and didn't have much walking to do. When we'd had enough, Paul walked me back out of the museum. We got back to the traffic lights and Paul suggested we walk to a multi-story bookshop. We hoped to find a chair I could sit in while Paul look for books, and I rested and hopefully regained some energy or at least conserve what little amount I had left.

We got to the bookshop and Paul steered me straight to the lift. He hoped that the 4th floor would be less busy and would have some empty armchairs to sit in. Other people got in the lift and upward we went. The lift stopped and I have no idea why, but I started to get out of the lift. Paul said, 'this is only the 2nd floor and we were going to go the 4th'. 'Never mind, there's an empty sofa over there. I'll sit on that', I told him.

It was a lovely comfy leather sofa, and Paul held my hands as I lowered myself down. I knew it was going to be a struggle to get back up again, but at that moment in time it didn't matter. Paul said he'd go and have a look around while I rested. I sat with my eyes closed for

98

some time. When I opened them, I took a look around me. To my left, there was a whole wall of bookshelves which were marked as 'Medical'. A while later Paul came back with 3 books he'd found and was going to take a look at. I asked him if he could go over to the medical books and see if he could find any on Fibromyalgia. It didn't take him long and he came back with a book for me to look at.

I started reading and by the time I'd got to the 3rd chapter, it was like I'd just read parts of my own life story. I carried on reading, fascinated by every word it had to say. I hadn't realised how long I'd been reading for. Paul suddenly said, we need to get up and go, the bookshop is closing in 15 minutes. Paul helped me out of the sofa and he went straight to the cashier to buy the books he'd found, plus my one of course. I wasn't going to leave without it.

We took a slow walk back toward the Theatre and fortunately we were allowed to go in, even though it was too early for the performances. Paul found me a seat in the bar room and we both had a soft drink. I was so looking forward to seeing Sammy and the rest of her group perform. I was also looking forward to being at home so I could climb into bed and crash.

It was time for the show. There were several groups from around the country. All of the performances were well presented and you could see how hard so many of the children had worked. Sammy's group came on to perform. Sammy was due to have a microphone, as were three or four others in her group of 20+ children. They performed brilliantly and I could see Sammy was putting her heart and soul into her singing. Tragically no-one could hear her. The microphone she'd been given was broken. Sammy was devastated, as were the team, as was her singing coach. Paul and I were devasted too. We knew how important the whole experience was for her and how much we had been looking forward to seeing her on such an important stage. I could feel the anger welling up inside me body and my energy draining away. I was finding it hard to focus on any of the remaining performances. I just wanted to give Sammy a huge hug and go home.

A few days later, Paul and I talked everything through and came to the only conclusion that was worth taking forward.

Sell the house.

Move to another location. Somewhere nearer a town and less isolated.

Buy a house and be mortgage free.

Take redundancy.

Take early retirement.

As much as I knew it was the right answer, I felt like I was failing. Failing to achieve my goal of 40 years work service. Failing to achieve my personal goal of delivering a significant global project. Failing my family, by making them move again. Failing to live up to my dad's expectations!

I spent several weeks going over and over the finances and working out if or how I could make it all work.

Eventually I reached a conclusion. We would move. We would find a house mortgage free. I could take redundancy and get an early pension that was enough for us to live on.

We put our house on the market quickly. We knew it could be a challenge finding a buyer as it was a house with an integral shop. A very bespoke property which wouldn't appeal to many people.

We got a few viewings which didn't lead to anything. After a few weeks, we got a viewing and they fell in love with the house. They made an offer and we accepted.

It wasn't straight forward. Our house wasn't built with a damp course. They didn't have such a thing in the 1700's. Their mortgage company wanted a full & detailed survey, which highlighted the property needed to be 'tanked' to prevent invasive flooding. Tanking would mean digging down through the floor of 3 rooms downstairs, put a liner in and then fill it in again. Fortunately, they still wanted to buy the house, but I had to take a significant reduction on the asking price.

I couldn't take the chance of not getting the house sold. Our future depended on it, so I agreed. A reduction of over £20,000. It was a devastating blow and would mean I would have less money to manage once I stopped working. That worried me a lot.

The sale was now full steam ahead, but where would we live?

I arranged, and took, a few days off work which coincided with one of Sammy's school holidays. We decided we liked the idea of living near the sea. We'd never done that before, so we booked a room in Weymouth. Why Weymouth? No specific reason. We'd stuck a pin in the map and it was closest! I arranged a couple of properties for us to view.

We saw the properties. I hated them all. The estate agents took us to see others. I hated them too. I hated the area. It all felt completely wrong. On our last morning, we were sitting in the breakfast room of the B&B, and were talking about what we'd do next and where we would start looking. In the corner of the room there were a couple of people having their breakfast. Paul had his back to them and heard a 'chink chink' sound. It was the exact sound my mum used to make when she was stirring her tea. Two chinks.

'Oh, my goodness', Paul said. 'Your mum is here'.

'That's tough', I said. 'I'm not living here, so I hope she's here for another reason'.

We all laughed and forgot all about it.

Back at home, Paul and I were looking for properties online. Friends of ours were moving to Hampshire, near the coast, so we started looking at houses in that area. It would be nice to move to somewhere with a couple of friends close by.

Both Paul and I found the same house. Paul had fallen in love with the kitchen and said, 'This is the house we are going to live in'.

I made arrangements for us to view it and Paul drove us down on the Saturday morning. There were several people viewing the same house that morning, so we felt like we were in some bizarre queuing system.

Paul and I were shown round the house and knew straight away it was the right house. Everything about it was right. It didn't need any work done to it so we could simply move in. It was exactly on budget. What made us realise it was exactly the right house was its address, which started with 'Weymouth'.

Now I understood why Mum had been with us in Weymouth on our last day. We went straight to the estate agent and put in an immediate offer of the asking price. There was no point in insulting the sellers. The house was worth what they were asking. They had priced it at the maximum they could without it going into the next price threshold that incurred higher fees. They had a couple of other people who had made exactly the same offer. None of us were prepared to increase the offer due to the increase of fees. Our offer was accepted because we were already a long way down the process of selling our house, so the timing fitted in with the family that were selling this one.

They say selling houses is one of the top 5 most stressful things in your life. Many things didn't go to plan and my health was being impacted every day as a result.

The higher the stress, the worse I got. My stress levels were escalating with work, the move and my own thoughts around everything. My memory was getting so poor, I couldn't even manage straightforward calls at work, let alone more complex ones.

We at last had a date for the move, which everyone agreed to. Paul was so concerned about my health that he made an appointment to see my GP. Paul drove me there and came in with me this time. The GP asked me a couple of simple questions and I burst into tears. I couldn't stop crying. Paul told the GP about how I wasn't coping with work, that we were moving and the stress of everything was making my health deteriorate. She agreed with Paul that I couldn't carry on working in this condition and signed me off work, with no end date. That sounded like a great plan, but to me, I was failing again.

We were due to move in the December but Sammy needed to stay in Wiltshire for 3 months beyond the move date, and a friend agreed for Paul and Sammy to live in their house for 3 months.

The night before the move I slept in our house with our 2 dogs, while Paul and Sammy slept at our friend's house. Paul was with me early the next morning for when the removal company arrived. Our entire home was packed into their lorry and off they went. We packed the last of our personnel effects into my car, and the 2 dogs. I hugged and kissed Paul and said I'd see him at the new house.

I drove from Wiltshire to Hampshire with two dogs in the back. It was reminiscent of the move from Surrey to Wiltshire in many ways. The difference was my health. I had taken 4 painkillers just before leaving so I had a chance of being able to do the drive. Paul drove down in Sammy's car and went direct to the Estate Agent to collect the keys.

I arrived at the new house 2.5 hours later. The removal van was already outside the house waiting. They were getting impatient. I was just grateful to have got there. Paul rang me to say he was at the Estate Agent. We were all waiting. Waiting for the solicitor to confirm everything was done, monies had moved and we could move in. We waited. Waited until 14:30 and then we got the call. Now we waited for Paul to get the keys and drive to our new house to let us all in. That took another 30 minutes and then it was all systems go.

I got the box of essentials unpacked and made everyone teas and coffees. I made sure the dogs were OK in the garden and put drinking bowls at the back door for them. It was much safer to keep them in the garden than watch them get stressed or under our feet as furniture got brought in. Everything went well and the van was emptied and everything moved into the house and garden by 19:00.

Paul also had to leave and drive back to Wiltshire, so Sammy wouldn't be on her own in a strange house.

I was now on my own in our new house, with two dogs. I got the dogs settled downstairs and went to bed. I didn't have any more energy to do more. It could all wait.

It felt so very strange when I got up the next morning. It was just me and two dogs. I had a list of essentials that needed to be done, not least get our internet connections up and working. That didn't go according to plan, despite my having made all the arrangements before the move. I had to jump through many hurdles to get even basic connections set up. After a few days I managed to get everything in place and was able to connect up for my work, even though I was still signed off.

I then spoke to my boss and told him I was going to apply for redundancy. He laughed and said he was surprised I hadn't done it already. There were no issues and everyone would be supporting my application. I applied the same day and in a matter of days got formal notification that I would be leaving on 31 December, 2014. It was great getting the confirmation and it lifted a weight, but I burst into tears. This was ending my career and everything I had worked for.

I unpacked a box at a time, often pushing myself too hard and ending up exhausted again. Paul and Sammy came down at weekends and pitched in with unpacking boxes. They were both amazed at how much I had managed to do and that it actually looked like a home.

Paul hugged me when I told him my leave date was confirmed. He was delighted that I wouldn't be working myself into the grave and could concentrate on getting my health to a better place. I had no idea what that would look or feel like. I just wanted to rest.

We had a simple Christmas in our new house, with Paul's mum, as always. Our friends came around on Boxing Day and we saw other friends and family over the following days. Straight after the Christmas break, Paul and Sammy were back in Wiltshire.

I created myself a routine in the house, and seemed to manage reasonably well. I didn't have the energy to walk the dogs during the week, so they had to make do with the back garden. Paul would take them out for long walks when he came down at the weekend.

My brother had arranged to come over from where he lives and stay with me for 3 weeks during February. That was something to look forward to and would mean I'd have someone to help me around the house. Except it wasn't as straightforward as that. I was due to collect him from Gatwick Airport, but had to shelve that idea as I'd got a call from Paul telling me his mum had broken her arm and the hospital were refusing to let her go back to her flat as she would be unable to look after herself. If it was OK, he would drive from Wiltshire to Surrey, pick her up from the hospital, get some clothes from her flat and then bring her straight down to me.

What else could I say, other than yes. I told my brother he would have to get the train from the airport when he landed at Gatwick, but I'd be able to pick him up from our local station. My brother wasn't well himself, and was suffering with mental health problems. The anxiety of the trip, and my not being at the airport to pick him up resulted in a major anxiety attack and paramedics were called. I got a phone call from my brother telling me what had happened and I spoke to the team, asking if he was well enough to travel on the train. We agreed they'd get him on the train and I would be at the other end when the train was due to arrive. My mother in law would be OK for an hour without me.

I drove to the station and got there much earlier than I needed to. I spoke to the station staff and explained what had happened to my brother. They were brilliant. They were all waiting on the platform with me when the train pulled in and waited until I gave them the thumbs up when I'd spotted my brother. They waited to make sure he was OK and made sure we got across the platforms safely. My brother was not in a good place, but at least he was now with me and safe.

My mum in law got absolutely pampered having both my brother and I waiting on her hand and foot. We took her down to a café on the seafront which she thoroughly enjoyed. Getting her washed and dressed was a challenge as she had a full cast from shoulder to hand which was bent at the elbow. We managed though. It all helped my brother in a way, as having someone else to focus on was good for him at that moment in time.

My levels of exhaustion were continually changing. Some days I found I could push myself that bit more and not have significant repercussions, but then I didn't have any major challenges to face. Looking after my mum-in-law was a challenge, but nothing I hadn't done before.

My brother went back to his own home and I carried on looking after my mum-in-law. When Paul and Sammy arrived at the end of March, I felt a bit overwhelmed. Suddenly my routine was completely thrown into disarray. I had become used to doing things in a certain way and going out to the seafront café amongst other places. Paul didn't find them to be that special and over time I simply stopped going.

It was lovely to have them both home for good and it made getting things done around the house so much easier and less work for me. I was able to rest so much more. It was lovely not having to do so much.

Age 55-56

I knew I had to do something about my weight, and get rid of my diabetes. Now I wasn't working, I had the chance to focus on it and do something about it. By chance I found an advert on Facebook for 'Beyond Diet' and signed up for it. I weighed 221 lbs.

My main project was getting the back garden into something of interest. It had a lawn and a border on the right-hand side, but apart from 3 trees, it had absolutely no plant life. The soil was hard and solid. Not a worm to be seen!

Little by little I dug the soil with a fork and spade. It was painstaking work and I could only do a very small amount at a time. Some days I didn't have the energy to do any. Over the months, I worked in a lot of compost, aeriated the soil and began putting perennial plants in.

Most of my time going out was to look for and find plants. I found one particular place which I enjoyed just to be able to sit amongst the plants and relax. I'd often go there and come home without a plant. It had become a form of social life. A life among plants. Very calming, but not so good on the conversation front.

My brother called with devastating news. His best friend Thomas, who we'd borrowed the flat from a few years before, had committed suicide. It was hard to take in everything he was saying. I'd known that Thomas and his girlfriend were looking to buy a home together, and there had even been talk of my brother moving into the house too. Now that was all gone. I had no idea that Thomas was struggling and my brother hadn't seen it coming either, even though they knew each other so well. Oh my, how on earth would my brother cope with this. He'd already lost an incredibly close friend, our parents and now this. Loss was something he struggled with deeply. I had no answers to give, just all the love I could muster.

My brother's mental health deterioration was rapid and concerning. During our conversations he was expressing paranoia over having a shower in his bathroom, to the point he hadn't used it in weeks. The flat didn't have a bath, so that was concerning me greatly. Paul and I agreed we'd go over for a week and fix the problems in the bathroom and decorate it as best we could. At the same time, I could give my brother as much mental help and support as possible. I knew he was seeing the psychiatrist regularly, so at least that was helpful. Paul worked like a trojan and I did as much as I could when I could. I was slow and methodical. I achieved far beyond anything I'd managed before, and an incredible amount in one week. All of the bathroom problems were fixed and the whole room painted. I made sure my brother ate food every day so his physical health got some support.

It was so incredibly painful to leave him at the end of the week. I knew he was far from right but I couldn't stay any longer. I'd spoken to some of his close friends and they were there to help him when he needed it. My whole body hurt and I was close to tears all the way home. Paul kept reassuring me he would be O.K and that I'd done everything I could. It just didn't feel like enough. It wasn't enough. I just knew it. I'd promised Mum. What more could I do? I needed care myself.

My brother's mental state was deteriorating. He'd been in an out of the psychiatric hospital which didn't seem to be helping that much. He was having psychotic episodes regularly. Talking to your brother and hearing him tell you he's having suicidal thoughts and doesn't see any reason to carry on, is just *unbearable*. All I could see was sheer hopelessness and watch him in tears. I'd be trying to talk to him normally while every muscle in my throat would be so tight I could barely breath. Silently crying inside. Telling him everything was going to be O.K. That he was much loved and there was a way forward. We just had to find it. We would find it. When each call ended, I'd be screwed up in a ball on the floor, sobbing and sobbing. Screaming in my head. Not knowing how to help him. Desperately asking Mum to help him. The hospital told him he was their 'most complex case'. My only piece of hope was that I'd seen him cry. To me it meant he must be feeling something.

My brother hit rock bottom again in a matter of days from being released and was back in hospital. Not long after that he got a major infection which had a huge impact on his overall health and well-being. I felt so inadequate. I didn't know what to do or how to fix the situation for him. I needed to find an answer. All I could see was my brother bumping along the bottom. I'd find out he'd been discharged and be worried sick about whether he was alright, or whether I needed to do something quickly.

In just a matter of a few weeks, he was admitted again to the psychiatric hospital. He had absolutely no ability to care for himself, he had no will or desire to even exist. This time the hospital decided to take more drastic action. They were going to give him ECT treatment. Our mum had ECT treatment many years before. That didn't fill us with any degree of confidence and I knew my brother was worried sick about what impact it would have on his memory. There didn't seem to be any alternative being suggested, so the hospital went ahead. He did experience some funny memory reactions, weird dreams and had trouble waking up, but after a few weeks his memory was back to normal.

My brother's communicative capability was the worse I'd seen and he was locked in a complete state of loneliness that we just couldn't penetrate. He'd been sent out of the hospital yet again with inadequate medicine and treatment that hadn't helped. He was sleeping a lot of the time, missing appointments because he couldn't even sit himself up. I, and some of his friends, were trying to tell him it was time to move on from the loss of his friend but that was a terrifying thought for him. It was heart breaking to see such little progress, despite the extreme treatment he'd had. With the medication he had been given, his brain was in overdrive, so he wasn't sleeping in any pattern and was just concentrating on the day to day priorities and not any of the next steps that were needed. The day to day priorities didn't even include looking after himself.

Five months after Paul and I had been there decorating the bathroom, I went back. This time with Sammy. My brother wasn't at the airport, as we'd hoped and expected. I tried a few times to call his mobile and eventually got to speak to him. He was so ill he couldn't even get out of bed. This was a twist I hadn't expected, but I knew how to get to the flat so that wasn't an issue. Getting in would be the issue, if he couldn't get up. He had full blow influenza. We got there, and Sammy carried our heavy case all the way up to the flat. Bless her, she knew I'd never manage it. It was enough for me to get myself up the stairs! Phew, he'd managed to open the door. I don't know how best to describe the environment we saw when we got there. There was almost no space to move around. There was furniture and boxes crammed into rooms. My brother had received over 5,000 films from Thomas' estate. They were in crates which overwhelmed his bedroom. You had to squeeze past them to get into the bed. Furniture from the bedroom was now in the living room. My brother was somebody who couldn't let anything go, through emotional attachment, but the problems in the flat were on a whole new scale. The flat was stifling. I had no idea how we were going to manage, but we rolled up our sleeves.

Sammy spent the whole week typing over 500 films, and key details, into a database, so we could start the task of getting rid of DVD boxes and putting them into special DVD cases that could take 1000 DVDs each. The task was painstaking. While Sammy was working on that, I was decorating the very small hall as my brother wanted its colour changed. On the third day, I managed to get him to come out and around the corner so he could look at paint colours. It took so long to choose. I tried making suggestions, but he wasn't open to any of them. The choices got made, even though he still wasn't sure what he wanted and making any decision was incredibly hard.

Later that day I started the job of painting. In-between painting, I was shopping and cooking for all of us. I have absolutely no idea how I managed to do so much. Pure adrenalin. Most days my brother just stayed in bed or sat in a chair to eat a small meal. I'm not sure how best to describe the colour scheme for the incredibly small square of hallway. Unusual would perhaps be the best answer. The walls were of a deep orange hue, with the doors being a mustard colour and paintwork a reddish brown. As unusual as it was, I quite liked it. On the last day, my brother got to see it and I could see he wasn't sure. Too late, it was done now. Once again, I had to leave him in what was now an incredibly chaotic and overwhelming flat, in a state of poor physical health and seeing him making no progress with his mental health. Sammy and I both flew home feeling very low, extremely exhausted and knowing we needed some recovery time.

The payback from my Fibro kicked in as soon as we were home. I did nothing for days. I just needed to recover. Thank goodness I didn't work anymore and had time to just vegetate. Thank goodness I had Paul, who could get the essentials done at home without me.

Just three months after my last visit to my brother, I flew back over again. This time I was on my own. My brother had wanted me to go alone as he felt so claustrophobic in his flat and couldn't stand the thought of any more people. My mission was to start clearing through and tidying up the flat so it became more bearable. My dearest brother was in a very dark place and I told him to take himself to the hospital if he didn't improve. I was there for 2 weeks this time and I spent time going through a few boxes, so we could start to get rid of things he didn't need. The pace was very slow, which suited me very much. I wasn't under the physical pressure I'd had before. My brother's emotional attachment to each and every item was severe and, on many things, I just had to let them remain without any comment. As much as I knew things needed to go, I also could see how painful the whole process was. It was also clear to me that he was still grieving the loss of Thomas and the fact that he wouldn't be moving home. The pain of it all was still too much to bear. We did manage to make some progress with a basement room my brother had and the space we freed up meant we could move some items down there from the flat. I also managed to get a couple of pieces of furniture sold which created some much-needed space. My brother was hugely appreciative of everything I'd done, but as always it didn't feel like it was enough. Leaving him was as painful this time as it had been each time before. He was incredibly anxious about me leaving. I was incredibly worried about what would happen once I'd gone. How would he cope. Would he cope. What if......

Within a couple of days of my leaving, my brother was re-admitted to the hospital. We'd speak every couple of days, so I could gauge how he was doing. I also sent and received messages from one of his friends, so we could compare notes. I had to have faith in the psychiatric team and hope they'd find an answer to help him!

Closer to home, my girlfriend told me about an old lady, who was related to her brothers' ex-wife's family. The family was concerned about her as she'd been put in a nursing home against her will. The nursing home was near both our homes, so I agreed to go along and see if she was OK. It was a distraction, which was something I needed.

Over the weeks, the stories we heard were so startling. The lady's sister and her sister's neighbour had put her into the home, cleared her flat of all possessions and were even collecting her pension but not passing it on. The family were in contact with the lady's solicitor, and we gave as much help as we could.

My visits to the lady became more and more frequent, such was our concern for her well-being. It became a routine for me to visit 3 times a week, and my girlfriend did the same. That left 1 day where we knew her sister and neighbour visited. We couldn't stop them visiting, but the care home staff kept a listening ear when they knew they were in the room just to make sure everything was OK.

I became more and more absorbed with it all, and then we were notified the care home was closing, so she would need to be found somewhere else to go. My girlfriend and I went to see various care homes and eventually found one that we thought was suitable. We met with the solicitor, as they managed the lady's financial affairs, and they agreed to the move.

I had already taken her to see it before the move day and agreed which room she would have. I packed up all her clothes, and few possessions and I took her in my car as it was the easiest for her to be seated in. We got her settled in her room and stayed for a while. Conversation with her was always difficult. She had great understanding and comprehension, but could say very little. Stringing words together rarely happened and we spent most of our time trying to piece together what we thought she wanted to say.

She'd only been there 6 weeks and we could see she was getting more and more agitated. It became clear she wasn't happy in the room she had. I took a walk around the care home with a couple of the staff, to see what other rooms they had available. By chance, one mentioned a room that someone was to have moved into, but wasn't now coming. They took me to see it and I knew immediately that she would be happier in it. I got them to put her in a wheelchair and we took her across to see it for herself. Yes, she loved it. The two staff members, and myself, switched the cabinets and cupboards from one room to the other. It was so easy. They were all on wheels. As soon as we'd finished, I wheeled her into the room which was now hers. It was clear for all of us to see that she was definitely happier, but only time would tell.

Visiting and making sure the lady was comfortable became like a new job for me. When she needed to go to the hospital for a pacemaker check, I went with her in the ambulance. We had found a niece who lived 25 minutes away and I picked her up so she could visit from time to time. I even took the lady to her niece's home on a couple of occasions.

I had completely changed my eating regime, and had lost over 14 pounds which made me start to feel more positive about my life and future, and more importantly my marriage. Even better, I got told by my GP that I was no longer in the diabetic range. In fact, I was outside of the pre-diabetic range. WOW. I got home and cried. Tears of absolute joy and happiness.

Some things in my life were definitely on the UP.

Age 57-58

Sammy and I made another trip to Denmark to visit my brother. In some ways my brother was better but was still very lost, still with a major fear of moving forward. At least the two of us could help with the practical things and hope that made a small difference.

Sammy was working on the film database while I spent time doing cleaning around the flat. Just a couple of days in and the database started playing up. Sammy carried on as best she could but then it crashed completely. There was nothing any of us could do. No matter what we tried it was hopeless. It was beyond anything we had the capability to fix. Sammy was devastated. She'd put in so much hard work and nearly 1000 films in total.

I contacted another friend to see if she had the details of the person, we needed help from and she managed to find them. I told my brother I would contact him, but that was a no go. My brother knew he'd have to contact the person who had given him the database in the first place, but neither of them had been in touch for such a long time. I could see it just wasn't going to happen! By the time we flew home, we had at least managed to get rid of some personal items and make a small dent in everything that needed to be done.

When we got back, Sammy was preparing herself for a new job which meant she would be taking a first step towards her dream of performing, but also being away from home for the first time.

Sammy's singing coach had worked hard with her, and her voice had grown exponentially. A seriously good Soprano. Every time I heard her sing, it brought goose bumps to my skin. She made my heart sing.

I made another trip to visit my brother. It was the hardest visit yet. He was in an incredibly low place. His energy level was dreadful and all I could do was feed him and help him with small scale things which were unbearable for him. I didn't have a clue what or how we could change things for him. As I had so much time to myself, I spent time testing out another idea for a database. I knew it wasn't entirely what my brother wanted, but it would give us another option if he couldn't get the database problem solved. I continued the work I'd done earlier in the year and carried on cleaning and sorting through as much as possible. I so desperately wanted to try and create a space that he would feel more comfortable with and feel safe in his own home. It was an uphill battle, because he hated the flat, where it was and everything about it. I knew this was being exacerbated by his own mental health, but was determined to keep trying.

After I'd returned home, he was re-admitted into the hospital. I was extremely worried about him. This time we got a completely new diagnosis. Schizotypal Personality Disorder. I researched it to death. I read every trait associated with it and realised my brother had every single one. No wonder he was such a complex case. No wonder the medication he was on wasn't right. They'd been medicating for Bi-Polar. He'd become very introvert and difficult to hold conversations with so medication changes were key, but so was making him see he had a future. In just a handful of weeks he'd been discharged and re-admitted several times. He had no energy at all and was completely helpless. At last they agreed their diagnosis of the last 3 years had been wrong, but he needed immediate help. He was just about functioning and couldn't keep his eyes open while he tried to talk. Occasionally the brother I'd known all my life would make brief appearances in the conversation, but was then gone again.

Before I knew what was happening, my brother had been discharged from the hospital. This time he'd had less than a day's notice. In fact, the head doctor had even woken him up to tell him he was going home. No-one else in the team even knew. They were speechless and apologised to my brother. Just 2 days before he'd been told he would be there for a further 3-4 weeks. I was so angry; my temper was raging.

I realised then that I needed to do something. I'd repeatedly asked Mum to help, but that hadn't done anything. Then, all of a sudden, the penny dropped. Mum hadn't helped because I was the one asking for my brother. My brother needed to ask for her help. Now I needed her help. I realised then that I needed to do what I do best. Write to the head doctor at the hospital my brother had been discharged from. I had no idea why they were treating such a severe case in this way, but was sure going to find out.

I spent a long time pondering over the right words. My mum had somehow made me realise I wasn't writing on my brother's behalf; I was writing on my own behalf. As his sister, his next of kin, the one family member he had to fight his corner.

I wrote the letter which covered my concern over the sheer number of diagnosis he'd had. That this had been the longest period of time seeing him in such an incredibly low state. That I understood the complexity of mental health, having had a mum who was paranoid schizophrenic and my brother's diagnosis which I'm sure had some connection. That there had been no sustained improvements in all of that time. That the team were not up to speed and the discharge had been out of line with the expectations of everyone. That I wanted to understand why he'd been discharged and the implications of them having done so on his health and welfare.

A friend of my brothers had found me two email addresses to send the letter to. One for the head doctor who had discharged him and another for a hospital board member.

Now my mum came into action, well at least that's how I see it. My letter to the doctor had gone to an email address she hadn't used in months and was meant to have been closed

111

down. On the day I sent the email, she had for some strange reason decided to go and look at it! My letter was there waiting for her. My brother was contacted and told to re-admit himself. My letter was mentioned to my brother once he was back in, but nothing more was said. I told him I'd read it to him when he was good and ready. There was no rush. He was back where he needed to be to remain safe.

It was time for Sammy to spread her wings and move to her new job. Paul and I helped her pack up my car. It was bursting at the seams. I felt sure I could do the long drive; I was in better health. I'd lost some weight, now being 188 lbs, and was able to move around that bit better. There was no mental stress and strain related to the trip, or at least I didn't think so.

The journey was going to take around 5 + hours. We were going to need many breaks along the way too. Sammy was nervous. I was nervous too. We spent much of the time chatting and singing together. The journey took much longer than expected but we eventually got there. The team she was meeting up with all came out to help her unpack and move everything into the flat where she would be living. I had arranged a Bed and Breakfast stay for one night, so I could sleep before starting my return journey. Leaving Sammy was so hard. I thought my heart was going to burst. My little girl had grown up.

The next morning, I rang Sammy to check if there was anything she needed before I drove home. Just the sound of her voice told me she wasn't O.K. I drove straight to the flat and went in to see what was wrong. We chatted for some time and I felt sure it was nothing more than nerves about living away from home. I reassured her that it was all fine and that I was just at the end of a phone call. I also had a chat with her Manager and he said the whole team were there to support her and she would be just fine. We agreed I would stay in the flat that night, just to give Sammy a bit more support.

In the morning, Sammy seemed a lot better. We hugged, kissed and I told her to ring me anytime if she needed to. I drove out of the road, stopped and burst into tears. I kept telling myself she would be fine, but was worried sick. At that moment, I suddenly felt the weight of the world on my shoulders. Had I done enough to prepare my daughter, had I done enough to help my brother. Had I done enough......

Sammy rang almost daily to start with and we chatted about what she was doing and how well her Manager thought she was doing. As the days went by and turned into weeks, the conversation centred more on other people in the team and how horrible they were toward her. We talked about how she could and would handle situations and the need to talk to her Manager. Sammy and the team all lived in the same flat, so there was nowhere she could go to get away from any fall outs they had.

Sammy was clearly struggling and we agreed she should speak to the local GP for some advice.

It was four months to the day when I got the phone call from Sammy when she said, 'I want it all to end'.

The scream inside my body felt like it was consuming me. In an incredibly calm voice I said, 'Where are you now, sweetheart'. 'I'm in the flat, in my room, Sammy told me. I told her, 'Dad and I are getting in the car now and are on our way. We are bringing you home. You know it's going to take us a few hours to get there. Stay in your room and don't go anywhere'. Sammy needed us NOW.

Paul had heard the conversation about us getting in the car and knew it was incredibly important. I told him word for word what Sammy had said. We both sobbed as Paul drove away from the house. Five and half hours later we were in Sammy's room. I almost didn't recognise my daughter as I climbed over all her stuff which was strewn around the room. It was clear she hadn't been coping. I got to her and pulled her close to me. Hugging and kissing her as she sobbed. Her whole body was shaking violently. Sammy agreed to come home with us so we could get her some help. We told her Manager what we were going to do and he was supportive.

It was an incredibly long night. Paul drove us all the way home again. He'd had no breaks or rest. Sammy slept in the back with me cuddling her all the way. When we got home, we got her straight upstairs to bed. Sammy was safe, she was home and we would take care of her.

I went to bed, and as tired as I was, I struggled to sleep. My mind was whirring. Memories came flooding back of my mum attempting suicide, her schizophrenia. I knew this wasn't the same, but the memories were triggered and flooding my mind.

The next morning, Sammy talked about what had happened. The lead up to it. How she was struggling to deal with the team. We talked about coping strategies she could use. We also made an emergency appointment to see the GP. The GP told us to self-refer to iTalk and put Sammy on anti-depressants.

Sammy was at home for a week and she had decided she wouldn't and couldn't go back. We agreed and we all went back to Wales, packed up all of her stuff and came home. Once again, Paul and I did the round trip in one go, only the return journey entailed Paul and I driving a car each.

I was physically and emotionally drained. The two months had been a roller coaster starting with natural nervous excitement, followed by apprehension then overwhelming sadness, regret, anxiety, stress, fear and so many more. How could I possibly move on from this?

Every day was a tentative step forward and sometimes an extreme step back. As the days turned into weeks, Sammy's health deteriorated. We had repeatedly tried to get iTalk to assist, but that felt like being on a slow boat to nowhere.

All of the things Sammy had once loved and enjoyed had gone. Sammy was going out and we were constantly worrying about where she was and whether she was O.K. I had a constant feeling of tightness around my chest. I felt sick and thought I was going crazy. I wanted my beautiful daughter back. This wasn't my daughter. Where had she gone. Every day was like walking on egg shells. I was in complete turmoil. I'd ask where she'd been and be told is was none of my business. Sammy's mental state was wrong. I could see that, but couldn't comprehend it.

The worst day of my life came next. My daughter came home, in a dreadful state. I had never seen her look so scared, traumatised and broken. I almost couldn't bear to ask what had happened. I knew I didn't want to hear the answer. Even before she'd opened her mouth, I wanted to scream and cry and walk away. Me, her mum, wanting to walk away. I knew I couldn't do that. I knew I didn't want to. I just knew that whatever was coming next was going to be horrific. It was horrific. My beautiful Sammy had been RAPED.

I held her tight, but I wanted to run. Run away from the horror of what she'd experienced. I wanted to fix it, but knew there was nothing I could do. I wanted to shut it all out as if it had never happened. I wanted to turn the clock back so she had never moved away and experienced so much in such a short space of time. I wanted to go and harm the person who had done this.

I tentatively asked questions that no mum wants to ask. I felt sick and wanted to push it all out of my mind. Paul didn't want to know any of the detail, he knew he wouldn't cope. I wasn't coping, but had no choice. I asked questions and challenged what she told me. I know I didn't support Sammy well enough. Not because I didn't want to, but because I couldn't. Emotionally I was falling apart. I had an overwhelming feeling of guilt and was going into denial. Denial was my way out so I didn't have to deal with it anymore.

The following weeks and months were horrendous. Sammy wasn't functioning well. In an emergency I took her straight to the hospital. I couldn't see any other option! My daughter needed help. I needed help. I was facing something I didn't know or understand. Sammy's emotions and reactions weren't even vaguely familiar. I'd managed mental health issues with Mum and my brother, but this was a whole new situation. We needed a professional to see Sammy. The hospital was of no help whatsoever and simply turned us away without any assistance. I felt helpless but wasn't going to stop finding help for my daughter.

I went online and started looking for a private psychiatrist. I didn't care what it was going to cost. We'd find the money somehow. If we could just get her seen, and find out what to do to help her, it would be a start.

I did find a psychiatrist, and got an appointment quickly. That appointment was the best thing I could have done to help my daughter Sammy. It was significant for me too. Sammy got her diagnosis of having 'Borderline Personality Disorder'. I put myself into a state of mental anguish because she'd inherited this from my family. I was to blame for everything that was happening to her. I couldn't fix this. I didn't know how to help her.

The psychiatrist had a meeting with Paul and I, a week later, to talk us through the diagnosis and that Sammy could learn to manage really well with help from a psychologist. It wasn't going to be an easy journey, and there was a lot to learn including new ways to interact with our own daughter. We weren't always going to get it right either. We got a recommendation for a psychologist. I felt so overwhelmed. This was so much to take in. So much to process. Why hadn't I seen it earlier. I'd become an expert with my mum, but this was so different.

As soon as I got home, I researched the diagnosis to death. I wanted to know and understand everything about BPD. As I was reading all the different traits, at a high level, I could see immediately which related to Sammy and which didn't. The hard part was trying to understand how to interact with my own daughter.

Time went by and every day I had to learn to deal with something new. Seeing and hearing my daughter screaming. Trying to hold her and almost being punched and screamed at to go away. I had never felt so out of my depth at being a parent, a mum who loved their daughter with every ounce of breath in their body but was being pushed away. Told they didn't understand. Spoken to with words that made me feel inadequate, unloved, unworthy.

Then came the next hurricane. Sammy's physical health hit a major hurdle. The screaming of BPD got joined with horrendous nausea and screaming with pain. Every night was spent with Sammy, her new boyfriend and I in the bathroom. Again, I couldn't help, but wanted Sammy to know I was there to support her. Over the following weeks, we spent 5 nights in Accident & Emergency at the nearest hospital. Series after series of tests showed nothing. Was my daughter experiencing physical pain from the emotional trauma? Was there something else happening here that I didn't know about? Sammy got her diagnosis which showed adenomyosis and an ovary stuck to the uterine wall. The subsequent operation resolved the immediate problem. They couldn't find endometriosis from the operation but suspected it was there and therefore couldn't rule out further surgery.

Sammy was now seeing her psychologist regularly, and doing really well learning the skills she needed. I desperately needed something to pull me out of the depths of sadness and feeling of being inadequate.

My brother's own psychiatrist, who wasn't part of the hospital, had been in contact with a psychiatric rehabilitation centre and my brother had been interviewed to see if it would benefit him. It meant being admitted for 6 months. The normal wait to get in was anything up to 2 years, but somehow, he got a place in a few short weeks. He was incredibly nervous but he knew this was almost a last chance.

Sammy was in a much more stable state, so Paul and I travelled over and stayed in his flat. It gave us some time to do a bit of sightseeing, which we'd missed on all the previous trips. We travelled to the centre to see where he was living and Paul and my brother even had a go at playing table tennis. We took him out for a day just so he could get the benefit of a change.

Shortly after we returned home, my brother had to attend a meeting with the council where he got told he was being put on early retirement pension. This was incredible news and was one less pressure we needed to worry about.

I started looking at a whole range of websites to see what I could find to help me. I'd given everything I'd got to helping everyone else, but I knew I needed to give myself some attention. Nothing seemed to resonate with me.

Then I found 'Mindvalley.com' and started a course to help improve my memory, called 'Superbrain' with Jim Kwik. It was a lot of fun and I learnt a lot, including being aware for ANT's (Automatic Negative Thoughts). I'd done something like that before and not heard it called ANT's, but that kept it in my mind in a much better way. The course also helped me create a structure for my day and got me on the road to journaling. It helped me detach myself from what had been happening around me. I needed that to keep myself in a stable state. In hindsight I wish I'd written them in my early journal. I would have liked to look back and see how far I'd come. If ANT's is something you get a lot of, I would recommend writing them down each day in a journal.

Another Masterclass got me meditating which included gratitude, forgiveness and 3-5 things that I had a vision for in 3 years' time. This was absolutely invaluable. I didn't have any vision. I didn't know the last time I had! I definitely wanted it to include getting rid of Fibromyalgia and pain. I wanted to be stronger so I could help Sammy and my brother.

I started a course on Energy Medicine (Donna Eden) and that proved to be helpful in shifting the fibro pain out of my body. Every day, without fail, I did Donna's Daily Energy Routine (DER) which, by the way, happens to be on YouTube along with many other routines with Donna and/or her daughters; Titanya and Dondi Dahlin, along with energy testing food to make sure it was suitable for my body at that moment in time.

Then I started listening to podcasts and hearing about having a Lifebook; to become the author of my best life. I had a very strong desire to do the course, but it was a lot of money. Paul knew how important improving my life was and asked his mum if she would pay for it. She did, and I started. During the stages of the course, I gradually worked on 12 categories of my life; Health & Fitness, Intellectual, Emotional Life, Character, Spiritual Life, Love Relationship, Parenting, Social, Financial, Career, Quality of Life and Life Vision. It helped me to start thinking differently and more importantly incorporate so many things into my life that would help me. I knew I needed help with my emotions. I got so excited, I started researching them. I read website after website. Document after document. I even read the handouts that my daughter was bringing home from her psychologist sessions.

There was a lot of great information, but I needed a simple structure that would help me to capture the emotions I had felt and was feeling and reflect what was working for me to move them from negative emotions to positive ones. During one of the *Lifebook* calls, Jon Butcher (owner of *Lifebook*) talked about recipes. I love cooking and my mind went straight to recipes and what they look like. A list of ingredients and a set of directions. I knew just what I needed to create. A recipe book for emotions. I would capture what was working for me, what was working for my daughter, my husband, my friends, the community of people I was doing personal development with. I was transforming my emotions and wanted others to be able to do the same; yes YOU.

Although I was working through my emotions, and ridding myself of a lot of the baggage from across the years, there were some deep routed negative beliefs that just didn't shift. Years ago, during my working career, I had done some development on writing down negative beliefs and re-writing them as positive statements. I tried that, and it worked for so many. Others still wouldn't shift.

Paul was 'Chair of Governors' at a local school and they were desperately looking for volunteers to help children with their reading. I jumped at the chance. One afternoon a week would be fine for me to manage. I got to read with several children and worked well with them all. Several had some extremely difficult circumstances with their home life. Their backgrounds were heart wrenching.

Two of the children I met with every week had some behavioural problems and I spent time with them just listening and providing them with support. We talked about their emotions and what was leading them to become angry. We talked about ways they could overcome the anger and even talked through ways of not getting angry in the first place. We were creating their recipes for overcoming anger. I found it hard coming home sometimes, and worried about a couple of them. I did feel a sense of excitement that my recipe idea was working.

Paul spoke to me about applying for a job as Clerk to the Governors of the school as they desperately needed someone. The existing Clerk was leaving the job. It would only be for 80 hours a year, so he thought it would be OK for me. Somehow, he persuaded me to apply. It turned out I was the only applicant, so got the job.

The 80 hours a year was so far from the reality of what the job needed. Previous Clerks, and the Governing Body, had simply not done everything they needed to do. I had a huge amount to get to grips with and even more to put in place. I was also doing a lot of personal development learning, which needed me to join calls every two weeks, do specific writing/work after the call as well as read and listen to podcasts.

My week was getting busier and busier. I was starting to become quite stressed, worrying about how I would get everything done. I found it hard and started to feel some of the same panic I'd felt before I'd left my previous job. This wasn't how it was meant to be. I knew something needed to change or drop. I didn't want to let anyone down.

There had been an incredible number of negative things that had happened in my life and I had been carrying the baggage with me for so long. It had taken its toll on my life and my health. This had to stop. I needed to turn it all around. I had to take control. I had to get rid of the remaining negative beliefs that were still plaguing me.

My girlfriend and I talked about the fact we were both struggling to keep the three times a week visits to the elderly lady we were visiting. She arranged, through the solicitor, for a company to provide carers to visit on a regular basis during the week which meant I could reduce my visits to once a week, at the weekend. This was a major help and freed up time for all the other commitments I had. The lady I visited seemed fine with the changes, so that was a relief.

Paul gave me as much support as he could for the Clerk job. Paul and I started working together to make a difference. The more structure we got into place, the easier the job would become.

My *Lifebook* was working on 12 categories of my life with many goals and an overriding life vision. I realised that for the school to really improve, it needed to focus on what outstanding looks like and aim for it with a Vision and 5-year plan too. Why not. I remember Sammy being taught at the age of 4, to reach for the stars. If you don't try, you will never know what you could have achieved.

Age 59

My own vision incorporates helping my family and others to learn, grow and flourish. I wrote the school's Vision and 5-year plan and included 'to learn, grow and flourish' within it.

I was overwhelmed with happiness when the Headteacher and Governing Body agreed to the plan. I felt like the personal development I'd done, in such a short space of time, was taking me at warp speed to where I wanted to get to.

I kept reading so many books, listening to podcasts and getting more and more insight into how I could overcome the final limiting beliefs. Writing down the limiting belief and re-writing it had been fine for most. The complex and deep-rooted ones from childhood needed something more. Then I heard a podcast interview, which had been provided as part of my *Lifebook* journey, which talked about only being able to remove negative beliefs if you are able to bring the emotion with it too. That made sense. If you don't capture the complex layers of mind and the body, the belief isn't removed. It's simply pushed down, but keeps raising its ugly head. Mine had raised their heads all my life.

During the podcast I closed my eyes and took a deep breath. In my mind, I took myself to a safe place. The first thing that came into my head was a painting a friend and I painted on my daughter's playroom wall when she was 9. It had hills, trees, a dog training centre with dogs, sheep and clouds that looked like elephants and a bear. Up on the top of the hill there was a church. Outside the church was a gravestone which had my dad's initials on it. Sammy liked that because it meant her Grandad, who she'd never known, was near. My safe place was inside that church. Then I had to feel what it felt like holding the negative belief I wanted to remove. I could feel the belief like I was back being 5 again, and understood all of the negativity it had caused throughout my life. I stood inside the empty church dressed as my 5-year old self. I looked in a mirror and could see myself back as I had been then. I knew it was a belief I didn't want anymore, so I took off my 5-year old clothes and let them fall. It felt so gratifying. I was giving myself permission to take the belief away and let it go. I pulled it out of every nook and cranny of my very being. I took so many deep breaths.

I chose the belief that felt good for me, that I am a strong and capable person, who can give so much value to the world. Tears rolled down my cheeks, as I went through the beliefs that had held me back. After that I looked in the mirror and saw myself, wearing my own clothes. Except I was lighter from having left the beliefs behind. I left the safe place, back as myself. As I left the church in the painting, the tears continued to flow. They were tears of absolute relief. I have never experienced anything so powerful. My negative belief was gone.

Note: This is my interpretation, and an abridged version, of the *Belief Clearing* podcast I listened to. I have provided a link for *Belief Clearing* in the reference section of this book. I highly recommend it.

I was becoming more and more in control of my life, my health and my future. My life was transforming.

I was transforming my life using powerful practices. Using them has allowed me to offload the negative emotions in my head. I can remember things from my past and have no negative emotion. I've finally left the baggage behind at the age of 59!

Of course, things happen in my life that are negative. The difference now is I move so quickly from whatever has happened so the negative emotion is gone almost before it started. I am conscious of my feelings. I even track my emotions each day which has been invaluable.

Being able to change emotions from negative to positive can have such a significant and powerful impact on your life.

It has for me.

It can for you too.

I know I may have some deep-rooted beliefs, associated with the things that have happened in my life, that haven't come to the surface yet. They form our character and can impact our lives in both positive and negative ways. Many beliefs are formed in our childhood and don't serve us well as we get older. The hard part is getting rid of them as they are so ingrained. Finding someone great like Lion Goodman, is a game changer for these.

With all the things I've listened to, people I've spoken with and books I've read, I have a zest for life I've never had before. One of the most recent books I've read is 'Conversations with God' (Book 1), by Neale Donald Walsch. I read it and not too far into the book I realised I had tears streaming down my face. They were tears of relief. I found some answers in the book on my spiritual beliefs. It also said, 'be & decide who you really are'.

I've decided who I really am.

The woman who has no limiting beliefs.

The woman who is now in control of her emotions and doesn't have them controlled by others.

A strong-minded woman who cares and wants to help others.

I want to help you.

✳ ✳ ✳

No matter who, what, why, where or when your

emotions and feelings came from,

free yourself of the burden of your past.

Create your recipes and manage your emotions.

Then, when you've created your recipe(s) for a life full of joy & happiness and/or love, you can make them part of your daily habits. Daily habits take time to become instilled into your way of life, so use a tracking method to help you, like I did, in my daily Journal.

The Cleansing

The day, bright and warm,
Relaxes me.
Lifting my face and closing my eyes to the sun's warmth
I feel a small, cold drop of water
Fall upon the flesh of my cheek.
Gray clouds swiftly black out
The sun's enlightening rays.
More drops,
Faster
They rain down
Breaking into miniscule particles
Splattered upon the cement.
One loses sight of those in the green grass.
I find shelter to keep the drops
From penetrating my now fragile clothing,
But I continue to watch.
Small droplets become sheets of water,
Graying my vision to what lies behind them.
Clouds move on,
Releasing the sun to shine.
Starting with a tiny crack in the gray sky
The sun eventually extends its full radiance.
Again I step into the light
Awaiting the embrace of warmth
Only to feel the cold and callous air.
Resuming my journey
The hardened wind slaps against my face,
My body.
It stops long enough for a shiver to creep along my spine.
I look to the sun
Shining brightly with no knowledge
Of the deceitful wind, or
The cooling from the rain.
I continue on
For who I am to stop the wind
Or make the suns warmth felt.
I pull my jacket closer
And reach my destination.

Dani Glaeser

PART 2: POWERFUL PRACTICES TO INVOKE POSITIVE EMOTIONS

~~Learning never stops~~ Never stop learning

My learning over the last year catapulted me forward to a life I had never imagined. It altered my thoughts, it changed my beliefs, it clarified my thinking, and more importantly changed how I felt and made me realise what I could still accomplish.

There have been some powerful practices that I learnt and really want to share with you. I've also read some amazing books, listened to podcasts from some of the world's masters. People who are the top of their game. Choosing the right people to listen to and learn from has been invaluable. You'll find a list of resources at the end of this book.

When I first started, I was quite sure the practices I'd learnt would work for me. Why would they. I was no-one special, and yet, the more I did them the more I reaped the reward and grew.

They helped me to move to, and remain in, a positive state of mind.

Now I am fully in control of my life, my purpose, my life vision & goals and most importantly, my own emotions & feelings. I have a joyful and happy mind.

The specific areas I want to take you through, which helped me so much are;

- ❖ Daily Structure
- ❖ Journaling
- ❖ Meditation: Compassion, Gratitude, Forgiveness, Vision for my future, Perfect Day, Blessing
- ❖ Limiting Beliefs/Reframing
- ❖ Brule's
- ❖ Health: Diet, Energy, Exercise/Fitness
- ❖ Emotions
- ❖ Emotions Recipe Card (general)
- ❖ Recipe Card Directions List
- ❖ Recipe Cards
- ❖ Journaling your Emotions and track how you're doing each day.
- ❖ Thank you and Reference List

Daily Structure

The first practice I built was a daily structure, which needed to incorporate all of the activities and actions I needed to manage in my day. What I'd learnt was the importance of the first hour of the day, which needed to focus on myself and my health. It didn't include looking at anything, including my mobile phone or iPad! That was a big change. It also was designed to get the body and mind active.

My lunchtime is later than some people, but simply accommodates a new routine of intermittent fasting.

The evening time was also crucial so that I got into a good routine which rested my mind and helped me remain calm before bed-time, with no interruptions from phones and computers.

The content of my day may be very different to your own. I'm retired, so my day doesn't include work in the way it would have done in the past. Having said that, I do now have a career, it's just different. We're all different. It's structuring that is important, making sure you include all the important elements into your day.

Journaling

During my personal development courses, it was suggested that I should do journaling. I'd had diaries in the past, but usually bought one, started writing each day, got bored and stopped.

Now I was learning a different purpose. I was tracking things I needed to do in a day, my Life Vision, my emotions, my beliefs, health & fitness and memories & moments. I also tracked some key things I'd learnt and needed to practice remembering.

This became an incredible way of capturing so much about the day. I found it allowed me to plan ahead, review in the morning and reflect/capture what happened at the end of each day. The more I got into journaling, the more I wrote down and the more positive I became. I wouldn't be without it now. I also found that through greater learning, my journal needed to evolve and change for my needs. There are plenty of places you can buy a journal, but I needed mine to be very specific, so I designed it myself. I can change it as and when I want to.

There are many components in my journal, but some are a 'must have' to help on your emotional journey;

Meditation: Here I can capture any specific thoughts that came to me during mediation, especially if they were different in some way. Also, which meditation I've done, where I might have experimented with something new and my thoughts about it.

Emotions: Later in this book I will take you through how I really go into journaling emotions. This is where I learnt what was happening and got to a place of being able to manage them. Over the months, I realised I was moving further away from negative emotions and that most of my days were just filled with joy & happiness, and love. It doesn't mean they never happen, but they are rare and often just fleeting. My journal now is much simpler. I have a section where I tick which emotion's I've experienced each day. If I've experienced any negative ones, I write at the bottom of the section what it was, and write more about it in the Memories and Moments section.

My recipe cards for Joy & Happiness and Love contain things that made me feel that way. I make sure every day includes several things that keep myself in these emotions and don't give way to negative ones. It was key to my being successful and once you've achieved it, there's no looking back.

Gratitude: This is covered by my meditation, but every day I write down specific things that I'm truly grateful for that day. I try and think beyond the ones I thought about in my meditation to make sure I'm expanding my thinking. The more gratitude you can build into your life, the more positive you feel.

Meditation

I learnt that meditation helps on so many levels, and through my personal development journey I started meditating. I'll cover meditation a bit later, but for now I want to share the practice I chose to work with;

'6 phase meditation' – Vishen Lakhiani

Phase 1 - Compassion

Learning to feel compassion for every living creature on this planet. I found this intriguing and visualised white heart emojis going around my house, my neighbourhood, my country and then the entire earth. As I get to the earth becoming covered and shining brightly, different animals pop into my mind as well as faces I've seen from around the globe. Repeatedly doing this has meant my outlook toward people has changed dramatically over time. It's opened my mind and heart to try and give compassion to everyone. That's been hard sometimes, but something I keep focussing on and is getting much easier as time goes by.

Phase 2 – Gratitude

Life is a gift. A gift from God, the universe, energy or whatever higher power resonates with each of us. Every day we experience a range of senses; sight, hearing, taste, smell, touch and all of our other senses – most of which we simply take for granted because, on the whole and for the majority of people, our body just does that stuff naturally. Being grateful for what we have can help to take away our negative feelings. Thinking of all the things you are grateful for during the day helps to lift your mood and become more positive in how you think. The act of thinking gratefully can even change how you feel. At times, I had a debilitating disability which reduced what I could do and meant I was in pain or exhausted on many days. I could have focussed on my limitations and what I couldn't do, but that would have resulted in negativity and diminished my outlook, which it did for quite some time. The more you practice at being conscious of the negative thoughts/ANTs (Automatic Negative Thoughts), and looking at the positive to counteract them, the more you can get rid of them. Now I focus on things I can do and enjoy. So much so, that I started pushing myself forward, that little bit more each day. I constantly think of the positive things I am doing, the things I am grateful for, and what more I can do to make things better. If there was something I couldn't do, I changed my words to 'I cannot do, yet'. Adding that one simple word, changes the whole thought process in the mind. All of this helped me to reduce or block out my pain levels and reduce them. I'll come back to this point later.

Just a fraction of the things I wrote down over the months, that I am grateful for;

- ❖ My neighbour chatting with me today.
- ❖ I had such a lovely breakfast this morning. I'll make that again another day.
- ❖ The sun is shining today – the sky looks beautiful. What a wonderful day.
- ❖ I saved money on my shopping today.
- ❖ Just being able to rest and have time to repair.
- ❖ I've had time today where I haven't been aware of any pain.
- ❖ My partner came shopping with me to help as I was so tired.
- ❖ The air/oxygen I have breathed today.
- ❖ Seeing my daughter smile today.
- ❖ The rain watering my garden for me.
- ❖ Making an elderly lady at a care home laugh when my dog jumped into her bed for a cuddle.
- ❖ My body feeling better now I've stopped eating certain foods.
- ❖ Watching lots of kites flying near the beach.
- ❖ Getting soaked on a hot summer's day.
- ❖ Able to just do nothing today.
- ❖ Learning so many new things.
- ❖ So much positive energy today.
- ❖ The phone call from my friend to see how I am.
- ❖ The mistakes I make are OK with the people they affect.
- ❖ Hearing my daughter sing, so glad she's feeling brighter today.
- ❖ All that I have learnt today.
- ❖ I woke feeling really bright today.
- ❖ I did some exercise today and feel better for it.
- ❖ I'm getting more and more energy every day.
- ❖ I haven't had any pain today.
- ❖ Feeling so well today.
- ❖ Seeing someone's face light up when I gave them some repaired clothes, because they needed mending.
- ❖ Having time out in nature with the river, trees and flowers.
- ❖ A comfortable home.
- ❖ Finding some new vegetables, we've not had before to try for dinner.
- ❖ Lovely food.
- ❖ Meeting so many lovely people today.
- ❖ Seeing a relative's health improve.
- ❖ The new friendships I have made with people around the world.
- ❖ I rode a bike, which I haven't been able to do for years.
- ❖ Learning new ways to make myself well naturally.
- ❖ Read another incredible book today which has helped me to make my life better.
- ❖ Life just keeps on getting better.

- ❖ Fantastic day and so much to look forward to.
- ❖ Rode further than planned on my bike.
- ❖ Making connections.
- ❖ I am growing.
- ❖ I'm getting well.
- ❖ Being appreciated by my family.
- ❖ Enlightenment, positivity, fun, life.
- ❖ My work mind is coping.
- ❖ Feeling so positive.
- ❖ To feel I am on the right path.
- ❖ I am able to provide help, love and support to others.
- ❖ A calm, loving, relaxed day.
- ❖ Able to share my joy, love and happiness with others.
- ❖ I've come so far.
- ❖ I have enough.
- ❖ I am blessed with everything I have.
- ❖ I have more than I need to be happy.
- ❖ So much beauty around me.
- ❖ Being able to create my reality.
- ❖ So many lovely people and being so kind.
- ❖ I feel so alive.
- ❖ I'm making fantastic progress.
- ❖ My social life is expanding.
- ❖ My whole life is expanding.

Phase 3 – Forgiveness

Why should I forgive people who hurt me as a child, who hurt me as an adult, who hurt the people I love? I will never forgive them. They are evil, hurtful people. They don't deserve forgiveness. Why shouldn't I hate them. I had stayed angry with so many people for so long. I had kept the pent-up feelings deep inside. Some days I'd be consumed by the anger and pain. Sometimes I'd become paranoid, by reliving the moments over and over again in my head and projecting them onto the people in my life. I'd let it affect my life, my relationships and ultimately my happiness. What I hadn't even begun to think about is how I would feel if I simply forgave them. How it would release so much negative energy in my own mind and body. How free I would feel once I'd done it. It took me time to forgive. During my meditation I would forgive the person for cutting me up on the motorway. That was easy. I wouldn't likely see them again. Then I'd forgive someone I hadn't seen in years. That was easy. I wouldn't likely see them again. I actually started to enjoy forgiving the simple ones, until I ran out of them.

Then I was faced with some of the more complex issues I had kept buried in my very being. The very core of who I am. I found that there were many days where I started going through the years of my life trying to work out who I needed to forgive. Several I knew without having to try; the teacher and headteacher who had beaten me, the doctor and then hospital who made my mum suffer in a mental hospital, the religion that meant I was different, the children that bullied me, the parents that didn't recognise my suffering, the people that treated my parents so badly, the partner(s) that cheated on me, the food industry that focusses on creating food that caused my ill health and will kill humankind if it doesn't change, the medical profession for their focus on ailments instead of the root cause, the governments for not managing the finances of our country to benefit the very people it serves. Some were deeply hidden, and by going through my life, year by year, others surfaced.

As I started forgiving the significant someone/something it became so incredibly emotional but it was also powerful. The more I allowed myself to learn to forgive, the quicker I released myself from negative emotions and thoughts. Some of my hurts were long standing and incredibly hard to forgive. As I attempted to forgive them, my thoughts and emotions took me straight back to the very thing I had been suppressing, trying to forget or had been hidden. It felt like I was going through it all over again. I'd start the forgiveness for a particular person, and have to stop and go to the next part of my meditation. I'd feel angry, distraught, exhausted, and had to do my best to distract my thoughts with other things, or go to sleep. Sleep just to stop the thoughts for a while. That was hard too. There were many nights I didn't really sleep. My good old brain would run like a tape machine on permanent loop. I wouldn't even try and bring that one to mind the next day, or the next or the next. I kept putting it off. It had become too raw, all over again. Some days I thought, 'who am I going to forgive today?' and a face I hadn't even thought of would pop into my mind. I would do my best to forgive that person and for some reason the ones that popped into my mind I found easier than those I had worked hard to bring forward. It's like my own mind was learning when to bring them forward. I learnt to trust it and left it to my own mind to help me. Some days nothing would pop in. I would bring to mind those I had already forgiven. If I felt emotions by forgiving them again, I knew I hadn't fully moved on. As time went by, I found my emotional reactions reducing. It took time, and some I had to forgive many times until they at last got released. I knew they'd been released when I brought them to memory and no longer had the emotional anguish that I'd previously felt. That feels so amazing. There were a couple that didn't budge and needed something more and were overcome using *Lion Goodman's Belief Clearing* approach.

In my meditation practice it challenged me to forgive the person/situation but also to imagine them forgiving me. WHAT! Why am I imagining them forgiving me! I don't care about them. They hurt me. I didn't hurt them. I'm not going to. I won't. I will for some, but not for others. I need to think about this one.

The reality is that in every situation where something occurred, it had taken two sides to create it. My side, and theirs or its. Recognising that, and allowing myself the freedom to forgive them and let them forgive me, truly released the emotional memory. I've forgiven everyone and every situation that I can remember now. That doesn't mean there won't be something that will pop into my mind. It just means there's none that I can actively remember and my mind isn't ready to bring them forward OR it means I truly have forgiven everyone/everything from my past. There will be stuff that crops up in my future, and I will be forgiving them/it much quicker now. I will not return to my days of holding onto anger. Life is too short and too valuable for that. I want to enjoy my life and reach my life vision.

Based on my journey, my message to anyone is to start out by forgiving things that are less important. They are easier to forgive. Over time I'm positive that you will be able to forgive the tough ones. Let them come to you when they and you are ready. If you need to, talk to a close friend or family if you're having difficulty at any time, while you are going through this process or use belief clearing like I did. There is no time limit on forgiveness, but remember the longer you hold on to the negative emotion, the longer you are holding yourself back.

Phase 4 – Vision (for my future, including joy, happiness, success, excitement)

Through the personal development I've been doing I have created my *Lifebook*. A 12-category smart *Lifebook*, thanks to *Jon & Missy Butcher* who own *Lifebook* and have provided invaluable learning through *Mindvalley.com*. This has moved my life forward exponentially. I have a complete Life Vision which I am working towards every day. I know exactly what it looks and feels like, so it's so much easier to go through this part of my meditation.

Phase 5 – Perfect Day (envisioning my day ahead)

I manage my day by using the journal which includes specific actions and activities I want to incorporate into my day. Having this structure has helped me incredibly. It makes envisioning my day easier and because I do this, I find my day runs well. On a rare occasion where I miss my meditation, I find my day doesn't always go according to plan.

Phase 6 – Blessing (from a higher power)

This felt very strange at first. I didn't believe in God! What is so great about this is you are connecting yourself to whatever higher power resonates with you. It could be a god, it could be energy, it could be the universe, it could be a loved one who has passed. It doesn't matter. What matters is feeling the connection. To start with I didn't really imagine anything, but I then I thought of my mum. Now I imagine my mum and dad on their wedding day. Their picture epitomises happiness. It gives me such a feeling of strength and joy, especially now that I've forgiven the past.

Limiting Beliefs/Re-framing

Many years ago, I'd been on a *National Health Service (NHS)* course for stress. We went through a number of personal expectations we had, which may/may not have developed out of beliefs we held about ourselves, and were causing stress at work. A couple of mine were;

I will always complete all of my work on time

I will give everything 100% effort

I can remember the lady running the session asking me what would happen if I wasn't feeling too well one day, or was asked to help someone else at work. What would happen?

Through the group discussion, I realised that I was setting myself up to fail. I was creating my own stress by having beliefs that I had placed on myself that didn't serve me well. I realised that it was OK to complete my work on time, most of the time. Just not all of the time. There needed to be room for exceptions or just 'circumstances' beyond my control.

I could only ever give 100% effort when everything was right, but there were and would be times when I couldn't. When factors stopped it from being possible, and that was OK.

We re-framed our beliefs;

- ❖ I will complete my work on time, when I am able to do so.
- ❖ I will give everything my best effort and taking account of surrounding factors that may impact me or my work.

Writing beliefs down and re-writing them is a powerful way of making changes to your life.

During the last year, through my meditation, journaling, the personal development courses, podcasts and reading, I identified so many beliefs. I needed to challenge them all and decide if they served me well or needed to be scrapped or re-written. As I then went on to write this book, pulling out year by year what had happened in my life, I pulled out even more.

Here's just some of my beliefs. More importantly I have shown what they are like now, after everything I've worked through to make the transformation in my life.

My beliefs then	and now
I'm naughty	I can be naughty when I want to be, and that's OK, so long as I don't negatively impact others around me
I'm deformed	I'm perfectly formed and I'm delighted because I'm left-handed
I'm not clever	I am extremely clever at all the things I am good at, which are many
God knows I am bad	*I'll cover this one later*
The devil has made me bad, so I won't live forever/I'm the devil's child	Nothing has made me bad. I'm not bad. I no longer believe in the devil. I appreciate as a human, I will not live forever, but now I have my spiritual beliefs defined, I am confident and comfortable with what comes next.
I'm no good at any sport	I don't need to be good at sport unless I want to be.
I'm slow and lose concentration	I work at a pace that's good for me and I concentrate really well when I am interested and inspired.
Learning is too difficult for me	I have learnt an incredible amount and if it's difficult, and I want or need to, I will find ways to overcome it.
My ability is not good enough/limited	My ability is good enough for what I want and need to do. There are no limits.
My dad never shows his love	My dad showed love in the way he knew how.
I'm not special	I'm very special to the family, friends and others I have in my life.
No-one likes me	I have so many people who like me. If people choose not to like me, that is fine.

My beliefs then	and now
I deserve to be lonely	I'm not lonely.
I hate my life	I love my life.
I'm fat	I was medically obese. Now I know how to manage my health and weight. I'm losing weight, and on my way to achieving my life goal.
I'm ugly	I'm not ugly. I am who I am and I love that.
I'm not good enough	I am good enough
I'm stupid	I am bright and intelligent.
No-one will love me	I am incredibly loved by the most important people in my life.
I'm not qualified or bright enough to do anything	I worked hard to get qualifications and succeeded, through being bright enough to do my job(s) well for so long.
I hate/don't care about my dad	I loved my dad and cared for him deeply.
I will never have a life of my own	I've lived my own life.
I'm better off dead	I love life and am excited about the years yet to come.
I don't believe in God	I have found my spiritual believes now, and know that 'until we meet again' was the right thing to write for my mum.
There is something wrong with me	There is nothing wrong with me
I'm not worth anything	I'm worth a lot, to so many.
I'm never ever going to be happy	I am incredibly happy, every day.
I'm never going to find someone special	I found someone truly special.

My beliefs then	and now
I am a jealous person	I was a jealous person, but not anymore.
I should have been with my dad when he died	I would like to have been with my dad when he died, but it was not meant to be.
I know my baby will be fine!	Yes, I did know. I felt at the time that my dad had given her to me. I had a sense of an energy at the time.
I am inadequate	I am adequate in all that I say and do.
I couldn't feed my baby. There was something wrong with me!	Yes, there probably was something wrong with me that could have been solved, but I put my priority on spending valuable time with her and don't regret that.
I'm hopeless at managing money	I've successfully managed to pay all bills across all the years, had holidays, our car and many other things. I wouldn't call that hopeless.
I can't stick to a diet	I couldn't stick to a diet until I found the right ones; a human diet.
I have to work hard	I can work as hard as I want to and rest when I need to.
I failed my family	I didn't fail my family. They have everything they need.
I must help my family whenever they need me to	I will help my family whenever I am able to.
There is no god	I do believe there is a higher force and energy across the universe. I felt my dad's energy when my daughter was born. I felt my mum's energy three weeks after she passed. I've felt my mum's energy help me on many occasions and I know the Universe is helping me when I ask for it. What I call the higher force is my work in progress.

My beliefs then	and now
I'll never have friends like my mum did	My friendship group is growing at a pace of knots, globally.
I don't believe in 'until we meet again', even though I wrote those words	'Until we meet again!'
I will and must always keep going	I will always push myself to achieve things, but I will also spend time taking care of myself so I can continue achieving now and in the future.
I am totally responsible for providing for my family. I'm the breadwinner	As a family we are collectively responsible for everything, and individually responsible for specific things. We agree our responsibilities and pull together to achieve them.
I love being successful	I love being successful and I don't apologise for that. It's who I am.
I love recognition and being appreciated	I love recognition and being appreciated and I don't apologise for that. It's who I am.
I made myself ill	I believe I was born with certain illnesses and I created others.
I will be ill for the rest of my life	I know I can rid myself of diabetes, because I've done it. I know I can rid myself of Fibromyalgia. Autoimmune illnesses are caused by the very food we put in our mouths. I changed all that. I eat what a human should eat. In the final stages of finishing this book, I can announce I am free of all fibro symptoms. This is truly mind blowing.
I had to keep working to pay the bills	I needed to work to cover the bills, but at any point could have made different decisions and choices.

My beliefs then	and now
I'm a life-long born carer	My character traits mean I love caring for people. I will always be that way and will help people when and wherever I can. I wouldn't have it any other way. I will care for myself too.
I didn't help my daughter enough	I gave my daughter total love, support and guidance. My daughter's life choices were her own to make.

B-rules

I learnt a saying from *Vishen Lakhiani, founder of Mindvalley.com; BRULES – Bullshit rules*. There are rules and beliefs we have been brought up with, or that society has dictated throughout time, that we often just accept and continue to live by.

They affect who we are and ultimately who we become. That may be OK, or maybe they are holding us back. It is not saying any of the rules or beliefs are right or wrong. What it's saying is; STOP, become conscious of them and ask yourself if they still hold true for you.

Every rule or belief that has been passed to you from birth, has formed the life you have now. As you understand your emotions and what drives them, you may well tease out rules and beliefs that are driving an emotion you are wanting to change. As you identify rules and beliefs in your life, write them down and decide if they resonate with you now, or not. Do they still hold true?

Here are some simple rules and beliefs just to get you thinking;

Self

- ❖ Your past defines your future.
- ❖ Once something bad happens in your life, it stays with you forever.
- ❖ Listen to your elders, they know best.
- ❖ You must wear your gender specific clothing.
- ❖ You must follow society's dress code to fit in.
- ❖ Your worth is based on material possessions.
- ❖ You have to be in a relationship.
- ❖ You must have hobbies and interests.

Children

- ❖ Children should/must be seen, not heard.
- ❖ Children should/must grow up quickly.
- ❖ Children should/must be and act like adults.
- ❖ Children should/must attain the education level for their age.

School

- ❖ You should/must go to school and get good exam results.
- ❖ You should/must go to college/university.
- ❖ School is the only place to learn.

- ❖ Home schooling means you will miss out on a proper education.
- ❖ You won't get a good job if you don't do well at school/college/university - and get top grades in your exams.

Work/Home

- ❖ You must get a good job, raise a family and provide for them.
- ❖ You must get a mortgage and buy a house.
- ❖ Some jobs are good and some are bad. Get out of the bad.
- ❖ You must be 100% in all that do you do.
- ❖ Don't apply for a job if you can't meet all their requirements.
- ❖ You have to work hard to earn money.
- ❖ Travellers don't contribute to society and should be frowned upon.
- ❖ A woman's work is in the home.
- ❖ Top 5 most stressful life events

Family

- ❖ You must continue and follow the traditions of your family.
- ❖ You must love your family, no matter what.
- ❖ Blood is thicker than water.
- ❖ Family must come first.
- ❖ You will do what your family tell you too.

Health

- ❖ You can only have certain foods at certain mealtimes.
- ❖ You must have 3 meals per day.
- ❖ You must have a specific number of fruit and vegetables per day.
- ❖ You are disabled for life.
- ❖ You can't change the health you inherited/were born with.
- ❖ People with learning disabilities have a negative impact on society.
- ❖ People with mental illness should be locked away.

Money

- ❖ Money is the root of all evil.
- ❖ Money is scarce.
- ❖ Children are entitled to inherit the wealth of their parents/family.

Superstition

- ❖ Walking under a ladder is bad luck.
- ❖ No open umbrellas inside.

- ❖ Failing to respond to a chain letter.
- ❖ Certain numbers; 4 ,9, 13, 17, 39, 666.
- ❖ Breaking a mirror.
- ❖ Priest in the street.
- ❖ Bad things happen in 3's

Social Conventions

- ❖ You must provide food to feed your guests
- ❖ You must invite family/friends to an event, even if you don't want to
- ❖ You must follow tradition;
- ❖ wedding - wear white, father walks the bride, men do speeches, go on honeymoon

Sex

- ❖ You must not have sex before marriage.
- ❖ No sex with the lights on
- ❖ No sexual positions, or acts like 'that'
- ❖ No sex while the children are awake
- ❖ No sex on a full stomach
- ❖ Orgasm is the goal of all sexual activity
- ❖ Everyone needs sex to be happy

Crime

- ❖ Once you commit a crime, you'll never change.
- ❖ No-one deserves a second chance.
- ❖ A leopard never changes its spots.
- ❖ Once a thief, always a thief.

Religion

- ❖ Once you've been brought up in a religion, they've got you for life.
- ❖ Turn the other cheek!
- ❖ An eye for eye!
- ❖ Eating certain meat means you will go to hell.

Health

Being diabetic was not what I had wanted to hear. I'd seen what my mum had gone through and the time I'd spent looking for food that didn't have sugar in it. The reality was I was morbidly obese, so it shouldn't have come as any surprise when I got told. At the time I put myself on a calorie-controlled diet. I'd done so many diets in the past, so I knew it was going to be extremely challenging. Diets don't really work that well. You lose some weight and them put it all back on and more. I did manage to lose 14 pounds, and kept it off.

Over the last year, my personal development has included really learning about health and fitness. I've read and learnt that a third of the world's population can eat whatever they like and their body will deal with it, the next third will need a bit or caution on some specific foods but will be able to work it out and manage well. Then there's the last third, who no matter what they do will put on weight just by looking at or thinking about food. That's me. Others in my family fall into the middle category. Thanks!

Beyond Diet

By chance I came across *'Beyond Diet'* and that helped me to lose 35 pounds. The key changes that got me there was cutting out all grains (including gluten free), no more dairy (of any kind), no more vegetable oil (excluding Olive Oil, which I only use sparingly for salad dressing. In cooking, I use coconut oil only) and no sugar (processed sugars for which there are over 60 different names!). I did keep in honey and maple syrup, but these were for occasional use only. It was this programme that reversed my diabetes. A one-off cost and loads of help with meal planning and recipe ideas. Everything I ate was cooked from scratch. Absolutely nothing processed. I knew everything that I was putting in my mouth and it was all natural. It also made some changes to the inflammation in my body, which was a great start. I hit a plateau for nearly two years. I couldn't work out what or why the weight wouldn't budge, so I decided to look for something different for a while.

That's when I came across *Mindvalley.com* and a whole range of personal development programmes.

Energy Medicine

I was attracted to the *Energy Medicine quest* as it gave me hope that I could improve my energy levels which were still incredibly low. I've learnt about all the energy systems in my body; my meridians, chakras, aura, as well as energy testing and pain chasing. This has been truly life changing.

I do a daily energy routine (DER) and trace my meridians in the morning and again during the day if I need to.

My entire routine reduces any stresses in the body. It's made my entire body resilient to illness. My family get ailments and they pass me by! The energy flow in my body is running naturally, and I can give it a boost when I need it. My body is getting used to the positive habits I'm installing and I will keep working on more routines from Donna in the future. Moving the stress out of the body enables joy and happiness to become natural.

One routine that really fascinates me is energy testing food and other items to make sure they agree with my body at that moment in time. Seeing the way your body reacts if it doesn't want something can be a bit unnerving to start with. I remember the first time I did this with my daughter. She freaked out when she felt her body move in a negative way, to the food I held in front of her. She was convinced I'd pushed her, until I repeated it with her eyes open, so she could see for herself.

What I find amazing is when I think I'm tired or exhausted, I can draw on energies within my body and feel refreshed and energised. It's almost magical. The universe and everything around us are energy, so finding ways to tap into it and refresh is absolutely the way to go.

My energy levels are incredible compared to where they had been, thanks to *Energy Medicine*.

Thank you, Donna.

Lifebook

There are 12 chapters in my *Lifebook* and I could write chapters and chapters on all of them, but that's not the purpose of this book. I do highly recommend it to everyone, and will include details in the references section at the end of this book.

It's truly life changing.

Particular chapters I would like to highlight are:

Health & Fitness: This challenged me to think about what I wanted for my Health and what I wanted my fitness level to be. It pushed me to go looking for answers and through reading, podcasts and an amazing community I interacted with, I was made to realise that I could overcome all of the health challenges - MYSELF.

I could heal my own body, and yes, I am!

Emotional Life: This made me get a deeper understanding of emotions and what I wanted my emotional life to look like. During calls doing my *Lifebook, Jon Butcher* talked about recipes, which drove me to create my own and the contents for part of this book.

Wildfit

Through *Mindvalley.com* I found 'Wildfit'. *Wildfit* focusses on the Human Diet. I decided to go for it because it in part aligned with what I'd already been doing but also because I was intrigued. It focussed on the diet we, as humans, are meant to eat and not what the food industry and so many 'experts' tell us we should eat. So, I completed the *Wildfit* programme. I instantly lost another 14 pounds.

I'm still on my weight loss journey, at 170 lbs, but am in total control now. I am able to remain stable with my weight or put myself into weight loss. I'm on target to reach my goal of 140 lb by June 2020. I know it's in my grasp.

More importantly have been the changes to my health. By eating the *Wildfit* way, I have seen dramatic improvements in my blood test results and gut biome health. Even my finger nails have changed!

If you're not in a good place with weight or what you're eating, getting it right will play a big part in your emotional well-being. It certainly did mine. We are not being helped by the food industry who are creating food that keeps people addicted to sugar, or contains ingredients that aren't even natural (or labelled as natural but aren't). It sickens me to think that my diabetes was being fuelled by the products I was buying which were being created by the food industry whose intent is on making a profit. A profit made from my ill health!

I've had blood tests and stool tests (gut biome) to see what's going on in my body. Before I started *Wildfit*, I had some blood test flags. Nothing to do with diabetes and not something that a GP blood test would have picked up, but negative results that needed fixing. I also had moderate gut biome. Since having changed to *Wildfit*, my blood test results are all but one positive and my gut biome is now 'above average'. Understanding what's going on inside my body has become so important. It's driven my health to new levels. I've been able to work on my fitness through exercise which I couldn't have imagined when I medically retired. I'm lighter than I was in my late 20's and I'm out every day riding a bike. 2-3 years ago, I struggled to walk very much without becoming exhausted!

I've been working the pain out of my body. It's taken time, but I'm nearly there now. I said earlier that I've not had any Fibro symptoms. I'm ecstatic. I don't know if it's gone completely yet, but I've proved that:

a human diet
+ a bit of exercise
+ my daily energy routine
+ having daily positive emotions
+ having my amazing Life Vision
= an exciting, pain-free, happy & loving life.

And finally, what I realised, during all my personal development is that every emotion we experience has a list of ingredients. The things that built up to the emotion in the first place. There will be lots of emotions where many people will have the same ingredients, but equally there are many whose list will be different. We are all unique, so cannot expect everyone to act the same way under the same circumstances. It's OK to not feel the same as someone else. It's OK to be affected by something in a different way to someone else. It's OK.

To really understand and manage our emotions, we need to be conscious of the ingredients and then have clear directions to follow which can lead us to a better place. It's not about stopping an emotion. We all need to experience the emotions, but it is about managing them. It's about taking control of your emotions instead of letting your emotions control you. Creating your personal recipe book, I am sure, will help you to gain that control. It did for me.

The more positive your thoughts,
the better your emotions will be.
Positive decisions and actions,
create amazing results.
You'll see!

Heidi C Tyler

PART 3: EMOTIONS

A myriad of information

Before we even get started, I'd just like to mention that the number of emotions we might experience depends on where you get your information from. There is a myriad of information and professional advice available and this chapter is not here to replace that.

What I found important for me was to understand the emotions I was experiencing. I learned, through research that there are 2 types of emotion.

Primary is the first emotion which arises from a significant event and will dissipate after a period of time. So, something happens and you suddenly feel a strong emotional feeling. It is this first reaction that is your primary emotion.

Secondary emotions stem from the primary emotion that preceded it, and can become more complex and difficult to manage. As the primary emotion dissipates, our feelings over the situation bring in other emotions. They are ones we have learned as we grew up. These relate to our feelings over a particular situation and can overshadow the primary emotion. If multiple come into play, it can create emotional overwhelm.

Depending on where you do your reading, you'll see references to a number of primary emotions. There are a myriad of charts and diagrams to choose from, so I am not going to recommend one. It's best you look and choose one for yourself. The lists can and do vary but typically the primary emotions include; *Anger, Fear, Joy, Sadness and Surprise*. There are a vast number of lists for secondary emotions too.

When I looked on *Wikipedia* for Emotions, I came across a reference to a book which listed 154 different worldwide emotions and feelings. You can see why it's mind boggling.

A piece of information I did glean was that understanding the emotion that came first is key for determining an appropriate course of action. That doesn't mean you don't deal with the others. They are still valid, but as mentioned before, they relate more to feelings we've learned rather than our primary response. Where there are several emotions (feelings) coming into play, understanding the mix of them will help you to work them through and create the right recipe(s).

Here's another thought.

There are only 2 emotions; Love and Fear and everything else is a mixture of feelings. This is something I've been listening to very recently and it does make sense. Perhaps that's why I gave the book the name I did, and before I'd even heard this view!

So perhaps my use of the word 'Emotion' should be considered in its wider context – EMOTIONS and FEELINGS.

Introduction

Emotions can come and go in a moment. Some stick around and create the mood we are in; happy, sad, angry, loving, surprised and so many more. They can be triggered by events, our own thoughts, behaviours as well as reactions to words and events outside our control, even smell. The physical changes we experience are many; heart rate changing, body temperature rising/falling (sweating), muscle tension/weakness (twitching, trembling). It's incredible, amazing and even scary to think that we have chemicals in our body which are helping to drive the physical changes we are experiencing.

Our emotional energy can be read by others too; like when we walk into a room and feel positive or negative vibes, or that someone is looking at us across a room. Animals pick up and sense emotional energy too. Our own behaviour is motivated by our emotions, as they are preparing us for the actions we are going to take. That's really important if we need to take action immediately.

Letting emotions overwhelm us creates our mood and may prevent us from conscious thought. That takes time and effort which is easy to push away. Overwhelming emotions can also lead us to a point where we simply cannot work out what to do next.

A key to my learning about emotions is that no-one causes you to feel the emotion. What's important to remember is the emotion itself is yours. It's already part of you and being brought to the fore by being activated through an event. The emotion you are feeling is yours to own and manage. Understanding the emotion and what created your reaction is key to your being able to successfully manage it. What we do with our emotions (action), or how we manage them (toward others and ourselves) is entirely up to us. We have that freedom. Sometimes that's easy, and sometimes it's incredibly hard.

Learning to recognise each emotion, what triggers it, how it made us feel, how to manage it and what actions to take, requires consciousness. Just being conscious of the emotion we are feeling is a significant step. A powerful tool to start out with is simply identifying and naming the emotion(s) we are feeling.

When we know which emotion(s) we are feeling, we need to make sure that our response to that emotion is appropriate, by looking internally at what triggered it. This helps us to grow as a person and even improve our own self esteem. Having emotional outbursts may feel like the right reaction at the time, but it often ends in even greater negative emotions.

Sometimes we think about something, and our thoughts run away with us. The emotion becomes greater than the thought that triggered it. Thinking through the action/event, what our thoughts were and whether our emotion aligns with it, will help make sense of it.

Making sure our response to an emotion is appropriate, including our response towards others, is essential too.

We need to experience a range of emotions, with the positive (e.g. happy) flowing steadily and other emotions (e.g. negative) causing small waves rather than tsunamis.

Our emotions also influence the way we communicate with other people; through our body language, facial expression or tone of voice. This may influence how other people react to us.

Sometimes we can be angry about something. Later on, we can be talking to someone and without realising, we pass across to them our feeling of anger. They get angry and respond back and the situation doesn't go how it was intended. All because the original emotion of anger wasn't released.

Writing down our emotions each day, in a journal, is a great way to bring consciousness into play. Capturing triggers, feelings, physical changes and memories of the outcome, help us to develop the recipes we use for our emotions and become the best version of ourselves.

It's important to recognise that we are not our emotion. The emotions we experience and feel are part of who we are, but we are more than that. We are so much more than the sum of our emotions. We are who we want to be-come.

In this book there are many 'emotion recipes.' If they help as they are, then that's great. Each of us may need alternative recipes, and want to create our own. That's great too.

What's important is that each of us find OUR recipes for success. Ultimately success for many of us is that we want to 'Be Happy', more of the time. That doesn't mean emotions of sadness, anger, guilt, shame won't ever happen to us, but we have the right recipes in place to help us get back to a state of happiness, as quickly as we can.

That does raise the question of what happiness is. We may search for happiness and wonder if we will ever find it! How many times have we heard others, or even ourselves, say; 'I'll be happy when……' Then the when happens, and it's back to, 'I'll be happy when….'. When never seems to come, because we are not clear about what we are searching for, or ultimately wanting in our lives.

I've included a page in this book specifically looking at 'Vision for Happiness'. It's a brief start, and can be a bit scary, but I found by working at it, it helps you find what you're looking for. My *Lifebook* has been invaluable for this.

All of this gives everyone an amazing opportunity to help others; working through their emotions, experiences, creating recipes for success and tapping into what their 'Vision for Happiness' could look like.

Now it's time to:

Be Brave

Be Confident

Be Forgiving

Be Grateful

Be Kind

Be Loving

Be Happy

Be You (the you, you want to be)

With love, *Heidi* ♥

My approach to overcome emotions

I will take you through the approach I used to overcome most of my emotions. Yes, there were some that didn't budge and they got handled through belief clearing, which I covered earlier. Belief clearing is best for some of the really deep-rooted and tough beliefs if they are what's driving your emotions. In the following pages, I will take you through;

Emotional journaling

The method I used to capture and understand what was going on with my emotions, using a simple set of questions. Before we go any further, let me list the emotions that are covered in this book;

Anger

Desire

Disgust

Emotional Overwhelm - I've included a recipe card for this. It happens to so many of us.

Envy

Fear

Frustration

Grief

Guilt

Hurt

Jealousy

Joy & Happiness

Love

Resentment

Sadness

Shame

Shock

Surprise

You will see the questions I used, and some simple examples to show you what it looks like.

Emotions Recipe Card

This is a simple generic card that gives an overview of emotions and shows the construct of the recipe cards that will follow.

Recipe Card Directions

This is a list of techniques that I have either used myself for my own emotions, have been used by my daughter, or have been used by others who have contributed to this book.

Are they an exhaustive list? No, but they will give you a fantastic start for your own emotional journey. Over time you will add more to the list yourself and that will be a fantastic achievement.

Recipe Cards

You will see a recipe card specific to each of the emotions listed above. The difference now is that you will see attributes specific to that emotion and some of the techniques shown in the Recipe Card Directions.

Now it's your turn

This is where you will be given instructions to start your emotional journey. It includes details on how to create an Emotion Recipe Card from scratch for any emotions not covered in this book.

Emotion journaling

As I started meditation, and my emotions came to the forefront of my mind, I realised I needed to capture as much as I could to understand what was going on. I found the following questions were invaluable. They helped me get my head around the emotion and really get to understand it. It's like looking at your own emotion from the outside, as a spectator, which allows you to then take hold of it and then manage it.

When I first started, I didn't have a good structure, but what you'll find in the following pages is the method I created as I got better at it and am now sharing with you.

What emotion did I feel today? You choose from the list of emotions (previously listed) and look at the Ingredients (triggers) and shopping list (associated words; covered later) so you can decide which emotion fits best with how you felt. You may relate to one or more of the shopping list items shown against a particular emotion. What is important to recognise is the emotion it relates to. An example would be 'anxiety', which is one of the shopping list items for 'Fear'. In your journal you could capture 'Fear' or 'Fear - Anxiety'.

What prompted the emotion? Then you write down what actually happened. As clearly and concisely as you can. Keeping it simple.

What did I feel about the situation/event? This is where you capture what came to mind at the time. The first thoughts that went through your mind. It's best to try not to add more detail, otherwise you may start embellishing it.

How did it make me feel – physically, how did I express that feeling? Make a note of the physical sensations & reactions you encountered.

What techniques did I use/will I use to manage the emotion? Look through the list of directions (covered later) and write down which ones you can/would use to manage the emotion.

Here are some examples;

What emotion did I feel? Example: Anger – Resentment

What prompted the emotion? Someone at work got the credit for my work.

What did I feel about the situation/event? It isn't fair.

How did it make me feel – physically / how did I express that feeling? Flushed, hot, tearful, grinding teeth.

What did/will I use to manage the emotion?

Smile

90 Sec Rule

Choose to see the good in people

Journaling

What emotion did I feel today? Sadness - Insecurity

What prompted the emotion? My child has left home today to start their own life

What did I feel about the situation/event? I won't see them for a long time. They'll be too busy to talk to me

How did it make me feel – physically/how did I express that feeling? Low energy, emptiness, unwell, wanting to sleep

What did/will I use to manage the emotion?

Honour your feelings

Breathe

Reflect

Meditate and/or pray

Do what makes you happy

What emotion did I feel today? Joy & Happiness – Delight.

What prompted the emotion? I saw children laughing as they were playing in their garden.

What did I feel about the situation/event? Reminded me of pleasant times when I was young.

How did it make me feel – physically/how did I express that feeling?

Smiling, sharing their joy/pleasure, put a kick in your step.

What did/will I use to manage the emotion?

Do what makes you feel happy

Brighten someone's day

Emotions Recipe Card

This is a generic recipe card. It's where you can see a whole range of emotions in the *shopping list*. This is not exhaustive, but does contain many that you will recognise, or be able to associate yourself with.

It then shows *ingredients* that go into making up an emotion, the *directions* to manage the emotion and the *journal notes* that help capture the essence of what has occurred.

This first card shows you how the subsequent recipe cards, for specific emotions, are constructed.

EMOTIONS RECIPE CARD

Ingredients

- VAST AND COMPLEX
- DIFFICULT TO DEFINE AND ENLIST ALL
- EMOTIONS EXPERIENCED BY HUMANS
- SPONTANEOUS FEELING ABOUT ANY PERSON, THING OR EXPERIENCE

Directions

Try one or more of the following;

- DO WHAT MAKES YOU HAPPY
- SMILE, IT'S MAGICAL
- TUNE INTO YOUR MIND/BODY
- EXERCISE
- MEDITATE
- CHOOSE TO SEE THE GOOD IN PEOPLE
- KNOW YOU ARE IN CONTROL
- FOCUS ON POSITIVE ENERGY
- NEGATIVE EMOTION - DON'T WALLOW
- EMBODY POSITIVE & EMPOWERING FEELINGS
- TALK ABOUT WHAT CAN GO RIGHT
- JOURNALING

Journal Note (Example)

- EMOTIONS ARE SUBJECTIVE
- THEY ARE BASED ON PERCEPTION
- THEY ARE UNIQUE TO EACH INDIVIDUAL
- SOME PEOPLE HAVE MORE OF ONE
- SOME MAY LACK IN OTHERS
- THE MORE EMOTIONS YOU EXPERIENCE, THE MORE COLOURFULLIFE IS
- EMOTIONS HELP US COMMUNICATE WHAT WE FEEL TOWARDS A SITUATION, PEOPLE, THINGS AND COPE WITH EVERYDAY LIFE

SHOPPING LIST

Acceptance
Affection
Aggression
Ambivalence
Anger
Apathy
Anxiety
Boredom
Compassion
Confusion
Contempt
Depression
Doubt
Ecstasy
Empathy
Envy
Embarrassment
Euphoria
Fear
Forgiveness
Frustration
Gratitude
Grief
Guilt
Hatred
Hope
Horror
Hostility
Homesickness
Hunger
Hysteria
Interest
Joy/Happiness
Loneliness
Love
Paranoia
Pity
Pleasure
Pride
Rage
Regret
Remorse
Sadness
Shame
Suffering
Surprise
Sympathy

And many more….

Recipe Card Directions List

There are 44 directions provided in the list. I recommend you read through them a few times, and give yourself time to reflect on them and become familiar with them. This will make it easier to recall them when you start working through a particular emotion later.

The Recipe Card Directions List contains additional information that is not shown on the recipe cards themselves. Simply because it would make it too busy and unlikely to fit.

Once you have become familiar with them, and start working with them, you will find what works best for you.

You can add more positive actions/activities to this direction list as you identify them. If you do have some great additions, I would love to hear from you via my website: www.amixtureoffeelings.com

Who knows, you may be included in future updates to this book.

90 Second Rule

- Take 90 seconds to;
  - Recognise the stress/anxiety and watch it happen
  - Is the fear/worry real? Feel it happen. Work it through
  - Take a slow breath, then let it go. Watch it go away.
  - If you need more than 90 seconds, that's just fine.

Allow yourself to feel your feelings

- Don't try to hide them
- Feeling embarrassed around people you like is completely natural

Be nice to people

- Share your happiness with others
- Acknowledge others and use their name, when possible
- Listen to what they have to say
- Be polite and courteous
- Show empathy and compassion
- Look out for the people around you

Breathe/Breathing, choose from the following

Relaxation Technique

- Take steps while in the moment of this stressful emotion helps you focus on something you can control – your breathing
- If feelings are overwhelming you, take shallow breaths.
- Try breathing in through your nose and out through your mouth.
- Pay attention to inhale/exhale
- It will restore your conscious attention for full relaxed breathing
- Let your breath flow as deep down into your belly as is comfortable, without forcing it.
- Breathe in gently and regularly. Some people find it helpful to count steadily from one to five. You may not be able to reach five at first.
- Then, without pausing or holding your breath, let it flow out gently, counting from one to five again if you find this helpful.
- Keep doing this for three to five minutes.

<u>Rectangle breathing</u>

- Breathe in for 3, hold for 1, out for 3, hold for 1.
- Trace this with your fingers or imagine the rectangle.
- Breathe in for 5, hold for 1, out for 5, hold for 1
- Repeat both until your breathing is steady

<u>Intense difficulty/crisis mode/panic attack breathing for fight or flight stage</u>

- Hold your breath for 30 seconds
- Catch breath for 30 seconds
- Repeat no more than 3 times
- The hold your breath for 30 seconds kicks in your bodies response to slow your heart rate.

Additional help can be gained from putting a cold ice pack on your forehead (with a barrier between, such as a towel or cloth). This tricks the body into thinking it is going under water and will respond naturally to keep you alive by reducing your heart rate.

Brighten someone's day

- Let others see your joy and happiness. It may brighten their day and make them smile. This is one way you can 'gift' to society.

Choose to see the good in people

- It will help you to see the good in yourself
- It will make you feel happier and more confident
- Speak words of kindness and love
- See others through the eyes of love and with compassion
- Be the one that finds the gold
- Train your mind to see the good in people
- Don't let others negativity impact you. Don't carry it around
- Remain above the negativity
- Be compassionate to their pain

Coach yourself, if it's difficult

- If your feeling self-conscious, use your internal voice to guide you
- It's only one feeling
- Give yourself encouraging words on how to go forward
- Raise your own self-awareness through personal development (identify what you can/want to improve or eliminate)

Consciousness/Subconscious programming

(contributor: Tamara Mihályi)

- Think, say and do things that feel good and right for you
- Gain knowledge and insight into the power of your consciousness
    - Alter your state of consciousness (e.g. meditation, prayer, yoga, trance)
    - Raise energetic vibration
    - Elevate to higher level of consciousness
- Raise your own awareness of what's happening around you
    - What is contributing to your negative beliefs (e.g. media messages, negative communication) that you can identify and eliminate
    - Develop your logical mind through empowering thoughts (listen to positive affirmations during the day/during sleep)

Do what makes you happy

If there are activities that make you happy, then do more of them. Here are just a few ideas;

- Taking walks in the countryside, by the ocean,
- Hiking, trekking
- Exercise, being in good health/great shape
- Arts; painting, photography, ceramics
- Creativity; turn your home into somewhere special
- Enjoying time with pets/animals
- Voluntary work
- Reading / create your own library
- Listening to music
- Create daily/weekly schedule
- Meditation
- Interaction with others/social interaction or engagement
- Playing games/imagination; table tennis, team games
- Looking at photos from holidays/your past
- Remember the good times
- Spend time with friends/enjoy time with people / meeting people
- Hobbies; up cycling, cooking, gardening, crafting, writing, creativity

- Time with loved ones; family, special friends
- Sensual time with partner
- Travel / Adventure
- Achievement; accomplishing goals/targets
- Learn something new today/everyday
- Visit people in care homes
- Save things that remind you of loved ones
- Singing/Humming
- Visiting museums/places of interest
- Peaceful / serene environment – sight, sound, touch, smell etc.
- Reviewing your strategy for happy living
- Update your *Lifebook* - stay on track and live your Life Vision
- Work on your dreams/goals that you've always wanted to achieve
- Being in the moment
- Appreciate your favourite things
- Explore new and different places, alone or with others
- Perform random act of kindness
- Create Vision Boards (physical or imaginary) – use imagination and visualisation to manifest your life, home, family, self etc.
- Play, with family, friends, children
- Teach children to read
- Volunteer in the community

Embody positive & empowering feelings

- Embrace who you are, not who you think you're supposed to be
- Be thankful for what you have
- Write down all the things you are grateful for
  - Today I am thankful for…
  - I really appreciate…
  - I felt happy today when…
  - I loved watching …
- Focus on what you want; life vision
- Have the courage to dream bigger. Dreams can come true
- Empower yourself and you'll overcome obstacles
- Surround yourself with positive people

Emotional Freedom Technique (EFT)

Choose from a number of techniques that provide you with release from the emotions you are feeling

- Acupuncture
- Energy Medicine
- Neuro-linguistic programming
- Tapping (Meridian Points)
- Thought Field Therapy (TFT)

Exercise

- Exercise is any activity that enhances or maintains your physical fitness.

Remember to build up gradually. Make sure you are medically fit before undertaking exercise. Speak to your health provider.

The following are just a few ideas you might like to explore;

- HIIT – High-intensity interval training
- 30 second burpees
- 30 second shuttles/high knees
- Push ups
- Half sits
- Squats
- Go to the gym
- Fartlek Training
- Dance
- Pilates/Yoga
- Cycling/Spinning
- Walking/Hiking
- Skipping
- Swimming

Five Senses Technique

- Sit in a comfortable position and focus on your breathing
- Isolate each of your five senses
- Spend one minute each focusing on the specific sensations of each
- Notice what you see, hear, taste, smell and touch

Focus on positive energy/elevate your energy to positive/be positive in your thinking

- Imagine your energy as two ends of a thermometer
- HOT = POSITIVE
    - Causes everything in that area of your life to be going smoothly
- COLD = NEGATIVE
    - Causes everything in that area of your life to be a series of problems and struggles and changes your circumstances
    - Elevate your energy to the positive, gradually changing your beliefs and your circumstance

Forgiveness

- Be kind and forgive yourself
- Take time and forgive others
- Forgiveness will release my negative emotion & thoughts

Forgive & Flow
(Contributor: Dani G)

- Imagine talking to each person who you felt had hurt you
- Tell them how you felt
- Thank them for their part in your life
- Imagine them filled with white light,
- Send them floating on a raft down a river, far away from yourself
- Wish them all the best

Get Help

FROM OTHERS

- Talk to trusted family, friends, professionals and positive peer groups about how you feel: a compassionate friend, neighbour, counsellor, therapist, priest, someone who can help you
- Ask them for help when you need it
- Seek out people who will take care of you when you're suffering
- Know there are people there who can help you
- Let people know you value their support
- Avoid people who are not compassionate

SELF HELP/DEVELOPMENT

- Self-help/Personal Development
    - seminars, videos, audios

Give Help

- Give someone the benefit of your passion and drive
- Give someone the use of your time
- Give someone the benefit of your skills and knowledge to benefit their need
- Be proactive in offering your help and assistance, rather than waiting to be asked
- Start a conversation with someone who might need help
- Be patient with people you are helping

Gratitude

- Gratitude creates positive emotions
- Let gratitude lift your mood and become more positive
- Spend time focusing on what you can do and enjoy.

Honour your feelings

- Don't hide the way you feel
- Your feelings are yours and they're valid
- Don't judge yourself harshly
- Let the tears flow, if necessary
- Write your feelings down (journal)

HUNA & HO'OPONOPONO

- Bring to mind anyone with whom you do not feel total alignment or support, etc.
- In your mind's eye, construct a small stage below you
- Imagine an infinite source of love and healing flowing from a source above the top of your head (from your Higher Self), and open up the top of your head, and let the source of love and healing flow down inside your body, fill up the body, and overflow out your heart to heal up the person on the stage. Be sure it is all right for you to heal the person and that they accept the healing.
- When the healing is complete, have a discussion with the person and forgive them, and have them forgive you.
- Next, let go of the person, and see them floating away. As they do, cut the aka cord that connects the two of you (if appropriate). If you are healing in a current primary relationship, then assimilate the person inside you.
- Do this with every person in your life with whom you are incomplete, or not aligned. The final test is, can you see the person or think of them without feeling any negative emotions. If you do feel negative emotions when you do, then do the process again.

Improve/create social life

- Make new friends
- Limit/remove negative engagement
- Find new social activities to engage with

Journaling

- Recognise and capture your emotions each day in a journal
- Writing gives you the chance to clarify your thoughts and feelings and understand yourself
- Reflect on your happiness and capture under gratitude

Know you are in control

- You cannot control every situation or outcome
- You can control your attitude and how you deal with it
- You can control how you feel
- No-one can make you feel negative, without your consent
- It's your choice, know you are in control

Magnitudometer (a made-up word)

- Write down the emotion you feel, e.g. Anger
- Write down what's made you feel the emotion, e.g. someone called me horrible names and said I was stupid
- Draw a line on a piece of paper, writing 0 at one end and 10 at the other
- Write numbers 1 to 10 along the line (shown below);

0
1
2
3
4
5
6
7
8
9
10

- Write what the worst possible situation would be in relation to the negative emotion (example: anger) next to number 10, e.g. someone hurt my family
- Write the next worst possible situation would be in relation to the negative emotion next to number 9, e.g. someone broke into my house
- Then the next for number 8, e.g. someone stole all my money
- Then the next for number 7, e.g. someone ran over my dog
- Then the next for number 6, e.g. someone stole all my computers
- Then the next for number 5, e.g. someone smashed my phone
- Then the next for number 4, e.g. my family forgot my birthday
- Then the next for number 3, e.g. I lost all my keys down a drain
- Then the next for number 2, e.g. someone scratched the paintwork on my car
- Then the next for number 1, e.g. my bank card won't work in the shop/ATM
- Then finally the next for number 0 - someone called me horrible names and said I was stupid

The importance of this exercise is to put what made you feel the negative emotion, e.g. Anger, into its degree of magnitude versus all the other things in your life that are far more important.

Meditate and/or Prayer

- Meditation and/or prayer can improve position emotions, satisfaction, health and happiness.
- It helps you decrease anxiety, stress and depression
- Use it to stop emotions getting too intense
- Be hopeful and positive
- The goal is to calm the mind
- It helps you control emotions by shifting focus
- Just 'being' can shift your mood
- Calm yourself and gain control
- Close your eyes and focus on breathing until you calm down
- Focus on your breath and off of the situation
- Create a sense of well-being, inner peace, love, safety and contentment
- Consider what you are thankful for (gratitude)
- Use a meditation practice, e.g.
  - 6 Phases of Meditation (Vishen Lakhiani)
    - Connection
    - Gratitude
    - Freedom from negative charges
    - Creative visualisation
    - Intentions for the day
    - Blessing
  - Use an alternative method, e.g.
    - Calm music
    - Simple cleaning of house

Mindfulness

- Give yourself time and space
- Observe/be in the present moment – as it is, without attempting to change it
- Live in the present moment
- Let any judgements pass by
- Carry on observing the present moment - as it is, without attempting to change it
- If your mind wanders, recognise that it happened
- Return to observing the present moment – as it is

Negative Belief/Automatic Negative Thoughts (ANTs) clearing

- Be conscious of them
- Write them down (journal)
- Look at them and write a positive to counteract the negative
- Keep reading and being conscious of the positive YOU wrote down

Note: Adding the word 'yet' to some negative thoughts turn it from negative to positive, as it gives you the opportunity to learn and grow;

- I am not good at writing – yet
- I am not good as a parent - yet
- I can't make friends – yet

Negative emotion – don't wallow

- Wallowing in the emotion embodies it
- Let yourself understand and experience the negative emotion (60-90 seconds) but don't wallow in it
    - Say 'I am feeling sad' or 'I am feeling angry'
    - Do not embody them
    - NEVER say 'I AM angry'
- Only embody positive and empowering feelings
    - 'I am happy'

No regrets

- You cannot change the past
- Do not focus on what you *could* have done or *should* have done
- Concentrate on what you can do

One Step at a Time
(Contributor: AbhiPriya Pawar)

- Take things slowly and carefully
- Do just a little at a time

Pause and consider how you feel

- Ups and downs are a normal part of life
- Remember you have the power to control your emotions

Progressive Muscle Relaxation

- Tense and relax different muscle groups
- Start with toes and work up the body to the head
- Tense each muscle group for five seconds and then spend the next 30 seconds slowly relaxing them

Reflect

- Focus on positive steps you can take to feel better
- Think of what you want before you say it
- Deal with problems when you are calm
- Give yourself credit when you are in control and dealing with things in a positive way
- Identify the source of the situation
- Plan your way forward

Root out any fixation/obsession

- Recognise and acknowledge it
- Restore by listening to both positive and negative points
- Talk to someone you trust if you need help

Share simple/special moments

- Something that moved your heart
- Something that touched your soul
- Relive the pure joy of a memory
- Pause for a moment and reflect on something special
- Focus on something good that happened

Show compassion

- Listen and communicate with sincerity, empathy, and kindness
- Provide positive interaction
- Acknowledge how they are feeling
- Be respectful of the wishes of others
- Think carefully before you speak
- Show them you care
- Show your own emotion to their situation
- Give a random act of kindness to someone
- Respect others for the way they are, no matter what

Smile, It's Magical

- It creates a sense of well-being, inner peace, love, safety and contentment
- Did you know it's impossible to have bad feelings if you're smiling?
- Smile in the mirror. Do it even if you don't want to.
- Force a smile on your face. TRY IT. IT WORKS. Hold until its genuine, until your laughing
- Just smile. Let it light you up
- Infect others with your smile. It's highly contagious.
- When you're feeling bad, just smile
- It can't help but make you feel better.

Surprises

- If it's great, enjoy it and celebrate
- Feel motivated and think of the surprise in a positive way, even if you didn't expect it!
- Even if it's negative, think positively about it, and search for something better
- Make small changes in your life. This will help you manage surprises;
  - Walk/drive a different way
  - Stop at different places
  - Eat something different for breakfast
  - Do something spontaneous – surprise yourself
- Learn to let things go to stop negative emotions as and when surprises occur
- Breath. Slow steady breathing to bring your mind and body under control
- Meditate and/or pray

Take a break to regain composure

- To express your feelings, be in emotional control
- If necessary, get some air
- Go for a walk
- Go to the bathroom/restroom
- Breathe

Talk about what can go right

- Focus on what you want to create, based on love, happiness, abundance & freedom.
- Talk about what can go right, instead of what can go wrong
- Avoid focussing on a future based on fear, pain, luck and problems
- It will take effort but you can focus on the best-case outcome
- Negative thoughts and emotions impact the body
- Choose to think positive thoughts

Tell them

- In a relationship – tell them how you feel, often
- Talk with people you like about your feeling. If necessary, use;
  - 'I really enjoy your company'
  - 'I always have so much fun with you'
  - 'I don't feel so happy when you don't respond to my texts'

Tune into your mind/body

- Do some physical activity, it will
  - Elevate your mood
  - Release stress
  - Release endorphins that create feelings of well-being
- Practice Mindfulness
- Meditate
- Healthy eating; avoid sugar, heavy carbs, dairy
- Practice Yoga
- Massage/rejuvenation therapy
- Act with the good
- Listen to the bad. If you act, it will be worse once you've crossed the line.
- Neurological therapy

Techniques for a more significant crisis

You may occasionally experience a more significant crisis and the following may be particularly helpful in these circumstances. These can be followed by other breathing techniques or short meditation. They are intended to create a temporary distraction to help bring your breathing under better control.

- Sit and look at a clock with a moving second hand (analogue) and count your breathing; in for 6 and out for 6, until you feel ready to move on
- Out loud; say 5 things you can see, 4 things you can hear, 3 things you can touch, 2 things you can smell and 1 thing you can taste
- Solve several complicated problems in your head (e.g. 357 divided by 7)
- Lie down, start with your toes and work all the way to your fingers by focussing on each muscle group, tensing every muscle and holding for 10 seconds. Do this once only as it takes about a minute to hold every muscle.
- Count things; anything you like; the cracks in the ceiling/walls, the number of light sockets in the room, the number of tiles on the wall or floor, the number of posters/pictures on the wall, how many cars you can hear passing by.
- Snap rubber band; snap the band on your wrist so it causes low level pain
- Squeeze an ice cube in one hand
- Distraction to focus the mind; clean a room in the house, go for a walk, call a friend, listening to music, build something, learn a new game, play a game with children
- Sensory awareness: can you feel - your eyelashes touching your cheeks, the sensation of your feet touching the ground, the bottom of your feet being rooted into the earth, your tongue moistening your lips, your face relaxing
- Concentrate on holding a particular yoga/meditation position for 60 seconds with your hands; palms facing upward

Visualisation Technique

(Contributor: Jordan River)

<u>Self</u>

- Take a deep breath
- Close your eyes
- Connect with your imaginary future self;
    - See yourself in detail?
    - How will you look?
- Connect with the way you will feel
    - How will you feel?
    - What will the impact be?
- Focus on the positive/success
- Connect with the feeling
- Open your eyes
- Take a deep breath

<u>Situation</u>

- Close your eyes
- Imagine the situation
    - What does it look like?
    - Imagine every step
    - How does it look?
- Connect with the way you feel about it
    - How do you feel?
    - What is the impact and outcome?
- Focus on the positive/success
- Feel the outcome
- Open your eyes
- Take a deep breath

Become conscious of the emotions

that arrive without thought

Heidi C Tyler

Recipe Cards

The following pages focus on just some of the key emotions and look to provide some ideas to help you with your journey of success. In the diagram below, you can see how the recipe card is constructed. More detailed instructions on how to create a Recipe Card from scratch, for an emotion not covered in this book, are shown in the '**Now it's your turn'** section.

INGREDIENTS: These are the ingredients common to the particular emotion.

When you create your own recipe card, you can choose to leave them all in or change them to just contain the ones that you feel are relevant to you, or re-write them entirely.

DIRECTIONS: The directions show a number of techniques that I've included, which could help with that particular emotion., which have been selected from the 'Recipe Card Instruction List'.

In the templates you can choose a card partially completed card which includes the ones shown, or a blank card so you can create your own and decide which techniques serve you best. Choose the order you feel they best work for you too.

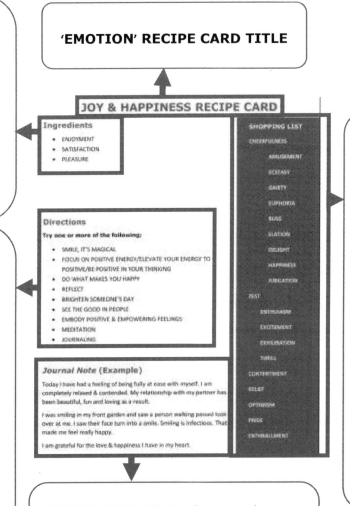

'**EMOTION' RECIPE CARD TITLE**

SHOPPING LIST: This list contains words specifically associated with the emotion shown.

There may be other words that you would use. Feel free to change the list if it suits you better. Just think carefully about the words you use so they are in context with the emotion.

JOURNAL NOTE: This is where you show a brief synopsis of your journal writing, as a reflection of what has happened and how you have worked it through using the directions you've used.

When you create your emotion card for Joy & Happiness, you will be selecting the 'directions' that consistently create Joy & Happiness for you.

If the emotion card is Anger, or indeed any of the negative emotions, then it would be beneficial if you consider picking a range of techniques that help you to manage and get the anger under control. Then pick techniques that help move you to a happier frame of mind.

The examples shown in the following pages are simply a starting point. How you construct your recipe card(s) is entirely up to you. Over time you may change them, until they feel right for you.

I recommend you start with 'Joy & Happiness' for your first recipe card and once you've created your own 'Joy & Happiness Recipe Card', it is worth printing out and have it pinned up in your home. Make it your 'go-to' emotion every day. Repeat it again and again, as often as you can, until it's instilled into your everyday life.

Mine is, so I hope you do the same.

If you want to create a recipe card for an emotion not shown in this section, instructions can be found later on advising how to go about doing them.

ANGER

Anger is a completely normal, and usually healthy, human emotion - when it's controlled effectively, but because anger is such an intense emotion, it can quickly get out of control and become destructive. There are so many things that can trigger anger; fear due to uncertainty, losing a job, failure, undermined at work by colleagues, being called names, derogatory remarks. The list is endless.

The card below shows key words associated with anger in the list of ingredients, and words shown in the shopping list that could be triggers for the emotion. In the directions, you will see actions/activities (which you will have seen in the previous section), which can help to reduce the anger and bring a person back to a calmer state.

The journal note captures some simple sentences that might be written showing what had triggered the emotion and how it changed having followed the directions.

ANGER RECIPE CARD

Ingredients

- INJUSTICE
- CONFLICT
- HUMILIATION
- NEGLIGENCE
- BETRAYAL
- VERBAL OR PHYSICAL ATTACK
- SILENT SULKING
- TENSION
- HOSTILITY
- EMPATHISING WITH ANOTHER

Directions

Try one or more of the following;

- SMILE, IT'S MAGICAL
- 90 SECOND RULE
- MEDITATE
- TUNE INTO YOUR MIND/BODY
- CHOOSE TO SEE THE GOOD IN PEOPLE
- NEGATIVE EMOTION - DON'T WALLOW
- TALK ABOUT WHAT CAN GO RIGHT
- EMBODY POSITIVE & EMPOWERING FEELINGS
- ELEVATE YOUR ENERGY TO POSITIVE
- KNOW YOU ARE IN CONTROL
- EXERCISE
- JOURNALING

Journal Note (Example)

I had a rush of anger at another person's work ethic. I practiced the 90 second rule today, and smiled. I smiled at others too. They smiled back. That made me feel happy

SHOPPING LIST

DISGUST
CONTEMPT
INDIGNATION
LOATHING
REVULSION
ENVY
JEALOUSY
EXASPERATION
FRUSTRATION
IRRITATION
AGITATION
AGGRAVATION
ANNOYANCE
GROUCHINESS
GRUMPINESS
RAGE
BITTERNESS
DISLIKE
FEROCITY
FURY
HATRED
HOSTILITY
LOATHING
OUTRAGE
RESENTMENT
SCORN
SPITE
VENGEFULNESS
WRATH
TORMENT

DESIRE

D esire is having a strong feeling of wanting or longing for something. This can be extremely positive if, for instance, your desire is to help others or yourself in some way or to achieve a long-term goal that brings satisfaction and enjoyment. A career perhaps. Conversely the desire becomes negative when it is for something you cannot or should not have; types of food, something that belongs to someone else. Without managing it effectively, the desire can become a fixation or an obsession which can run out of control.

The card below shows key words associated with desire in the list of ingredients, and words shown in the shopping list that could be triggers for the emotion. In the directions, you will see actions/activities (which you will have seen in the previous section), which can help to manage the desire effectively.

The journal note captures some simple sentences that might be written showing what had triggered the emotion and how it changed having followed the directions.

DESIRE RECIPE CARD

Ingredients

- STRONG FEELING OF;
  - o WANTING TO HAVE SOMETHING
  - o WISHING FOR SOMETHING TO HAPPEN
- LONGING OR HOPING FOR OR WANT (SOMETHING)
  - o PERSON
  - o OBJECT
  - o OUTCOME
- EXCITING HOPE OR DESIRE
- HAVE OR DO SOMETHING YOU KNOW YOU SHOULD AVOID
- SOMETHING THAT SEDUCES OR HAS THE QUALITY TO SEDUCE
- MISS/REGRET SOMETHING

Directions

Try one or more of the following;

- BREATHE/BREATHING
- COACH YOURSELF IF ITS DIFFICULT
- ROOT OUT ANY FIXATION/OBSESSION
- EMBODY POSITIVE & EMPOWERING FEELINGS
- FIVE SENSES TECHNIQUE
- VISUALISATION TECHNIQUES
- REFLECT
- GET HELP
- MAGNITUDOMETER
- MINDFULNESS
- KNOW YOU ARE IN CONTROL
- FOCUS ON POSITIVE ENERGY/ ELEVATE YOUR ENERGY TO POSITIVE/BE POSITIVE IN YOUR THINKING
- HONOUR YOUR FEELINGS
- TUNE INTO YOUR MIND/BODY
- EXERCISE

Journal Note (Example)

I went to a party and saw someone there that I have lusted after for so long. I knew they had a partner and nothing could come of it. I took some deep breathes and reflected on my thoughts and feelings. I worked through on a scale of 1-10 how he fitted in with my ideal partner, and realised he scored much lower than I expected. It was lovely to see him but now I don't have the fixation any more.

SHOPPING LIST

APPEAL

ATTRACTION

ALLURE

ENTICEMENT

SEDUCTION

COVET

EAGERNESS

FANCY

HANKERING

CRAVING

LONGING

LUSTING

WANTING

YEARNING

HUNGER

NEED

TEMPTATION

DESIRE

URGE

IMPULSE

INCLINATION

WISH

DISGUST

D isgust is a strong negative feeling of aversion or disapproval. It can invoke a sickening feeling of revulsion, loathing or nausea. You may be disgusted at the behaviour of others or how something has been done, but equally disgusted at yourself for an action you have taken.

The card below shows key words associated with disgust in the list of ingredients, and words shown in the shopping list that could be triggers for the emotion. In the directions, you will see actions/activities (which you will have seen in the previous section), which can help to reduce the disgust and bring a person back to a more comfortable state.

The journal note captures some simple sentences that might be written showing what had triggered the emotion and how it changed having followed the directions.

DISGUST RECIPE CARD

Ingredients

- OFFENSIVE OR REVOLTING OBJECT, PERSON OR BEHAVIOUR
- SMELL, TOUCH, VISION OR TASTE
- ANIMALS AND INSECTS
- BODY FLUIDS AND EXCRETIONS
- BODILY VIOLATION (LIKE BLOOD AND MUTILATION)
- DEATH AND CORPSES DEATH
- SPOILED FOOD
- POOR HYGIENE

Directions

Try one or more of the following;

- ALLOW YOURSELF TO FEEL YOUR FEELINGS
- BREATHE/BREATHING RELAXATION TECHNIQUE
- DO WHAT MAKES YOU HAPPY
- REFLECT
- TAKE A BREAK TO REGAIN COMPOSURE
- TUNE INTO YOUR MIND/BODY
- CHOOSE TO SEE THE GOOD IN PEOPLE
- KNOW YOU ARE IN CONTROL
- GET HELP
- REFLECT
- MEDITATE AND/OR PRAYER
- JOURNALING

Journal Note (Example)

I went into a neighbour's house today. Their kitchen was so dirty and there was stale food on plates and dirty crockery everywhere. You could see insects crawling all over the food. It was vile. I couldn't get rid of the smell in my nose.

When I go again tomorrow, I will help by doing some washing up for them.

SHOPPING LIST

CONDESCENSION

DERISION

REPULTION

- ANTIPATHY
- CONTEMPT
- DISLIKE
- HATE
- INDIGNATION
- LOATHING
- RESENTMENT
- REVULSION
- SCORN
- SPITE

REPEL

- AVERSION
- ABHORRENCE
- ABOMINATION
- DETEST
- DISDAIN
- REVOLT

VILE

- DISTASTE
- REPUGNANT
- SICKENING

EMOTIONAL OVERWHELM

Emotional Overwhelm is when you become overloaded with lots of different emotions at the same time. They become strong and intense. Overpowering even. When this happens, it becomes difficult to manage. Your mind, body and emotions become muddled and confused. Having multiple actions or activities arising all at the same time can very quickly create overwhelm and simply not being able to function to work through them.

The card below shows key words associated with emotional overwhelm in the list of ingredients, and words shown in the shopping list that could be triggers for the emotion. In the directions, you will see actions/activities (which you will have seen in the previous section), which can help to reduce the emotional overwhelm and bring a person back to a more comfortable and manageable state.

The journal note captures some simple sentences that might be written showing what had triggered the emotion and how it changed having followed the directions.

EMOTIONAL OVERWHELM RECIPE CARD

Ingredients

- BURY OR DROWN BENEATH A HUGE MASS OF SOMETHING
- A STRONG EMOTIONAL EFFECT

Directions

Try one or more of the following;

- ALLOW YOURSELF TO FEEL YOUR FEELINGS
- HONOUR YOUR FEELINGS
- BREATHE/BREATHING
- COACH YOURSELF, IF IT'S DIFFICULT
- EMBODY POSITIVE & EMPOWERING FEELINGS
- FOCUS ON POSITIVE ENERGY/ELEVATE YOUR ENERGY TO POSITIVE/BE POSITIVE IN YOUR THINKING
- MINDFULNESS
- MEDITATE AND/OR PRAYER
- REFLECT
- JOURNALING

Journal Note (Example)

I had so much work to do and had no time to spare. I needed to be a really important meeting and my work was pivotal for the team. I'd driven over 100 miles for the meeting and got a phone call to say my husband had collapsed. I had to drive all the way home. My mind was raising and I felt so overwhelmed with the enormity of everything. To keep myself calm I did lots of deep breathing. The drive gave me time to focus on what was important; my husband. I was mindful of my need to focus on my driving and decided I would ring my boss when I got home. My boss could ring me if they needed anything, although I realised the team would likely manage even though I wasn't there. When I got home, my husband had already visited the doctor and tests were being organised. We spent valuable time together talking about what had happened. My boss didn't call me, so they did manage!

SHOPPING LIST

DEFEAT

OVERCOME

OVERTRHOW

CONQUER

DESTROY

DROWN

SUBMERGE

INUNDATE

WASTE

ASTONISH

PUZZLE

BEWILDER

CONFOUND

ENVY

Envy is a complex, socially repugnant emotion made up of a mix of inferiority feelings, hostility, and resentment. It can be because you have reached a conclusion on what someone else has that creates a desire in yourself to have the same. This could be their perceived financial wealth, physical appearance, relationships, social standing, intelligence or any number of attributes.

The card below shows key words associated with envy in the list of ingredients, with words shown in the shopping list that could be triggers for the emotion. In the directions, you will see actions/activities (which you will have seen in the previous section), which can help to overcome envy and enable a person to feel perhaps more joyful, happy and accepting.

The journal note captures some simple sentences that might be written showing what had triggered the emotion and how it changed having followed the directions.

ENVY RECIPE CARD

Ingredients

- COMPARISON (BETWEEN SELF AND ANOTHER)
- DESIRE (SOMETHING SOMEONE ELSE HAS)
  - STATUS
  - MONEY/WEALTH
  - POWER
  - SUCCESS
  - FAMILY TIES
  - INTELLIGENCE

Directions

Try one or more of the following;

- SMILE, IT'S MAGICAL
- 90 SECOND RULE
- NEGATIVE EMOTION - DON'T WALLOW
- BE POSITIVE IN YOUR THINKING
- UNDERTAKE POSITIVE ACTIVITIES
- ELEVATE YOUR ENERGY TO POSITIVE
- KNOW YOU ARE IN CONTROL
- DO WHAT MAKES YOU HAPPY
- REFLECT ON YOUR HAPPINESS
- CHOOSE TO SEE THE GOOD IN PEOPLE
- EMBODY POSITIVE & EMPOWERING FEELINGS
- MEDITATE
- EXERCISE
- JOURNALING

Journal Note (Example)

My neighbour has just got a new car and I want one! I took a deep breath and reflected on what I already have. My priorities are different to theirs. I washed and cleaned my own car, inside and out, which now looks lovely and gave me some exercise. My neighbour's are lovely people, so I knocked on their door and told them how lovely their new car is.

SHOPPING LIST

COVET

CRAVE

ENVY

BEGRUDGE

RESENT

DESIRE

LONG FOR

WANT

YEARN

IDEALISE

JEALOUSY

BITTER

GREED

FEAR

Fear is caused by a perceived danger or threat that occurs which causes a change in metabolic and organ functions and ultimately a change in behaviour. It can result in a person fleeing, hiding, or freezing from perceived traumatic events. Irrational fear is called a phobia.

The card below shows key words associated with fear in the list of ingredients, and words shown in the shopping list that could be triggers for the emotion. In the directions, you will see actions/activities (which you will have seen in the previous section), which can help to overcome the fear and enable a person to become calmer.

The journal note captures some simple sentences that might be written showing what had triggered the emotion and how it changed having followed the directions.

FEAR RECIPE CARD

Ingredients

- IMPENDING DANGER
- SURVIVAL MECHANISM
- REACTION TO NEGATIVE STIMULUS
- MILD CAUTION OR EXTREME PHOBIA
- TRIVIAL OR SERIOUS

Directions

Try one or more of the following;

- BREATH/BREATHING - RELAXATION TECHNIQUE
- TAKE A BREAK TO REGAIN COMPOSURE
- COACH YOURSELF, IF IT'S DIFFICULT
- MEDITATION AND/OR PRAYER
- FIVE SENSES TECHNIQUE
- FOCUS ON POSITIVE ENERGY/ELEVATE YOUR ENERGY TO POSITIVE/BE POSITIVE IN YOUR THINKING
- GET HELP
- KNOW YOU ARE IN CONTROL
- REFLECT
- PROGRESSIVE MUSCLE RELAXATION
- TALK ABOUT WHAT CAN GO RIGHT
- JOURNALING

Journal Note (Example)

I felt fearful today because I had let my finances get out of control. I did deep breathing and meditation which helped me to focus. I faced the problems I was having and was able, with help, to find a way forward.

SHOPPING LIST

NERVOUSNESS

ANXIETY

APPREHENSION

DISTRESS

DREAD

EDGINESS

JUMPINESS

TENSENESS

UNEASINESS

WORRY

HORROR

ALARM

FRIGHT

HYSTERICAL

MORTIFICATION

OVERWHELMED

PANIC

SHOCK

TERROR

FRUSTRATION

Frustration often occurs when we are angry, annoyed or disappointed in some way. It's a mix of emotions and can be caused by feelings of uncertainty and insecurity which stems from a sense of inability to fulfil needs. If our needs are blocked, we become frustrated. Frustration may be directed at ourselves or others.

The card below shows key words associated with frustration in the list of ingredients, and words shown in the shopping list that could be triggers for the emotion. In the directions, you will see actions/activities (which you will have seen in the previous section), which can help to overcome the frustration and enable a person to become more contented.

The journal note captures some simple sentences that might be written showing what had triggered the emotion and how it changed having followed the directions.

FRUSTRATION RECIPE CARD

Ingredients

- UNABLE TO CHANGE OR ACHIEVE SOMETHING
- PREVENTION OF THE PROGRESS, SUCCESS, OR FULFILMENT
- FEELINGS OF UNCERTAINTY AND INSECURITY
- NEEDS ARE CONSTANTLY IGNORED OR UNSATISFIED

Directions

Try one or more of the following;

- BREATHE/BREATHING
- REFLECT
- TAKE A BREAK TO REGAIN COMPOSURE
- TALK ABOUT WHAT CAN GO RIGHT
- TUNE INTO YOUR MIND/BODY
- DO WHAT MAKES YOU HAPPY

Journal Note (Example)

It was lovely having friends to stay but I had so much to do to finish my project but kept being constantly interrupted. I could feel myself becoming more and more frustrated. I realised that spending time with them and talking about my project would get some new insights, but also taking a break would mean I could go back to it afresh, once they'd gone home. We all had a lot of fun together, going out for walks by the sea and letting the children play in the sand.

SHOPPING LIST

ANGER
BITTERNESS
    RESENTMENT
DEFEAT
    BLOCK
    COLLAPSE
    COUNTER
DISAPPOINTMENT
    DEPRESSION
    DISSATISFACTION
DISCOURAGEMENT
DISCONTENT
FAILURE
IRRITATION
    AGGRAVATION
    ANNOYANCE
    EXASPERATION
OBSTRUCTION
    HAMPERING
    HINDERING
    SCUPPERING
QUASHING
    CRIPPLING
    CRUSHING
VEXATION

GRIEF

Grief is such a strong emotional response to loss. It can have physical effects on the body and/or trigger other emotions such as sadness or loneliness. There are considered to be five stages of grief which need to be managed well by taking care of yourself, seeking support, and giving yourself time to heal. The five stages are: denial, anger, bargaining, depression and acceptance.

The card below shows key words associated with grief in the list of ingredients, and words shown in the shopping list that could be triggers for the emotion. In the directions, you will see actions/activities (which you will have seen in the previous section), which can help to overcome the grief and enable a person to reach acceptance.

The journal note captures some simple sentences that might be written showing what had triggered the emotion and how it changed having followed the directions.

GRIEF RECIPE CARD

Ingredients

- LOSS OF SOMEONE OR SOMETHING IMPORTANT TO YOU, TO WHICH A BOND OR AFFECTION WAS FORMED
  - PARTNER
  - FAMILY MEMBER
  - JOB
  - BELOVED PET
  - FRIENDSHIP/SOCIAL INTERACTION
  - PERSONAL DREAM/GOAL
  - ROMANTIC RELATIONSHIP
  - HEALTH

Directions

Try one or more of the following;

- BREATHE/BREATHING
- ALLOW YOURSELF TO FEEL YOUR FEELINGS
- HONOUR YOUR FEELINGS
- GET HELP
- NO REGRETS
- MEDITATION
- COACH YOURSELF, IF ITS DIFFICULT
- FOCUS ON POSITIVE ENERGY/ELEVATE YOUR ENERGY TO POSITIVE/BE POSITIVE IN YOUR THINKING
- KNOW YOU ARE IN CONTROL
- DO WHAT MAKES YOU HAPPY
- TALK ABOUT WHAT CAN GO RIGHT
- GRATITUDE

Journal Note (Example)

I became so ill, I had to stop working. I loved my job. I don't know what I'm going to do. I had over 10 years left to work and now it's all gone. I found some meditation which helped me so much, and some personal development training. It's been amazing. My whole life has changed now. I am so grateful I found a way forward.

SHOPPING LIST

AFFLICTION
ANGUISH
AGONY
ANGST
DISTRESS
HEARTBREAK
PAIN
SUFFERING
TORMENT
BEREAVEMENT
LOSS
DEJECTION
DESPONDENCY
MORTIFICATION
MOURNING
GRIEF
LAMENT
SORROW
PINING
REGRET
REMORSE
SADNESS
BLUES
DESOLATION
DESPAIR
DESPONDENCY
GRIEF
HEARTACHE
MISERY
SORROW
WOE

GUILT

Guilt can be a thought, or an emotional experience which happens when a person believes or realises, accurately or not, that they have compromised their own/other standards of conduct.

The card below shows key words associated with guilt in the list of ingredients, and words shown in the shopping list that could be triggers for the emotion. In the directions, you will see actions/activities (which you will have seen in the previous section), which can help to overcome guilt and enable a person to feel positive.

The journal note captures some simple sentences that might be written showing what had triggered the emotion and how it changed having followed the directions.

GUILT RECIPE CARD

Ingredients

- SOMETHING YOU DID OR DIDN'T DO
- SOMETHING YOU THINK YOU DID/DIDN'T DO
- DIDN'T DO ENOUGH TO HELP PERSON/PEOPLE
- CONSIDERED BY OTHERS TO BE DOING BETTER THAN THEM/SOMEONE ELSE

Directions

Try one or more of the following;

- ALLOW YOURSELF TO FEEL YOUR FEELINGS
- HONOUR YOUR FEELINGS
- PAUSE AND CONSIDER HOW YOU FEEL
- REFLECT
- ROOT OUT ANY FIXATION/OBSESSION
- TAKE A BREAK TO REGAIN COMPOSURE
- MEDITATE AND/OR PRAYER
- GET HELP
- COACH YOURSELF, IF IT'S DIFFICULT
- TALK ABOUT WHAT CAN GO RIGHT
- TELL THEM
- DO WHAT MAKES YOU HAPPY
- EMBODY POSITIVE & EMPOWERING FEELINGS
- SMILE, IT'S MAGICAL

Journal Note (Example)

My boss asked me to work late and I said yes. When I got home, I found out my little girl had been poorly most of the day and crying for me. I should have said 'no' and then she wouldn't have had so long without me. I felt like it was all my fault. Once I'd taken time to honour my feelings and reflect on it all, I realised I can't change what happened, but I can change how I manage going forward. I will learn to say no. I told my daughter how I felt and how I will be changing things in future. My time with her is more precious. I don't have to work late!

SHOPPING LIST

ANGER

ANXIETY

DEPRESSION

EMPTINESS

ENVY

GUILT

LONELINESS

RAGE

REGRET

REMORSE

SADNESS

SHAME

HURT

Hurt in the context of emotion, is a psychological, mental or emotional pain. It is an unpleasant feeling or suffering which stems from a non-physical origin. You may feel hurt because of opinions, behaviour, actions or words of others who don't hold the same view as you. The hurt may be down to your own insecurity or personal issues.

The card below shows key words associated with hurt in the list of ingredients, and words shown in the shopping list that could be triggers for the emotion. In the directions, you will see actions/activities (which you will have seen in the previous section), which can help to overcome hurt and enable a person to feel positive.

The journal note captures some simple sentences that might be written showing what had triggered the emotion and how it changed having followed the directions.

HURT RECIPE CARD

Ingredients

- PAIN CAUSED BY SOMEONE WE INTERACT WITH;
  - INSULT
  - REJECTION
  - JUDGEMENT
  - IGNORED BY
  - DIFFERING VIEWS
- BELIEF IN WHAT OTHERS SAY AND THINK

Directions

Try one or more of the following;

- FIVE SENSES TECHNIQUE
- MINDFULNESS
- REFLECT
- TELL THEM
- FORGIVENESS
- JOURNALING

Journal Note (Example)

My partner was told something that I'd apparently said which wasn't true. They should have realised it wasn't something I would say, but instead they challenged me about it. I could believe they would even consider it to be true. I was incredibly upset by the whole situation. I gave myself time to think it all through and told them how it had made me feel. I forgave them of course.

SHOPPING LIST

AFFLICTION
    MISFORTUNE
    TROUBLE
ANGUISH
    DISTRESS
    PAIN
    TORMENT
    UPSET
    WOE
DETRIMENT
    DAMAGE
    DISADVANTAGE
    HARM
    INJURY
    TRAUMA
DISBELIEF
GRIEF
    MISERY
    SADNESS
    SORROW
    SUFFERING
    WRETCHEDNESS
IMPAIR
    MAIM
    WOUND
MALTREAT
    ABUSE
    TORTURE

JEALOUSY

Jealousy in general, centres around thoughts and feelings of insecurity and fear which can generate a host of emotions including anger & fear. Jealousy differs from envy as it relates to losing something, whereas envy relates to wanting something. Jealousy tends to mean taking precautionary measures which can quickly run out of control.

The card below shows key words associated with jealousy in the list of ingredients, and words shown in the shopping list that could be triggers for the emotion. In the directions, you will see actions/activities (which you will have seen in the previous section), which can help to overcome jealousy.

The journal note captures some simple sentences that might be written showing what had triggered the emotion and how it changed having followed the directions.

JEALOUSY RECIPE CARD

Ingredients

- LACK OF SELF CONFIDENCE
- POOR SELF IMAGE
- FEAR
- INSECURITY

Directions

Try one or more of the following;

- REFLECT
- ROOT OUT ANY FIXATION/OBSESSION
- TELL THEM
- GET HELP
- TAKE A BREAK TO REGAIN COMPOSURE
- DO WHAT MAKES YOU HAPPY
- EMBODY POSITIVE & EMPOWERING FEELINGS
- FOCUS ON POSITIVE ENERGY/ELEVATE YOUR ENERGY TO POSITIVE/BE POSITIVE IN YOUR THINKING
- MEDITATE AND/OR PRAYER
- TUNE INTO YOUR MIND/BODY
- EXERCISE
- SMILE, IT'S MAGICAL

SHOPPING LIST

ANGER

FEAR

DISGUST

INADEQUATE

HELPLESS

INSECURITY

JEALOUS

LACK

RESENTMENT

Journal Note (Example)

My partner constantly talks of other women being gorgeous and sexy. They never say that to me. Why can't I look like them? What's wrong with me? I plucked up the courage to tell my partner how I felt. They were mortified I had been feeling like this. We spent hours talking about everything that was positive about me and our relationship. We're making some changes in the things we do together too. I can't wait.

JOY & HAPPINESS

Joy & Happiness are both emotions where you have feelings of contentment or satisfaction. Joy & Happiness are positive or pleasant emotions which can range from contentment to intense joy. They could be separated and each have their own recipe card, but in this instance, they have been combined. Happiness is about the self's pleasure. Happiness may dwell on materialistic, worldly pleasure while joy is derived from soul satisfying, emotional well-being.

The card below shows key words associated with joy & happiness in the list of ingredients, and words shown in the shopping list that could be triggers for the emotion. In the directions, you will see actions/activities (which you will have seen in the previous section), which can help to move into or remain in the joy & happiness emotion.

The journal note captures some simple sentences that might be written showing what had triggered the emotion and how it was achieved having followed the directions.

JOY & HAPPINESS RECIPE CARD

Ingredients

- ENJOYMENT
- SATISFACTION
- PLEASURE

Directions

Try one or more of the following;

- SMILE, IT'S MAGICAL
- FOCUS ON POSITIVE ENERGY/ELEVATE YOUR ENERGY TO POSITIVE/BE POSITIVE IN YOUR THINKING
- DO WHAT MAKES YOU HAPPY
- REFLECT
- BRIGHTEN SOMEONE'S DAY
- SEE THE GOOD IN PEOPLE
- EMBODY POSITIVE & EMPOWERING FEELINGS
- MEDITATION
- JOURNALING

Journal Note (Example)

Today I have had a feeling of being fully at ease with myself. I am completely relaxed & contended. My relationship with my partner has been beautiful, fun and loving as a result.

I was smiling in my front garden and saw a person walking passed look over at me. I saw their face turn into a smile. Smiling is infectious. That made me feel really happy.

I am grateful for the love & happiness I have in my heart.

SHOPPING LIST

CHEERFULNESS

AMUSEMENT

ECSTASY

GAIETY

EUPHORIA

BLISS

ELATION

DELIGHT

HAPPINESS

JUBILATION

ZEST

ENTHUIASM

EXCITEMENT

EXHILIRATION

THRILL

CONTENTMENT

RELIEF

OPTIMISM

PRIDE

ENTHRALLMENT

LOVE

Love encompasses a range of strong and positive emotional and mental states. Often love refers to a feeling of strong attraction and emotional attachment. Its effects and impact are far reaching. Love often involves caring for, or identifying with, a person or thing. You can "love" material objects, animals, or activities too.

The card below shows key words associated with love in the list of ingredients, and words shown in the shopping list that could be triggers for the emotion. In the directions, you will see actions/activities (which you will have seen in the previous section), which can help capture the emotional and mental state of Love.

The journal note captures some simple sentences that might be written showing what had triggered the emotion and how it was achieved having followed the directions.

LOVE RECIPE CARD

Ingredients

- FEELING OF PROFOUND ONENESS
- PLATONIC
- ROMANTIC
- RELIGIOUS OR FAMILIAL
- BONDING
- FRIENDSHIP
- ALTRUISM
- PHILANTHROPY

Directions

Try one or more of the following;

- WHAT TYPE OF LOVE ARE YOU FEELING?
  - AFFECTION, LONGING, LUST
- ENJOY THE MOMENT
- TELL THEM?
- ROOT OUT ANY FIXATION/OBSESSION
- ALLOW YOURSELF TO FEEL YOUR FEELINGS
- TAKE A BREAK TO REGAIN COMPOSURE
- COACH YOURSELF, IF ITS DIFFICULT
- BREATHE
- MEDITATION
- JOURNALING

Journal Note (Example)

I have such a warm feeling of love for Dad now, who I had been angry with for so long. I thought of them during my meditation. I worked it through and cleared my belief by handing it back to them. I feel so much better now and I thanked them.

SHOPPING LIST

AFFECTION

ADORATION

ATTRACTION

CARING

FONDNESS

LOVE

LIKING

SENTIMENTALITY

LONGING

LUST

AROUSAL

DESIRE

INFATUATION

OBSESSION

PASSION

RESENTMENT

Resentment is bitterness and anger that someone feels about something. It can be triggered by an emotionally disturbing experience felt again or relived in the mind. It can arise from misunderstandings, like feeling resentment over a dirty look you thought was directed at you but really wasn't. It's usually best to root out resentment early.

The card below shows key words associated with resentment in the list of ingredients, and words shown in the shopping list that could be triggers for the emotion. In the directions, you will see actions/activities (which you will have seen in the previous section), which can help overcome the feeling of resentment.

The journal note captures some simple sentences that might be written showing what had triggered the emotion and how it was achieved having followed the directions.

RESENTMENT RECIPE CARD

Ingredients

- SENSE OF INJUSTICE OR WRONGDOING
  - NEGATIVE TREATMENT BY OTHERS
  - FEEL LIKE OBJECT OF DISCRIMINATION OR PREJUDICE
  - FEELING USED OR TAKEN ADVANTAGE OF
    HAVING ACHIEVEMENTS GO UNRECOGNISED
  - REJECTION OR DENIAL BY ANOTHER
  - BEING PUT DOWN OR EMBARRASSED BY OTHERS

Directions

Try one or more of the following;

- BREATHING RELAXATION TECHNIQUE
- MEDITATION AND/OR PRAYER
- FIVE SENSES TECHNIQUE
- PROGRESSIVE MUSCLE RELAXATION
- TUNE INTO YOUR MIND/BODY
- CHOOSE TO SEE THE GOOD IN PEOPLE
- NEGATIVE EMOTION - DON'T WALLOW
- TALK ABOUT WHAT CAN GO RIGHT
- EMBODY POSITIVE & EMPOWERING FEELINGS
- ELEVATE YOUR ENERGY TO POSITIVE
- KNOW YOU ARE IN CONTROL
- EXERCISE
- JOURNALING

Journal Note (Example)

Someone I worked with threw a shoe at me and told me I would never achieve anything, in front of other team members. I had worked incredibly hard and previously had my work recognised by the Manager. I resented the treatment from this team member.

SHOPPING LIST

ANGER

DISPLEASURE

FURY

INDIGNATION

IRE

IRRITATION

MALICE

PIQUE

RAGE

VEXATION

WRATH

BITTERNESS

GRUDGE

RANCOUR

UMBRAGE

GALL

HUFF

HURT

ILL WILL

ANIMOSITY

SADNESS

Sadness is an emotional pain. It is often caused by a feeling of being unhappy, especially because something bad has happened. Sadness is associated with, or characterized by, feelings of disadvantage, loss, despair, grief, helplessness, disappointment and sorrow. People deal with sadness in different ways, and it is an important emotion. It can help to motivate you to deal with your situation.

The card below shows key words associated with sadness in the list of ingredients, and words shown in the shopping list that could be triggers for the emotion. In the directions, you will see actions/activities (which you will have seen in the previous section), which can help to overcome sadness.

The journal note captures some simple sentences that might be written showing what had triggered the emotion and how it was achieved having followed the directions.

SADNESS RECIPE CARD

Ingredients

- FEELING OF LOSS
- DISADVANTAGE
- MAY LEAD TO DEPRESSION
- QUIET
- LESS ENERGETIC
- WITHDRAWN TO ONESELF
- SLOPING BODY
- STUCK OUT LIPS
- DOWNCAST APPEARANCE OF THE HEAD

Directions

Try one or more of the following;

- HONOUR YOUR FEELINGS
- TAKE A MOMENT TO PAUSE AND CONSIDER HOW YOU FEEL
- BREATHE
- REFLECT
- MEDITATE AND/OR PRAY
- GET HELP
- JOURNALING
- DO WHAT MAKES YOU HAPPY
- SMILE, IT'S MAGICAL

Journal Note (Example)

My dog died today. She has been with me my whole life. I've not had a day without her. I stayed with her until she was gone. My mum packed up all the doggy toys, bedding and food. Now I have no pet to cuddle or stroke. The house feels empty.   I could feel her during my meditation.   It would be brilliant if I could teach dogs. I'm going to find out how to do that and then focus on getting there. She would love that. YAY.

SHOPPING LIST

SUFFERING

AGONY

HURT

ANGUISH

DISAPPOINTMENT

DISMAY

DISPLEASURE

SHAME

GUILT

REMORSE

REGRET

NEGLECT

INSECURITY

ALIENATION

HOMESICKNESS

EMBARRASSMENT

HUMILIATION

SYMPATHY

PITY

SHAME

Shame is a self-conscious emotion associated with a negative evaluation of the self. It makes you feel like a bad person and regret what you did. The way we may talk to others and make them feel bad, is because we are trying to shame them.

The card below shows key words associated with shame in the list of ingredients, and words shown in the shopping list that could be triggers for the emotion. In the directions, you will see actions/activities (which you will have seen in the previous section), which can help to overcome the emotion of shame.

The journal note captures some simple sentences that might be written showing what had triggered the emotion and how it was achieved having followed the directions.

SHAME RECIPE CARD

Ingredients

- SELF-AWARENESS
- BLAMING YOURSELF
- PERSONALITY TRAIT
- SELF-ESTEEM

Directions

Try one or more of the following;

- ALLOW YOURSELF TO FEEL YOUR FEELINGS
- HONOUR YOUR FEELINGS
- PAUSE AND CONSIDER HOW YOU FEEL
- REFLECT
- TAKE A BREAK TO REGAIN COMPOSURE
- MEDITATE AND/OR PRAYER
- GET HELP
- COACH YOURSELF, IF IT'S DIFFICULT
- TALK ABOUT WHAT CAN GO RIGHT
- TELL THEM
- DO WHAT MAKES YOU HAPPY
- EMBODY POSITIVE & EMPOWERING FEELINGS
- SMILE, IT'S MAGICAL

SHOPPING LIST

SELF CONSCIOUS

UNWORTHY

UNLOVABLE

DISTRESS

EXPOSURE

DISHONOUR

DISGRACE

CONDEMNATION

MISTRUST

POWERLESSNESS

WORTHLESSNESS

Journal Note (Example)

I bought shame on myself and the whole family. I stole something and got caught. I took something that I thought would look lovely on me but couldn't afford. I spoke to a really close friend who told me how lovely I am and that it's what's on the inside that matters. I realised it was a stupid thing to do. If I need something to make me feel better, I'll make it in future. I went and apologised to the shop. They were so genuine and grateful. The Manager actually smiled. They decided not to press charges as I had taken the time to go and see them. That make me smile. I feel so much better.

SHOCK

Shock emotionally speaking, is when you get a surge of strong emotions which bring about a physical reaction, causing hormone changes in the body (fight or flight response). This may be in response to an unexpected or stressful event. Understanding the cause of the shock and taking steps/actions to overcome it are key to preventing it becoming more severe.

The card below shows key words associated with shock in the list of ingredients, and words shown in the shopping list that could be triggers for the emotion. In the directions, you will see actions/activities (which you will have seen in the previous section), which can help to overcome the shock.

The journal note captures some simple sentences that might be written showing what had triggered the emotion and how a calm state could be achieved.

SHOCK RECIPE CARD

Ingredients

- CANNOT THINK STRAIGHT
- EXPERIENCING PHYSICAL SIDE EFFECTS
- FEEL STRANGELY EXHAUSTED
- MIND CAN'T MAKE SENSE OF THE SITUATION
- FEARFUL

Directions

Try one or more of the following;

- BREATHE/BREATHING RELAXATION TECHNIQUES
- TAKE A BREAK TO REGAIN COMPOSURE
- GET HELP
- MEDITATE AND/OR PRAYER
- REFLECT
- SHARE SIMPLE/SPECIAL MOMENTS
- KNOW YOU ARE IN CONTROL
- NO REGRETS
- GRATITUDE
- JOURNALING

Journal Note (Example)

The police had come to my house to see me. I was in the shower and my husband came to get me. I said they could wait, but he said it was urgent. They told me my Dad had died during the night. I felt very faint and had to sit down. I didn't understand as no-one had rung me. How could this be true. I realised later that my phone was unplugged. I spent time talking with family and coming to terms with what had happened and why.

SHOPPING LIST

UNEXPECTED

DISTURBANCE

EVENT

EXPERIENCE

SURPRISE

TRAUMA

UPSET

SURPRISE

Surprise is a brief mental state. Something that a person might feel if something unexpected happens. The unexpected could be positive, negative, neutral, pleasant or unpleasant depending on what it is and a person's perception. It can happen when we are startled by something happening nearby, or something we see which has caught us unaware.

The card below shows key words associated with surprise in the list of ingredients, and words shown in the shopping list that could be triggers for the emotion. In the directions, you will see actions/activities (which you will have seen in the previous section), which can help to manage/overcome the emotion of surprise.

The journal note captures some simple sentences that might be written showing what had triggered the emotion and how it was achieved having followed the directions.

SURPRISE RECIPE CARD

Ingredients

- UNEXPECTED RESULT
- MOMENTARY RAISING OF EYEBROWS
- HORIZONTAL LINES ON THE FOREHEAD
- OPEN MOUTH OR DROPPED JAW
- STRETCHED SKIN BELOW THE EYEBROWS
- WIDE OPEN EYELIDS

Directions

Try one or more of the following;

- LOVE SURPRISES!
  - IF ITS GREAT, ENJOY IT AND CELEBRATE
  - FEEL MOTIVATED AND THINK OF THE SURPRISE IN A POSITIVE WAY, EVEN IF YOU DIDN'T EXPECT IT
  - EVEN IF IT'S NEGATIVE, THINK POSITIVELY AND SEARCH FOR SOMETHING BETTER.
  - MAKE SMALL CHANGES INTO YOUR LIFE. THIS WILL HELP YOU MANAGE SURPRISES;
    - WALK/DRIVE A DIFFERENT WAY
    - STOP AT DIFFERENT PLACES
    - EAT SOMETHING DIFFERENT FOR BREAKFAST
    - DO SOMETHING SPONTANEOUS - SURPRISE YOURSELF
  - LEARN TO LET THINGS GO TO STOP NEGATIVE EMOTIONS AS AND WHEN SURPRISES OCCUR
  - BREATH. SLOW STEADY BREATHING TO BRING YOUR MIND AND BODY UNDER CONTROL
  - MEDITATE AND/OR PRAY

Journal Note (Example)

I got my payslip today. It was not what I expected. My pay was lower with no explanation of why. All my financial plans for the month were out the window! I rang my Mum to get help. Mum spent time going through the payslip and worked everything out. When Mum explained it, I understood, but we both agreed the company could have been more open about their payroll practices. I wrote to the boss and they are going to change the contract details because of it. It doesn't change my payslip but it's made me feel better that I did something positive. Mum's helping me with a bit of money to help me through my first month.

SHOPPING LIST

ASTONISHMENT

ASTOUND

AWE

BEWILDER

CONFOUND

CONFUSE

DAZZLE

FLABBERGAST

OVERWHELM

PERPLEX

RATTLE

AMAZEMENT

CONSTERNATION

WONDERMENT

CURIOSITY

DISAPPOINTMENT

JOLT

SHOCK

STARTLE

MIRACLE

REVELATION

Now it's your turn

Copy 'My emotion' template (shown in the templates section).

Write down an answer to the following questions.

Select and write down what emotion you felt, from the following list?

Anger

Desire

Disgust

Emotional Overwhelm

Envy

Fear

Frustration

Grief

Guilt

Hurt

Jealousy

Joy & Happiness (I recommend you start with this one. See my NOTE further down)

Love

Resentment

Sadness

Shame

Shock

Surprise

You could be feeling happy and be excited about something. Looking at the 'Joy & Happiness' card you will see 'excitement' is in the 'shopping list'. In your journal you could capture 'Joy & Happiness' or 'Joy & Happiness - Excitement'.

What prompted the emotion? Write down what actually happened. As clearly and concisely as you can. Keep it simple and keep it confined.

What did you feel about the situation/event? Capture what came to mind at the time. The first thoughts that went through your mind. Try not to add more detail, otherwise you may start embellishing it.

How did it make you feel – physically, how did you express that feeling? Make a note of the physical sensations & reactions you encountered.

What directions did/will you use to manage the emotion? Look through the list of directions I have provided and write down which ones you used, or will use, to manage the emotion.

NOTE: Sometimes it's hard to know where to start. If it helps, think back to something that made you happy. It doesn't matter when it happened. What's important is being conscious of it and writing it down. Once you've done one, think of another. Keep going if you can. It's lovely to bring back happy memories, no matter what they are. To someone else they may seem small or insignificant. To you they may be the most important thing in the world. This is your journal. You capture what is important to you. It's you that matters. No-one else. Once you've done some happy ones, its perhaps time to venture into some of the negative ones. As a starting point think of something from the past, that you no longer have a deep emotional feeling or attachment to. This should allow you to go through it without the deep emotion and be able to capture the facts relating to it. Something that made you sad in the past, but doesn't affect you the same way now, could be the loss of a family pet from childhood. Thinking back on it, could inadvertently bring up emotions. If that happens use the appropriate 'Recipe Card' and follow the directions. Thinking of things from the past can trigger emotions without warning. You might like to use the 'Surprise Recipe Card' too if that happens.

The more practice you get in consciously thinking of your emotions, and working them through using journaling and recipe cards, the better you will be able to manage them.

Some Examples

Here are some very simple examples of feeling an emotion and what you might capture.

What emotion did I feel? Example: Anger - Resentment

What prompted the emotion? Someone at work got the credit for my work.

What did I feel about the situation/event? It isn't fair.

How did it make me feel – physically / how did I express that feeling? Flushed, hot, tearful, grinding teeth.

What can/will I use to manage the emotion?

Smile

90 Sec Rule

Forgiveness

Choose to see the good in people

Journaling

What emotion did I feel today? Sadness - Insecurity

What prompted the emotion? My child has left home today to start their own life

What did I feel about the situation/event? I won't see them for a long time. They'll be too busy to talk to me

How did it make me feel – physically/how did I express that feeling? Low energy, emptiness, unwell, wanting to sleep

What can/will I use to manage the emotion?

Honour your feelings

Breathe

Reflect

Forgiveness - self

Gratitude

Meditate and/or pray

Do what makes you happy

What emotion did I feel today? Happiness – Delight.

What prompted the emotion? I saw children laughing as they were playing in their garden.

What did I feel about the situation/event? Reminded me of pleasant times when I was young.

How did it make me feel – physically/how did I express that feeling?

Smiling, sharing their joy/pleasure, put a kick in my step.

What can/will I use to manage the emotion?

Do what makes you feel happy

Brighten someone's day

Select a Recipe Card Template

You can either copy one of the partially completed recipe cards or you can copy a blank recipe card.

Partially completed recipe card template:

Choose from one of the cards appropriate to the emotion you wish to create;

Anger

Desire

Disgust

Emotional Overwhelm

Envy

Fear

Frustration

Grief

Guilt

Hurt

Jealousy

Joy & Happiness (I recommend you start with this one. See my NOTE further down)

Love

Resentment

Sadness

Shame

Shock

Surprise

Go through the list of directions, and write down which ones would help you the most to manage the emotion.

Each time you experience this emotion, use your recipe card to work your way through it. If you find it helped you, then use it again. If it didn't, don't despair. Work through which parts you felt helped and which ones didn't. Go back through the list of directions and see what other actions/activities you could incorporate that would make it better. Keep tweaking the recipe until you do succeed. It does take time, but you will, so keep going. If you come up with extra things you'd like to add to the list of directions, just go ahead and add them. That's what this process is all about. Finding your recipe for success.

Once you've applied the recipe, **capture a journal note** that reflects the situation and the outcome that occurred. If it wasn't entirely successful, capture that and keep the recipe. It may prove useful to look back on them in the future.

REPEAT for each emotion, or just the emotions you specifically want to focus on.

<u>Blank recipe card template</u>

Select the blank recipe card template.

Write specific words under 'shopping list' which have meaning for you. You can copy some from the templated recipe and/or create some of your own*. It's your recipe, so it's entirely up to you.

Write a few key points under 'ingredients'*. This could be the specific triggers that occurred and triggered the emotion. It's your recipe, so it's entirely up to you

Go through the list of directions I have provided and write down which ones would help you the most to manage the emotion. If there are actions/activities that you want to include that aren't on the list, just go ahead and add them. This is yours to own and manage in a way that works for you.

Each time you experience this emotion, use your recipe card to work your way through it. If you find it helped you, then use it again. If it didn't, don't despair. Work through which parts you felt helped and which ones didn't. Go back through the list of directions and see what other actions/activities you could incorporate that would make it better. Keep tweaking the recipe until you do succeed. It does take time, but you will, so keep going. If you come up with extra things you'd like to add to the list of directions, just go ahead and add them. That's what this process is all about. Finding your recipe for success.

Once you've applied the recipe, **capture a journal note** that reflects the situation and the outcome that occurred. If it wasn't entirely successful, capture that and keep the recipe. It may prove useful to look back on them in the future.

REPEAT for each emotion, or just the emotions you specifically want to focus on.

*I recommend you read 'Creating a Recipe Card from scratch (below)

Creating a Recipe Card from scratch

Select the blank recipe card template

Emotion: Decide on the emotion you want to create: e.g. Loneliness and put it in the Emotion Card heading

Ingredients: Research the causes for that emotion by searching (e.g. google). Check a number of sources to make sure you pick up, as much as possible, all of the key causes.

Looking at a number of sites, for loneliness, I picked out;

- feel empty, alone, and unwanted
- difficult to form connections with other people
- physical isolation; moving to a new location
- low self-esteem
- social or psychological problem: chronic depression
- loss of any important long-term relationship: breakup, divorce, death

Put the causes under the heading of 'ingredients'.

Shopping List: Research the definition of the emotion. Use a variety of sources, including dictionary and thesaurus. Looking at a number of sites, for loneliness, there is an extensive list of words. I've shown some key words, but also associated words that can be used. With so many possibilities, it's best to just select the ones that resonate with you.

Alienation	Disaffection, Estrangement, Indifference, Separation, Coolness, Divorce, Remoteness, Withdrawal
Desolation	Anguish, Dejection, Despair, Gloom, Melancholy, Sadness, Sorry, Woe, Wretchedness
Heartache	Agony, Bitterness, Despair, Grief, Heartbreak, Misery, Pang, Sadness, Suffering, Torment, Affliction, Dejection, Depression, Despondency, Distress, Hurting, Remorse, Torture
Solitude/Solitariness	Confinement, Desert, Detachment, Emptiness, Isolation, Loneliness, Lonesomeness, Quarantine, Reclusiveness, Retirement, Seclusion, Separateness, Silence, Solitariness, Withdrawal
Aloneness	Friendlessness, Solitude
Forlornness	Alienation, Desolation, Heartache, Solitude, Aloneness, Seclusion
Remoteness	Separation
Seclusion	Hiding, Remoteness, Solitude, Aloneness, Aloofness, Privateness, Separation
Withdrawal	Disengagement, Abandonment

Once you've finalised the list of words, you can **place them into the recipe card under the heading 'Shopping List'.**

Directions List: Select the relevant actions/activities and add them to your recipe.

Journal Note: Once you've applied the recipe, capture a journal note that reflects the situation and the outcome that occurred. If it wasn't entirely successful, capture that and keep the recipe. It may prove useful to look back on them in the future.

Awareness

Emotions are messengers

opportunities wrapped in waves

of energetic feelings.

What do they want to tell us?

Will we listen?

Will we answer their call?

If you push them down,

they rise up

stronger

louder

consuming.

Take the time to listen.

See them for what they are

Sacred tools of awareness.

Dani Glaeser

TEMPLATES

Emotions Journal Template

What emotion did I feel?

What prompted the emotion?

What did I feel about the situation/event?

How did it make me feel – physically / how did I express that feeling?

What can/will I use to manage the emotion?

Partially completed recipe card templates

ANGER RECIPE CARD

Ingredients

- INJUSTICE
- CONFLICT
- HUMILIATION
- NEGLIGENCE
- BETRAYAL
- VERBAL OR PHYSICAL ATTACK
- SILENT SULKING
- TENSION
- HOSTILITY
- EMPATHISING WITH ANOTHER

Directions

Journal Note

SHOPPING LIST

DISGUST
CONTEMPT
    INDIGNATION
    LOATHING
    REVULSION
ENVY
    JEALOUSY
EXASPERATION
FRUSTRATION
IRRITATION
    AGITATION
    AGGRAVATION
    ANNOYANCE
    GROUCHINESS
    GRUMPINESS
RAGE
    BITTERNESS
    DISLIKE
    FEROCITY
    FURY
    HATRED
    HOSTILITY
    LOATHING
    OUTRAGE
    RESENTMENT
    SCORN
    SPITE
    VENGEFULNESS
    WRATH
TORMENT

DESIRE RECIPE CARD

Ingredients

- STRONG FEELING OF;
  - WANTING TO HAVE SOMETHING
  - WISHING FOR SOMETHING TO HAPPEN
- LONGING OR HOPING FOR OR WANT (SOMETHING)
  - PERSON
  - OBJECT
  - OUTCOME
- EXCITING HOPE OR DESIRE
- HAVE OR DO SOMETHING YOU KNOW YOU SHOULD AVOID
- SOMETHING THAT SEDUCES OR HAS THE QUALITY TO SEDUCE
- MISS/REGRET SOMETHING

Directions

Journal Note

SHOPPING LIST

APPEAL

ATTRACTION

ALLURE

 ENTICEMENT

 SEDUCTION

COVET

EAGERNESS

FANCY

HANKERING

 CRAVING

 LONGING

 LUSTING

 WANTING

 YEARNING

HUNGER

NEED

TEMPTATION

 DESIRE

 URGE

 IMPULSE

 INCLINATION

WISH

DISGUST RECIPE CARD

Ingredients

- OFFENSIVE OR REVOLTING OBJECT, PERSON OR BEHAVIOUR
- SMELL, TOUCH, VISION OR TASTE
- ANIMALS AND INSECTS
- BODY FLUIDS AND EXCRETIONS
- BODILY VIOLATION (LIKE BLOOD AND MUTILATION)
- DEATH AND CORPSES DEATH
- SPOILED FOOD

Directions

Journal Note

SHOPPING LIST

CONDESCENSION
DERISION
REPULTION
 ANTIPATHY
 CONTEMPT
 DISLIKE
 HATE
 INDIGNATION
 LOATHING
 RESENTMENT
 REVULSION
 SCORN
 SPITE
REPEL
 AVERSION
 ABHORRENCE
 ABOMINATION
 DETEST
 DISDAIN
 REVOLT
VILE
 DISTASTE
 REPUGNANT
 SICKENING

EMOTIONAL OVERWHELM RECIPE CARD

Ingredients

- BURY OR DROWN BENEATH A HUGE MASS OF SOMETHING
- A STRONG EMOTIONAL EFFECT

Directions

Journal Note

SHOPPING LIST

DEFEAT

OVERCOME

OVERTRHOW

CONQUER

DESTROY

DROWN

SUBMERGE

INUNDATE

WASTE

ASTONISH

PUZZLE

BEWILDER

CONFOUND

ENVY RECIPE CARD

Ingredients

- COMPARISON (BETWEEN SELF AND ANOTHER)
- DESIRE (SOMETHING SOMEONE ELSE HAS)
  - STATUS
  - MONEY/WEALTH
  - POWER
  - SUCCESS
  - FAMILY TIES
  - INTELLIGENCE

Directions

Journal Note

SHOPPING LIST

COVET

CRAVE

ENVY

BEGRUDGE

RESENT

DESIRE

LONG FOR

WANT

YEARN

IDEALISE

JEALOUSY

BITTER

GREED

FEAR RECIPE CARD

Ingredients

- IMPENDING DANGER
- SURVIVAL MECHANISM
- REACTION TO NEGATIVE STIMULUS
- MILD CAUTION OR EXTREME PHOBIA
- TRIVIAL OR SERIOUS

Directions

Journal Note

SHOPPING LIST

NERVOUSNESS

ANXIETY

APPREHENSION

DISTRESS

DREAD

EDGINESS

JUMPINESS

TENSENESS

UNEASINESS

WORRY

HORROR

ALARM

FRIGHT

HYSTERICAL

MORTIFICATION

OVERWHELMED

PANIC

SHOCK

TERROR

FRUSTRATION RECIPE CARD

Ingredients

- UNABLE TO CHANGE OR ACHIEVE SOMETHING

- PREVENTION OF THE PROGRESS, SUCCESS, OR FULFILMENT

- FEELINGS OF UNCERTAINTY AND INSECURITY

- NEEDS ARE CONSTANTLY IGNORED OR UNSATISFIED

Directions

Journal Note

SHOPPING LIST

ANGER

BITTERNESS

RESENTMENT

DEFEAT

BLOCK

COLLAPSE

COUNTER

DISAPPOINTMENT

DEPRESSION

DISSATISFACTION

DISCOURAGEMENT

DISCONTENT

FAILURE

IRRITATION

AGGRAVATION

ANNOYANCE

EXASPERATION

OBSTRUCTION

HAMPERING

HINDERING

SCUPPERING

QUASHING

CRIPPLING

CRUSHING

VEXATION

GRIEF RECIPE CARD

	SHOPPING LIST
Ingredients	**SHOPPING LIST**

Ingredients

- LOSS OF SOMEONE OR SOMETHING IMPORTANT TO YOU, TO WHICH A BOND OR AFFECTION WAS FORMED
  - PARTNER
  - FAMILY MEMBER
  - JOB
  - BELOVED PET
  - FRIENDSHIP/SOCIAL INTERACTION
  - PERSONAL DREAM/GOAL
  - ROMANTIC RELATIONSHIP
  - HEALTH

Directions

Journal Note

SHOPPING LIST

AFFLICTION
ANGUISH
    AGONY
    ANGST
    DISTRESS
    HEARTBREAK
    PAIN
    SUFFERING
    TORMENT
BEREAVEMENT
    LOSS
DEJECTION
    DESPONDENCY
MORTIFICATION
MOURNING
    GRIEF
    LAMENT
    SORROW
PINING
REGRET
REMORSE
SADNESS
    BLUES
    DESOLATION
    DESPAIR
    DESPONDENCY
    GRIEF
    HEARTACHE
    MISERY
    SORROW
    WOE

GUILT RECIPE CARD

Ingredients

- SOMETHING YOU DID OR DIDN'T DO
- SOMETHING YOU THINK YOU DID/DIDN'T DO
- DIDN'T DO ENOUGH TO HELP PERSON/PEOPLE
- CONSIDERED BY OTHERS TO BE DOING BETTER THAN THEM/SOMEONE ELSE

Directions

Journal Note

SHOPPING LIST

ANGER

ANXIETY

DEPRESSION

EMPTINESS

ENVY

GUILT

LONELINESS

RAGE

REGRET

REMORSE

SADNESS

SHAME

HURT RECIPE CARD

Ingredients

- PAIN CAUSED BY SOMEONE WE INTERACT WITH;
  - INSULT
  - REJECTION
  - JUDGEMENT
  - IGNORED BY
  - DIFFERING VIEWS
- BELIEF IN WHAT OTHERS SAY AND THINK

Directions

Journal Note

SHOPPING LIST

AFFLICTION
MISFORTUNE
TROUBLE
ANGUISH
DISTRESS
PAIN
TORMENT
UPSET
WOE
DETRIMENT
DAMAGE
DISADVANTAGE
HARM
INJURY
TRAUMA
DISBELIEF
GRIEF
MISERY
SADNESS
SORROW
SUFFERING
WRETCHEDNESS
IMPAIR
MAIM
WOUND
MALTREAT
ABUSE
TORTURE

JEALOUSY RECIPE CARD

Ingredients

- LACK OF SELF CONFIDENCE
- POOR SELF IMAGE
- FEAR
- INSECURITY

Directions

Journal Note

SHOPPING LIST

ANGER

FEAR

DISGUST

INADEQUATE

HELPLESS

INSECURITY

JEALOUS

LACK

RESENTMENT

JOY & HAPPINESS RECIPE CARD

Ingredients

- ENJOYMENT

- SATISFACTION

- PLEASURE

Directions

Journal Note

SHOPPING LIST

CHEERFULNESS

AMUSEMENT

ECSTASY

GAIETY

EUPHORIA

BLISS

ELATION

DELIGHT

HAPPINESS

JUBILATION

ZEST

ENTHUIASM

EXCITEMENT

EXHILIRATION

THRILL

CONTENTMENT

RELIEF

OPTIMISM

PRIDE

ENTHRALLMENT

LOVE RECIPE CARD

Ingredients

- FEELING OF PROFOUND ONENESS
- PLATONIC
- ROMANTIC
- RELIGIOUS OR FAMILIAL
- BONDING
- FRIENDSHIP
- ALTRUISM
- PHILANTHROPY

Directions

Journal Note

SHOPPING LIST

AFFECTION

    ADORATION

    ATTRACTION

    CARING

    FONDNESS

    LOVE

    LIKING

    SENTIMENTALITY

LONGING

LUST

    AROUSAL

    DESIRE

    INFATUATION

    OBSESSION

    PASSION

RESENTMENT RECIPE CARD

Ingredients

- SENSE OF INJUSTICE OR WRONGDOING
  - NEGATIVE TREATMENT BY OTHERS
  - FEEL LIKE OBJECT OF DISCRIMINATION OR PREJUDICE
  - FEELING USED OR TAKEN ADVANTAGE OF HAVING ACHIEVEMENTS GO UNRECOGNISED
  - REJECTION OR DENIAL BY ANOTHER
  - BEING PUT DOWN OR EMBARRASSED BY OTHERS

Directions

Journal Note

SHOPPING LIST

ANGER

DISPLEASURE

FURY

INDIGNATION

IRE

IRRITATION

MALICE

PIQUE

RAGE

VEXATION

WRATH

BITTERNESS

GRUDGE

RANCOUR

UMBRAGE

GALL

HUFF

HURT

ILL WILL

ANIMOSITY

SADNESS RECIPE CARD

Ingredients

- FEELING OF LOSS
- DISADVANTAGE
- MAY LEAD TO DEPRESSION
- QUIET
- LESS ENERGETIC
- WITHDRAWN TO ONESELF
- SLOPING BODY
- STUCK OUT LIPS
- DOWNCAST APPEARANCE OF THE HEAD

Directions

Journal Note

SHOPPING LIST

SUFFERING

AGONY

HURT

ANGUISH

DISAPPOINTMENT

DISMAY

DISPLEASURE

SHAME

GUILT

REMORSE

REGRET

NEGLECT

INSECURITY

ALIENATION

HOMESICKNESS

EMBARRASSMENT

HUMILIATION

SYMPATHY

PITY

SHAME RECIPE CARD

Ingredients

- SELF-AWARENESS
- BLAMING YOURSELF
- PERSONALITY TRAIT
- SELF-ESTEEM

Directions

Journal Note

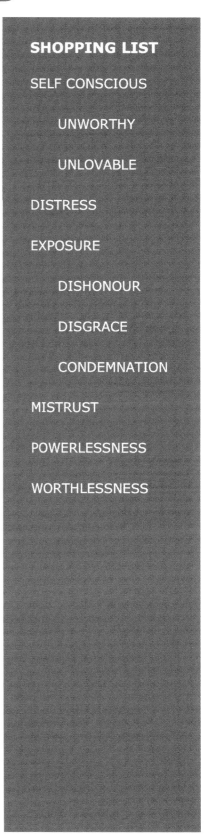

SHOPPING LIST

SELF CONSCIOUS

UNWORTHY

UNLOVABLE

DISTRESS

EXPOSURE

DISHONOUR

DISGRACE

CONDEMNATION

MISTRUST

POWERLESSNESS

WORTHLESSNESS

SHOCK RECIPE CARD

Ingredients

- CANNOT THINK STRAIGHT

- EXPERIENCING PHYSICAL SIDE EFFECTS

- FEEL STRANGELY EXHAUSTED

- MIND CAN'T MAKE SENSE OF THE SITUATION

- FEARFUL

Directions

Journal Note

SHOPPING LIST

UNEXPECTED

DISTURBANCE

EVENT

EXPERIENCE

SURPRISE

TRAUMA

UPSET

SURPRISE RECIPE CARD

Ingredients

- UNEXPECTED RESULT
- MOMENTARY RAISING OF EYEBROWS
- HORIZONTAL LINES ON THE FOREHEAD
- OPEN MOUTH OR DROPPED JAW
- STRETCHED SKIN BELOW THE EYEBROWS
- WIDE OPEN EYELIDS

Directions

Journal Note

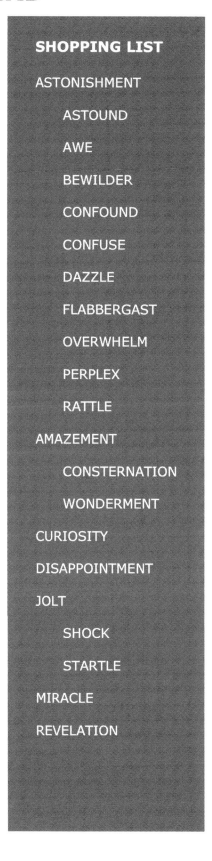

SHOPPING LIST

ASTONISHMENT

ASTOUND

AWE

BEWILDER

CONFOUND

CONFUSE

DAZZLE

FLABBERGAST

OVERWHELM

PERPLEX

RATTLE

AMAZEMENT

CONSTERNATION

WONDERMENT

CURIOSITY

DISAPPOINTMENT

JOLT

SHOCK

STARTLE

MIRACLE

REVELATION

Blank recipe card template

RECIPE CARD

Ingredients

Directions

Journal Note

My Own Journal

My journal covers so much these days, but what I love is that I can change it whenever I want to.

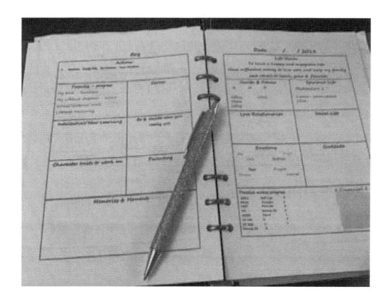

Actions for the day – where I hand write any specific actions, meetings/personal development calls, video calls with friends, visits I've got arranged and mustn't forget.

Project(s) progress – A list of projects I'm currently focussing on and can mark to show which ones I've done that day

Career notes – where I write down what I've done for the Governors and school which will help them move forward in their journey

Intellectual /New Learning – things I've read or heard that have helped /interested me

Character – capturing how I'm doing against a particular character trait that I want to make better or stop doing.

Parenting – capturing how I'm doing in my relationship with my daughter, working hard to make positive connections every day

Memories & Moments – writing down snippets of what's happened during the day

Health & Fitness – tracking my weight and what fitness activity I've done that day

Spiritual Life – noting that I've meditated that day and writing down anything specific that came to me during that time

Love Relationship – writing down how my relationship with my husband and loved ones is going. Things that have made me smile and feel good about the relationship(s) and myself.

Social Life – writing down who I've specifically gone out of my way to contact and that I care about. This covers phone calls, visits, video calls, as well as some social media updates with specific personal development groups.

Emotions – tracking what emotions I've felt during the day. Where they are negative, I review them in detail, as explained in 'Journaling your Emotions'.

Gratitude – what I've been grateful for that day. Some days that's easy and others I have to dig a bit deeper to bring them to my mind.

Practice makes progress – a list of things I particularly want to practice and get better at, including things I want to remember.

£Financial – things I've spent money on (outside of the normal day to day bills) and whether it was budgeted (green) or not (red).

A Vision of Happiness – My Life Vision

During the amazing *Lifebook Program*, which I am completely indebted to, I created my Life Vision. I went through an incredible amount of internal searching across all of the categories that we covered. I learnt and gained a ton of ideas from some truly amazing people too.

I highly recommend it.

I have a Vision for each and every category – all 12 of them:

1. I am radically changing my **Health & Fitness**. I'm fitter and healthier at nearly 60 than I was in my 20's.

2. I am Learning and Growing, every day and improving my **Intellectual Life.** There are so many incredible books to read.

3. I've fixed my **Emotional Life** through clearing the old, and managing the new. My Emotions are in control

4. I'm getting rid of **Character** traits that don't serve me and creating new ones that do.

5. I completely understand my **Spiritual Life** and am connecting and manifesting every day**.**

6. I have the best **Love Relationship** – ever!

7. I am constantly looking at new and better ways to manage my **Parenting Life,** so I serve my family well.

8. My **Social Life** has completely changed. I have friends all around the world and talk to several every week.

9. I've got a grip on my **Financial Life.**

10. I've created an amazing **Career** for myself, even though I'm retired.

11. My **Quality of Life** has changed, for good.

12. All of which adds up to my **Life Vision.**

To have a happy and enjoyable life.

Have sufficient money to live well and help

my family and others to

'Learn, Grow and Flourish'.

PART 4: EMOTIONS AND RECIPES SHARED BY OTHERS FROM AROUND THE WORLD

People who contributed

The chart below shows the people who have contributed with their own emotional stories and their associated recipe cards. We hope you find these are a useful resource to help you create your own. The grammar and spelling used in these stories is verbatim.

Name	Country	Emotion Journal	Recipe Cards
AbhiPriya Pawar	India, Pune	Happiness beyond limits Anger, Anxiety, Fear, Sadness and depression Forgiveness	Joy & Happiness Anger Fear Sadness Hurt
Anne	Denmark	Anger Happiness & Love	Anger Joy & Happiness Love
Dani G	USA	Anger Intense Grief Jealousy Resentment	Anger Shock Grief Jealousy Resentment
Mary Grace	Pasay, Philippines	Anger – Frustration	Anger
Kathryn Cartwright	United States	Anger	Anger
Ingeborg Betuker, Certified Coach	Aux en Provence, France	Joy & Happiness	Joy & Happiness
Joana Loren Felisarta	Philippines	Guilt	Guilt

Name	Country	Emotion Journal	Recipe Cards
Jordan River	Chicago, Illinois, USA	Temptation	Desire
JW	California, USA	Sadness	Sadness Frustration
Maddy	New Zealand	Anger	Anger Frustration Guilt
Nora	Austria	Resentment Anger	Resentment Anger
Patricia	Canada	Joy & Happiness	Joy & Happiness
Santa	Aalborg, Denmark	Anger Frustration Overwhelm	Anger Frustration Emotional Overwhelm
Susie Earl, Licensed Health Coach	Washington State, USA	Joy Sadness	Joy & Happiness Sadness
Tamara Mihályi	Hungary	Grief – Sadness Guilt Fear - Insecurity	Grief Guilt Fear
Y. Sim	Dublin, Ireland	Hurt	Hurt
Yvette Ryan	Ireland	Overwhelmed	Emotional Overwhelm

AbhiPriya Pawar – Joy & Happiness

AbhiPriya Pawar's story below is showing the emotion of Happiness and is shown in her recipe card on the following page.

Name (& title if applicable)	AbhiPriya Pawar
Country/Location	India/Pune
What emotion did you feel today?	Happiness beyond limits
What prompted the emotion	A message from my dream boy with whom I always wanted to get married from the day I realised that I want to get married now, that his parents are agrees for our marriage proposal and call from his parents to my uncle regarding further discussion and formality regarding our marriage.

My parents were looking for my marriage since more than last 5-6 years. I was always wanted to settle in my professional life first and hence never serious about marriage at my 23rd.

Days were passing by and one thing I realised with time and through life experience and also as few of my friends used say "Marriages made in heaven". They say that I will get married to a person who is made for me and when my time come,

Before that if anybody trying to force it on me or however you try to ignore, it won't work. So, don't take tension and focus on your goals, achieve your dreams, work to fulfil all your desire.

Though family pressure was always there since last 8 years, I enjoyed my journey, lots of good things happened in my life related to my social, career life.

So that pressure used to get delegated behind all. Still one incident happened in Jan 2018 which made my life to take 180 degree change that time I got little bit serious about my future personal life so called Marriage. I registered my profile on online matrimonial site. Proposals were coming but I did not like a single proposal. ☹ Days, months were passing by, parents pressure was again started increasing day by day. And one proposal came on 29th July 2018. I was so surprised and astonished reading his profile that I felt vibe that he is the one who is made for me and |

	for whom I was waiting for in my life since long. I did not had his full name neither his contact number not his address nothing. But in his profile he had mentioned about his work. I googled it and from his company website I came to know his full name, I searched him on Facebook by his name and contacted him. We talked on WhatsApp for 2 days. The vibrations, vibes, cuteness, integrity, honesty and his nature made me to fall in love with him. With those two days of conversation i realised what I wanted in my life, who I was looking for in my life! My life purpose got cleared. I got vibrations that he is the one made for me. We both made for each other. There were lots of challenges getting him and his parents to agree for our marriage. But by god's grace things started working out and in last week of April 2019 I received a message from him that his parents were calling my parents for our marriage. That moment when I saw message blinking on my iPhone's screen and the happiness I felt was beyond eighth cloud. I was totally surprised with God's blessing and my believe in him got stronger than I was before. I was glowing brighter with his love. My happiness had no limits. That was the one of the day I won't forget ever in my life. 🖤
What did you feel about the situation/event?	I was very happy. It was like dream come true for me. I have been through lots of thick's and thins. Almost 9 months I was patiently and eagerly waiting for him. My believe in God got more stronger than before. I started believing in God's magical power because it was totally God's grace that I received marriage proposal from Abhi and his family. Though I had did lot of hard work to achieve it, it was all our destiny and God's blessings made things to work out for us.
How did it make you feel – physically/how did you express that feeling?	I was extremely happy. Though I was topper, ranker in my academics. I never felt happiness being topper but in life I felt I had achieved something which was just a dream for me. It was breakthrough for me. It was mid feelings. I was too happy at the same time my eyes were full of tears. I was in office, I immediately went to washroom, started crying with pleasure. It was beyond my imagination. I started pleasing God for all the magic he had brought in my life. My face was started glowing. My friends started asking me about my happiness. It was memorable moment of my life.
What did you use to manage the emotion?	I started cried in happiness. I started pleasing God for all his blessing and his magic.

	I called my uncle and explained everything about it to him over call.
	Journaling
	Gratitude
	Prayer
	Mindfulness
	Vision boards
	Meditation
	Imagination and **visualisation**
	Applying the secrete
	Fasting
	Following Ralph Smart on YouTube as he give lot of clarity on different aspects of things we see in our day to day life
	Following Jai Madaan's tips on YouTube, Instagram and Facebook
	Implementation of Neurology in achieving things I wish/want in my life.

JOY & HAPPINESS RECIPE CARD
- AbhiPriya Pawar

Ingredients

- ENJOYMENT
- SATISFACTION
- PLEASURE

Directions

- JOURNALING
- GRATITUDE
- MEDITATION & PRAYER
- MINDFULNESS
- DO SOMETHING THAT MAKES YOU HAPPY (VISION BOARDS)
- TALK ABOUT WHAT CAN GO RIGHT (THE SECRET)
- TUNE INTO YOUR MIND & BODY (FASTING)
- GET HELP (YOU TUBE: RALPH SMART & JAI MADAAN, IMPLEMENTATION OF NEUROLOGY)

Journal Note

A message from my dream boy with whom I always wanted to get married from the day I realised that I want to get married now, that his parents are agreed for our marriage proposal and call from his parents to my uncle regarding further discussion and formality regarding our marriage.

We talked on WhatsApp for 2 days. The vibrations, vibes, cuteness, integrity, honesty and his nature made me to fall in love with him. With those two days of conversation i realised what I wanted in my life, who I was looking for in my life! My life purpose got cleared. I got vibrations that he is the one made for me. We both made for each other.

SHOPPING LIST

CHEERFULNESS

AMUSEMENT

ECSTASY

GAIETY

EUPHORIA

BLISS

ELATION

DELIGHT

HAPPINESS

JUBILATION

ZEST

ENTHUIASM

EXCITEMENT

EXHILIRATION

THRILL

CONTENTMENT

RELIEF

OPTIMISM

PRIDE

ENTHRALLMENT

AbhiPriya Pawar – Anger, Fear, Sadness

AbhiPriya Pawar's story below is showing the emotions of Anger, Fear and Sadness and are shown in her recipe cards on the following pages. Anxiety, as a feeling, could have a specific recipe card created but has been incorporated into the other recipe cards in this instance. Depression is a feeling which, due to its complexity, has not been separated. The actions and activities that AbhiPriya undertook, helped her toward overcoming these feelings.

Name (& title if applicable)	AbhiPriya Pawar
Country/Location	India/Pune
What emotion did you feel today?	Full mixture of Anger, Anxiety, Fear, Sadness and Depression
What prompted the emotion?	My parents and family stubbornness, rudeness and act of non-compassionate nature towards their only daughter As I mentioned in first emotional story, my happiness towards my future life was extra ordinary and beyond cloud. Our marriage about to happen in May-June 2019, but my parents and brothers oppose this proposal just because we were sharing two different native place. Apart from this all things were perfect and everything was good. Groom's family were agree with all, my uncle and aunt was very happy with this proposal. Along with me my uncle and aunt tried a lot convincing my parents about this proposal. But at last they did not agree to it. But I wanted my parents let me to get married to Abhi. With their blessings I wanted to get married to him and be a part of his family. But my parents did not listen a single word of mine. Instead of that they started emotionally blackmailing me. They locked me inside home. Did not allowed me to step out of home to office or any means. My books were been tore off. They did not allow me to use mobile, laptop or anything. They orally, physically abuse me. They forcefully tried to make me ready for any other marriage proposal. They used to give me one time food every single alternate day. They started warned me of of getting murdered. They informed in my office that I don't want to go to office whereas truth was that they were not allowing me to go to office.

	Initially I thought they will get convinced. They will understand that their daughters happiness should be important for them rather than anything else. Looking my seriousness about this proposal they will be agree to make both of us get married. But I was wrong.
	I went through all of these just because I thought they will get changed. But it did not happened. Since April last week of 2019 till first week of June 2019 I had not seen rays of sun, I was locked inside home. My world had totally changed in that one and half month.
	They did not change at last, even for me he is lifeline, I wanted to get married to him only, if not he I was like I won't marry to anyone. That also my parents were not ready to listen. And I already had assumed him my husband in my imagination. The fact is that we haven't seen each other nor hear each other's voice once in last 9 month but I was totally connected to his soul. He is my inspiration, my resin to live, laugh and love. My first and last love. My motivation. I adore, respect, follow and love from bottom of my heart. After his entry in my life I became my best version.
	My parents even called up his parents and insulted his parents thinking that if they do this then his parents themselves break/regect our proposal.
	And at last they won. 😔
What did you feel about the situation/event?	I was totally depressed. My believe in God got broken. I started ignoring God. Stopped praying.
	Stopped all fasting. My believe on parenthood totally got broken.
	I started to be alone, started ignoring and avoiding people around me.
	It made me so crashed and broken that I used to cry hours and hours.
	It was like my life stopped at that moment.
How did it make you feel – physically/how did you express that feeling?	I was in deep depression state. I used to sleep whole day. Due to lack of food and nutrients I was physically very week. In that one and half month I lost more than 10 Kgs, my hair started fallen which was never a case in my life. I got deep dark circles under my

	eyes. I was not even able to walk few steps. In closed cabin or washrooms I used to cry a lot for hours and hour.
	People started observing depression symptoms in me. They started advising me to go under phycologist's consultation. Post one month I was able to go to office but my concentration, self esteem I found lost somewhere else. I used to be physically present at office but whole time my mind under to wonder somewhere else. I was not at work for more than one month, during my absence client escalations had happened. I was been removed out of project. It was like my entire life was scattered.

I gave a fare chance to my parents and family but being super orthodox minded they never changed. They continued their behaviour. Again in month of June end they locked me inside home. This time I decided to take outside help as I had already lost personal life whatever career I would have build for my safety and independence I wanted to save. I informed to NGO and took their help to escape out of that situation. I was been in shelter provided by NGO for two months. I used to work with them. I wanted to change all surrounding people, circumstances, work, company everything to change my mind and my life.

I changed my job.being and 8 years of experienced professional Preparing and cracking an interview in these situation was a big challenge for me.

I gone under some psychological consultations.

My all cloths, identity, educational and professional documents were at home, my parents refused to give me those. It was like I had to start everything from zero. In this journey two of my friends were there for me to support me morally. Even my company supported me by all means they could. |
| **What did you use to manage the emotion?** | *Mindvalley* Quests
Starting *Lifebook* and *Lifebook mastery*
Going out in nature, hiking, trekking
I started gym first time in my life
Contribute in social activities
Being part of NGOs to help those who are in need
Yoga
Making new friends
Explore new and different places alone
Implement – 'one step at a time' process
Live/be in present moment
Work for society, be in service |

	Start working on your old dream/goal which you always wanted to achieve Learn everyday something new Possess and learn any art Visit art gallery Play with children Visit old age home, share some moments with people stay there Do some kind act to three people everyday selflessly Read books and build own library Go full body massage and rejuvenate therapy Pass on smile to strangers on road everyday **Journaling** **Gratitude** **Prayer** **Mindfulness** Vision boards **Meditation** Imagination and **visualisation** Applying the secrete Fasting Implementation of Neurology in achieving things I wish/want in my life

ANGER RECIPE CARD - AbhiPriya Pawar

Ingredients

- INJUSTICE
- CONFLICT
- HUMILIATION
- NEGLIGENCE
- BETRAYAL
- VERBAL OR PHYSICAL ATTACK
- SILENT SULKING
- TENSION
- HOSTILITY
- EMPATHISING WITH ANOTHER

Directions

- GET HELP (FROM OTHERS)
- GET HELP (SELF HELP/DEVELOPMENT)
- HONOUR YOUR FEELINGS
- DO WHAT MAKES YOU HAPPY
- EXERCISE
- GIVE HELP
- IMPROVE/CREATE SOCIAL LIFE
- BRIGHTEN SOMEONE'S DAY
- GRATITUDE
- MINDFULNESS
- MEDITATION & PRAYER
- JOURNALING

Journal Note

I wanted my parents let me get married to Abhi. Abhi is my inspiration, my reason to live, laugh and love. My motivation. With their blessing I wanted to get married to him and be part of his family, but my parents didn't listen to a single word of mine. My parents and family were stubborn, rude and non-compassionate toward me. They would not allow me to marry Abhi. They even called up his parents and insulted his parents thinking that if they do this then parents themselves break/reject our proposal. And at last they won. I decided to take outside help as I had already lost personal life. Whatever career I would build for my safety and independence I wanted to save. I got help from NGO. I wanted to change all surrounding people, circumstances, work, company. Everything to change my mind and my life. I changed my job. I got psychological help. I had to start everything from zero. In this journey two of my friends were there for me, to support me morally. Even my company supported me by all means they could.

SHOPPING LIST

DISGUST

CONTEMPT

INDIGNATION

LOATHING

REVULSION

ENVY

JEALOUSY

EXASPERATION

FRUSTRATION

IRRITATION

AGITATION

AGGRAVATION

ANNOYANCE

GROUCHINESS

GRUMPINESS

RAGE

BITTERNESS

DISLIKE

FEROCITY

FURY

HATRED

HOSTILITY

LOATHING

OUTRAGE

RESENTMENT

SCORN

SPITE

VENGEFULNESS

WRATH

TORMENT

FEAR RECIPE CARD - AbhiPriya Pawar

Ingredients

- IMPENDING DANGER
- SURVIVAL MECHANISM
- REACTION TO NEGATIVE STIMULUS
- MILD CAUTION OR EXTREME PHOBIA
- TRIVIAL OR SERIOUS

Directions

- GET HELP (FROM OTHERS)
- HONOUR YOUR FEELINGS
- GIVE HELP
- IMPROVE/CREATE SOCIAL LIFE
- MINDFULNESS
- MEDITATION & PRAYER
- JOURNALING

Journal Note

My parents started emotionally blackmailing me, locking me inside home. They orally, physically abused me. They forcefully tried to make me ready for any other marriage proposal. They used to give me one-time food every single alternate day. They started warned me of getting murdered. They informed in my office that I don't want to go to office whereas truth was that they were not allowing me to go to office. Since end of April to beginning of June 2019 I had not seen rays of sun. I was locked inside home. My world had totally changed in that one and half month. I was totally depressed. My believe in God got broken. I started to be alone. I decided to take outside help, for my safety and independence. I informed NGO and took their help to escape out of the situation. I was been in shelter provided by NGO for two months. I work with them.

SHOPPING LIST

NERVOUSNESS

ANXIETY

APPREHENSION

DISTRESS

DREAD

EDGINESS

JUMPINESS

TENSENESS

UNEASINESS

WORRY

HORROR

ALARM

FRIGHT

HYSTERICAL

MORTIFICATION

OVERWHELMED

PANIC

SHOCK

TERROR

SADNESS RECIPE CARD - AbhiPriya Pawar

Ingredients

- FEELING OF LOSS
- DISADVANTAGE
- MAY LEAD TO DEPRESSION
- QUIET
- LESS ENERGETIC
- WITHDRAWN TO ONESELF
- SLOPING BODY
- STUCK OUT LIPS
- DOWNCAST APPEARANCE OF THE HEAD

Directions

- GET HELP (FROM OTHERS)
- GET HELP (SELF HELP/DEVELOPMENT)
- HONOUR YOUR FEELINGS
- DO WHAT MAKES YOU HAPPY
- EXERCISE
- GIVE HELP
- IMPROVE/CREATE SOCIAL LIFE
- BRIGHTEN SOMEONE'S DAY
- GRATITUDE
- MINDFULNESS
- MEDITATION & PRAYER
- JOURNALING

Journal Note

I gave a fare change to my parents and family but being super orthodox minded they never changed. They continued their behaviour. All my clothes, identity, educational and professional documents were at home, my parents refused to give me those. I have to start everything from zero. In this journey two of my friends were there for me, to support me morally.

SHOPPING LIST

SUFFERING

AGONY

HURT

ANGUISH

DISAPPOINTMENT

DISMAY

DISPLEASURE

SHAME

GUILT

REMORSE

REGRET

NEGLECT

INSECURITY

ALIENATION

HOMESICKNESS

EMBARRASSMENT

HUMILIATION

SYMPATHY

PITY

AbhiPriya Pawar – Forgiveness

AbhiPriya Pawar's story below is showing the emotions as Forgiveness which, based on her story, is to overcome the significant and deep Hurt she has experienced and is shown in her recipe card on the following page.

Name (& title if applicable)	AbhiPriya Pawar
Country/Location	India/Pune
What emotion did you feel today?	Forgiveness
What prompted the emotion?	My parent's and family member's behaviour
	As I mentioned in second emotional story,
	The circumstances I have been through since last week of April 2019 till date, I
	Been through lot of trauma, physically and emotionally I saw different dimensions of me.
	I realised whatever happened was may be for my best.
	Though whatever happened, was because of my parents and brother, I don't wanted to think a single thing about them nor even wanted any revenge or had any guilt about them.
	I had forgiven them but at the same time I don't wanted them to be a part of my life in future as I have seen their all faces.
	And whatever situation I had been through, I choose to be happy and be responsible for my own life.
What did you feel about the situation/event?	Whenever I used to think or whoever something memorise me about that phase of my life, I automatically started crying. And that is what I wanted to stop. Hence I decided to not to think about them and forget and forgive them for my
	Goodness.
What did you use to manage the emotion?	*Mindvalley.com* Quests Starting *Lifebook* and *Lifebook mastery*

	Going out in nature, hiking, trekking
	I started gym first time in my life
	Contribute in social activities
	Being part of NGOs to help those who are in need
	Yoga
	Making new friends
	Explore new and different places alone
	Implement – 'one step at a time' process
	Live/be in present moment
	Work for society, be in service
	Start working on your old dream/goal which you always wanted to achieve
	Learn everyday something new
	Possess and learn any art
	Visit art gallery
	Play with children
	Visit old age home, share some moments with people stay there
	Do some kind act to three people everyday selflessly
	Read books and build own library
	Go full body massage and rejuvenate therapy
	Pass on smile to strangers on road everyday
	Journaling
	Gratitude
	Prayer
	Mindfulness
	Vision boards
	Meditation
	Imagination and **visualisation**
	Applying the secrete
	Fasting
	Implementation of Neurology in achieving things I wish/want in my life

HURT RECIPE CARD - AbhiPriya Pawar

Ingredients

- PAIN CAUSED BY SOMEONE WE INTERACT WITH;
  - INSULT
  - REJECTION
  - JUDGEMENT
  - IGNORED BY
  - DIFFERING VIEWS
- BELIEF IN WHAT OTHERS SAY AND THINK

Directions

- ALLOW YOURSELF TO FEEL YOUR FEELINGS
- HONOUR YOUR FEELINGS
- FORGIVENESS
- MINDFULNESS
- GRATITUDE
- MEDITATION & PRAYER
- DO WHAT MAKES YOU HAPPY
- JOURNALING

Journal Note

I have been through a lot of trauma; physically and emotionally I saw different dimensions of me. I realised whatever happened was maybe for my best. Though whatever happened, was because of my parents and brothers, I don't want to think a single thing about them, nor even wanted any revenge or had any guilt about them. I have forgiven them but at the same time I don't want them to be part of my life in future as I have seen all their faces. Whatever situation I have been through, I choose to be happy and be responsible for my own life.

SHOPPING LIST

AFFLICTION
- MISFORTUNE
- TROUBLE

ANGUISH
- DISTRESS
- PAIN
- TORMENT
- UPSET
- WOE

DETRIMENT
- DAMAGE
- DISADVANTAGE
- HARM
- INJURY
- TRAUMA

DISBELIEF

GRIEF
- MISERY
- SADNESS
- SORROW
- SUFFERING
- WRETCHEDNESS

IMPAIR
- MAIM
- WOUND

MALTREAT
- ABUSE
- TORTURE

Anne – Anger

Anne's story below is showing the emotion of Anger, which is shown in her recipe card (following page).

Name (& title if applicable)	Anne
Country/Location	Denmark
What emotion did you feel today?	Anger
What prompted the emotion?	My 3 young children were arguing, fighting and shouting at each other at bedtime
What did you feel about the situation/event?	I felt irritated and out of control. I felt bad to get angry at them and unable to help them deal with their emotions.
How did it make you feel – physically/how did you express that feeling?	Tight feeling in chest, wanting to shout, irritation, taking over their feelings, upset voice instead of calming
What did you use to manage the emotion?	**90 second rule** **Breathe** **Honour your feelings** **Know you are in control** **Mindfulness** – observe the present moment **Do what makes you happy** - Singing/humming

ANGER RECIPE CARD - Anne

Ingredients

- INJUSTICE
- CONFLICT
- HUMILIATION
- BETRAYAL
- VERBAL OR PHYSICAL ATTACK
- TENSION
- HOSTILITY

Directions

- 90 SECOND RULE
- BREATHE
- HONOUR YOUR FEELINGS
- KNOW YOU ARE IN CONTROL
- MINDFULNESS – OBSERVE PRESENT MOMENT
- DO WHAT MAKES YOU HAPPY – SINGING & HUMMING

Journal Note

My 3 young children were arguing, fighting and shouting at each other at bedtime. I could feel myself becoming angry which made me feel bad. I took time to bring myself back under control and return to a happier frame of mind by singing and humming, which the children enjoy.

SHOPPING LIST

DISGUST
  CONTEMPT
    INDIGNATION
    LOATHING
    REVULSION
ENVY
    JEALOUSY
EXASPERATION
FRUSTRATION
IRRITATION
    AGITATION
    AGGRAVATION
    ANNOYANCE
    GROUCHINESS
    GRUMPINESS
RAGE
    BITTERNESS
    DISLIKE
    FEROCITY
    FURY
    HATRED
    HOSTILITY
    LOATHING
    OUTRAGE
    RESENTMENT
    SCORN
    SPITE
    VENGEFULNESS
    WRATH
TORMENT

Anne – Joy & Happiness, Love

Anne's story below is showing the emotion of Happiness and Love. They have been separated into two cards, Joy & Happiness and Love, which are shown on the following 2 pages.

Anne could create a single recipe card that covers both of these, but is showing them separately to show their differences.

Name (& title if applicable)	Anne
Country/Location	Denmark
What emotion did you feel today?	Happiness and Love
What prompted the emotion?	My 3 young children were playing together and helping each other dress up to make a theatre play
What did you feel about the situation/event?	I felt happy, proud and love.
How did it make you feel – physically/how did you express that feeling?	Warm feeling in chest, smiling, contentment
What did you use to manage the emotion?	**Brighten someone's day** **Choose to see the good in people** **Tell them**

JOY & HAPPINESS RECIPE CARD - Anne

Ingredients

- ENJOYMENT

- SATISFACTION

- PLEASURE

Directions

- BRIGHTEN SOMEONE'S DAY

- CHOOSE TO SEE THE GOOD IN PEOPLE

- TELL THEM

SHOPPING LIST

CHEERFULNESS

AMUSEMENT

ECSTASY

GAIETY

EUPHORIA

BLISS

ELATION

DELIGHT

HAPPINESS

JUBILATION

ZEST

ENTHUIASM

EXCITEMENT

EXHILIRATION

THRILL

CONTENTMENT

RELIEF

OPTIMISM

PRIDE

ENTHRALLMENT

Journal Note

My 3 young children were playing together and helping each other dress up to make a theatre play. I felt happy and proud.

LOVE RECIPE CARD - Anne

Ingredients

- FEELING OF PROFOUND ONENESS

Directions

- BRIGHTEN SOMEONE'S DAY

- CHOOSE TO SEE THE GOOD IN PEOPLE

- TELL THEM

SHOPPING LIST

AFFECTION

ADORATION

ATTRACTION

CARING

FONDNESS

LOVE

LIKING

SENTIMENTALITY

Journal Note

My 3 young children were playing together and helping each other dress up to make a theatre play. I love them so much.

Dani G – Anger & Shock

Dani G's story below is showing the emotion of Anger, but her story also relates to Shock. You will see her two recipe cards on the following 2 pages:

- **Anger** which relates to the disappointment and frustration.
- **Shock** shows the sensations that Dani G felt.

Dani G could create a single recipe card that covers both of these, but is showing them separately to show their differences. An additional card could be created specifically for Frustration.

Name (& title if applicable)	Dani G
Country/Location	USA
What emotion did you feel today?	Anger
What prompted the emotion?	My husband was admitted to the Hopkins for an emergency biopsy and evaluation. During this stressful time, we were not at our home, but staying with others. One of the people we were staying with, who I thought I had a good relationship with and cared about us, would take every opportunity to tell me or anyone listening how much our situation had inconvenienced and stressed her and her family, how angry she was, and just vent and moan. She also did this when my husband returned from the hospital, and made inappropriate comments around my kids.
What did you feel about the situation/event?	I was shocked. I couldn't understand how she could be so filled with venom and so inconsiderate. It completely changed my view of her; she lost all my trust. I was also angry with myself for not saying something at the time. I hesitated saying anything, as I didn't want to cause more stress for my husband.
How did it make you feel – physically/how did you express that feeling?	My whole body became exhausted. I was feeling so emotional from my husband's situation that I was still processing, that I just felt weak and wiped.
What did you use to manage the emotion?	**Get Help.** I ended up seeing a therapist. My therapist advised me that anger was a cover for what I was really feeling. She showed me a magnet and asked me to evaluate what I was really feeling: shame, anxiety, sadness, fear,

	frustration, guilt, disappointment, worry, embarrassment, jealousy, hurt, anxiety. I discovered that I was feeling disappointment and frustration. I **honoured my feelings** and I **journaled** about the situation. When I got to the point where I realized this was just who she was, I accepted the relationship and her. And made a list of reasons why I was grateful for what happened. **DG5 Forgive and flow**. I imagined talking to each person who I felt had hurt me, told them how I felt, thanked them for their part in my life, imagined them filled with white light, and then sent them all floating on a raft down a river and away from me, wishing them all the best.

ANGER RECIPE CARD - Dani G

Ingredients

- INJUSTICE
- CONFLICT
- HUMILIATION
- NEGLIGENCE
- BETRAYAL
- VERBAL OR PHYSICAL ATTACK
- SILENT SULKING
- TENSION
- HOSTILITY
- EMPATHISING WITH ANOTHER

Directions

- GET HELP
- HONOUR YOUR FEELINGS
- JOURNALING
- FORGIVE AND FLOW

Journal Note

Someone I trusted didn't behave in a way that I was expecting. It left me shocked and angry. I realized this was just who she was, and I accepted the relationship and her. I made a list of reasons why I was grateful for what happened.

SHOPPING LIST

DISGUST
 CONTEMPT
 INDIGNATION
 LOATHING
 REVULSION
ENVY
 JEALOUSY
EXASPERATION
FRUSTRATION
IRRITATION
 AGITATION
 AGGRAVATION
 ANNOYANCE
 GROUCHINESS
 GRUMPINESS
RAGE
 BITTERNESS
 DISLIKE
 FEROCITY
 FURY
 HATRED
 HOSTILITY
 LOATHING
 OUTRAGE
 RESENTMENT
 SCORN
 SPITE
 VENGEFULNESS
 WRATH
TORMENT

SHOCK RECIPE CARD - Dani G

Ingredients

- CANNOT THINK STRAIGHT
- EXPERIENCING PHYSICAL SIDE EFFECTS
- FEEL STRANGELY EXHAUSTED
- MIND CAN'T MAKE SENSE OF THE SITUATION
- FEARFUL

Directions

- GET HELP
- HONOUR YOUR FEELINGS
- JOURNALING
- FORGIVE AND FLOW

Journal Note

Someone I trusted didn't behave in a way that I was expecting. It left me shocked and angry. I realized this was just who she was, and I accepted the relationship and her. I made a list of reasons why I was grateful for what happened.

SHOPPING LIST

UNEXPECTED

DISTURBANCE

EVENT

EXPERIENCE

SURPRISE

TRAUMA

UPSET

Dani G – Grief

Dani G has a story of Grief which is shown in her recipe card on the following page.

Name (& title if applicable)	Dani G
Country/Location	USA
What emotion did you feel today?	Intense Grief
What prompted the emotion?	This happened as a result of a series of events, the main one being when my husband got diagnosed with POEMS syndrome. I had to grieve the life we had, that my husband was ill, and that we had to move forward and find a new "normal". The other events were based on people we cared about who acted in ways that were hurtful to us, narcissistic, and some flat out lied to us and attempted to make us feel bad for inconveniencing them by constantly telling us. After recognizing my anger was a cover for grief and disappointment, I grieved the relationship I thought we had, while accepting the truth of who they really were (as opposed to who we thought they were), and recognizing, it was time to stop investing our time and energy in them.
What did you feel about the situation/event?	Devastated – thinking about my husband dying, having people who I thought cared about us leave us, not understanding how some people could treat us in the way they did. This was followed by anger directed at those people who I felt had hurt us. After sitting with it, I was able to recognize the grief.
How did it make you feel – physically/how did you express that feeling?	I felt nauseous, like I had been punched in the gut, dizzy. When I was angry I vented, and when I recognized the grief, I just let myself feel it and cry as I processed it.
What did you use to manage the emotion?	**Get Help.** I ended up seeing a therapist. Who advised me to create a grief ritual and mourn the loss of what was and those people in our live who left or whose actions proved to us. I also did a lot of work with my therapist and my inner child. And I ended up asking friends for help and support and space to process.

	I honoured my feelings and I **journaled** about the situation. **Breathing techniques** **DG1 – Letter Infusion and Burning**. I would write each person a letter with pen and paper, where I told them exactly how I felt – no censoring. While writing I cried, cursed, mourned the loss of what we had before, infusing the letter with all my anger, frustration, sadness, pain, or any other emotion I needed to. And then, I ripped it up and burned it. I imagined that the fire was clearing and transforming my emotions, helping me to process them. I had to do this multiple times depending on the person. **DG2 – My personal grief ritual for loss**. I imagined having a funeral ceremony for them. I imagined myself walking along a beach to a line of easels with frames covered in black cloth. I would walk up to it, face it, remove the black cloth and view their portrait. I would then touch the portrait and fill it with all of the grief I was feeling. I would take a moment to remember all the "good times" and then grief their loss. Depending on the person, I might infuse the portrait with love. And then, I would burn it and stay with it until the ashes were taken by the wind. I also did this when I found out my hubby was diagnosed with POEMS. I imagined a painting that was disjointed and had the word POEMS on it. I let myself grieve, let it burn, and let it go.

GRIEF RECIPE CARD - Dani G

Ingredients

- LOSS OF SOMEONE OR SOMETHING IMPORTANT TO YOU, TO WHICH A BOND OR AFFECTION WAS FORMED
  - HEALTH
  - FRIENDSHIP/SOCIAL INTERACTION

Directions

- GET HELP

- HONOUR YOUR FEELINGS

- JOURNALING

- BREATHING TECHNIQUES

- DG1 – LETTER INFUSION & BURNING

- DG2 – GRIEF RITUAL FOR LOSS

Journal Note

I was devastated about my husband's illness, when people who I thought cared about us left us. I couldn't understand how people could treat us that way. I recognised I was grieving the loss of those friendships and the life I'd had before the illness.

I asked friends to help and support and allow me space to process the situation and be able to mourn the loss.

SHOPPING LIST

AFFLICTION
ANGUISH
   AGONY
   ANGST
   DISTRESS
   HEARTBREAK
   PAIN
   SUFFERING
   TORMENT
BEREAVEMENT
   LOSS
DEJECTION
   DESPONDENCY
MORTIFICATION
MOURNING
   GRIEF
   LAMENT
   SORROW
PINING
REGRET
REMORSE
SADNESS
   BLUES
   DESOLATION
   DESPAIR
   DESPONDENCY
   GRIEF
   HEARTACHE
   MISERY
   SORROW
   WOE

Inner Freedom

Give me the ocean's solace,
The tune of the crashing waves,
Bathe my skin in the sun's warmth,
And let me succumb to the soft sands.
Moonlit walks along the shore,
And early mornings watching
The sun rise along the water's edge –
This is the song of my heart.

When this world becomes too busy,
When the work becomes too much,
Away my mind goes to sandy beaches,
Soothing waters, and calming rhythms
Of the earth's blood.

Always with this picture
Be kept within my mind
To bring me from the ever present
Reality of careless drivers,
Unkind people,
And those really awful days
When nothing seems to go the way I want it to.

So until my lungs again
Breathe in the salty air,
And my skin is damp with ocean mist,
I will take a breath,
Close my eyes,
And return to the place where my spirit is free.

Dani Glaeser

Dani G - Jealousy

Dani G has a story of Jealousy which is shown in her recipe card on the following page.

Name (& title if applicable)	Dani G
Country/Location	USA
What emotion did you feel today?	Jealousy
What prompted the emotion?	A friend of mine had posted on Facebook about how she and her husband were working out together, and how well her kids were doing.
What did you feel about the situation/event?	I felt so sad and jealous – because my husband can't work out due to his health issues, and then I started comparing myself as a parent to her.
How did it make you feel – physically/how did you express that feeling?	Exhausted and sad.
What did you use to manage the emotion?	**Allowed myself to feel it** **Honour my feelings** **Journal about them**. During this, I remembered that Gretchin Rubin has once mentioned that jealousy is simply a signal of something you want, and how badly you want it. So I was able to then: **Tune into my mind and body.** Discovered that I was sad because she could do things with her husband that I couldn't. Just because we couldn't go and work out together, we could sit with each other while he did therapy, or make time to talk to one another each day. **Tell them.** I had a great talk with my kids, who really were not even interested in what her kids had done or were doing. My eldest informed me, "Mom, that might be great for her, but it is not me. I wouldn't enjoy that at all!" Her words of wisdom helped me feel so much better.

JEALOUSY RECIPE CARD - Dani G

Ingredients

- LACK OF SELF CONFIDENCE

- POOR SELF IMAGE

- FEAR

- INSECURITY

Directions

- ALLOW YOURSELF TO FEEL YOUR FEELINGS

- HONOUR YOUR FEELINGS

- JOURNALING

- TUNE INTO YOUR MIND/BODY

- TELL THEM

SHOPPING LIST

ANGER

FEAR

DISGUST

INADEQUATE

HELPLESS

INSECURITY

JEALOUS

LACK

RESENTMENT

Journal Note

A friend was posting on Facebook about how she and her husband were working out together, and how well her kids were doing. I felt so sad and jealous, because my husband can't work out due to his health issues, and then I started comparing myself as a parent. I realised that just because we couldn't go out, we could still sit with each other while he did therapy, or make time to talk to each other. Talking with my children gave me such beautiful words of wisdom which helped me to feel so much better.

Dani G - Resentment

Dani G has a story of Resentment which is shown in her recipe card on the following page.

Name (& title if applicable)	Dani G
Country/Location	USA
What emotion did you feel today?	Resentment
What prompted the emotion?	I had a long day where I had been working or doing or caring for someone all week, and seeing my family on their computers and playing – something in me snapped.
What did you feel about the situation/event?	I was feeling resentful for being a care giver and all that I was doing, and feeling as though I was not getting help.
How did it make you feel – physically/how did you express that feeling?	Angry. I had a headache. I wanted to curl up and cry.
What did you use to manage the emotion?	**Allowed myself to feel it** **Honor my feelings** **Tuned into my mind and body**. Discovered I needed self-care – rest, a good book, a hot cup of tea **Went for a walk** **Told my therapist** who recommended I tell them via a letter – because they weren't hearing what I needed **Told them** by writing a letter in which I told my family I needed help and listed what they could do to help me.

RESENTMENT RECIPE CARD - Dani G

Ingredients

- SENSE OF INJUSTICE OR WRONGDOING
    - NEGATIVE TREATMENT BY OTHERS
    - FEEL LIKE OBJECT OF DISCRIMINATION OR PREJUDICE
    - FEELING USED OR TAKEN ADVANTAGE OF
    - HAVING ACHIEVEMENTS GO UNRECOGNISED
    - REJECTION OR DENIAL BY ANOTHER
    - BEING PUT DOWN OR EMBARRASSED BY OTHERS

Directions

- ALLOW YOURSELF TO FEEL YOUR FEELINGS

- TUNE INTO YOUR MIND AND BODY

- EXERCISE

- GET HELP

- TELL THEM

Journal Note

I had a long day where I had been working and caring for someone all week. I saw my family on their computers and playing. I snapped. I resented being a care giver and I was not getting any help.

I realised I needed to give myself some care through rest, reading and a cup of tea. I went for a walk and wrote letters to my family to let them know what I needed and how they could help me.

SHOPPING LIST

ANGER

DISPLEASURE

FURY

INDIGNATION

IRE

IRRITATION

MALICE

PIQUE

RAGE

VEXATION

WRATH

BITTERNESS

GRUDGE

RANCOUR

UMBRAGE

GALL

HUFF

HURT

ILL WILL

ANIMOSITY

Ingeborg Betuker – Joy & Happiness

Ingeborg Betuker has a story that reflects Joy & Happiness which is shown in her recipe card on the following page.

Name (& title if applicable)	Ingeborg Betuker, certified Life Coach
Country/Location	Aix en Provence, France
What emotion did you feel today?	Joy & happiness
What prompted the emotion	My gratefulness and love for all the people in my life, for my community, gratefulness for everything I am
What did you feel about the situation/event?	I felt strong connectedness with myself and the universe, and with the present moment
How did it make you feel – physically/how did you express that feeling?	It made me smile, laugh, it made me conscious and mindful about life and time.
What did you use to manage the emotion?	**Be nice to people** **Have compassion for their life** **Give help** **Give smile** **Share simple moments**

JOY & HAPPINESS RECIPE CARD
- Ingeborg Betuker

Ingredients

- ENJOYMENT

- SATISFACTION

- PLEASURE

Directions

- BE NICE TO PEOPLE

- SHOW COMPASSION

- GIVE HELP

- SMILE, IT'S MAGICAL

- SHARE SIMPLE/SPECIAL MOMENTS

SHOPPING LIST

CHEERFULNESS

AMUSEMENT

ECSTASY

GAIETY

EUPHORIA

BLISS

ELATION

DELIGHT

HAPPINESS

JUBILATION

ZEST

ENTHUIASM

EXCITEMENT

EXHILIRATION

THRILL

CONTENTMENT

RELIEF

OPTIMISM

PRIDE

ENTHRALLMENT

Journal Note

I am so grateful, and have so much love for all the people in my life, my community and everything that I am.

I feel such a strong connection with the universe and the present moment.

It makes me smile, laugh and makes me conscious about life and time.

Joana Loren Felisarta - Guilt

Joana Loren Felisarta has a story of Guilt which is shown in her recipe card on the following page.

Name (& title if applicable)	Joana Loren Felisarta
Country/Location	Philippines
What emotion did you feel today?	Guilt
What prompted the emotion?	I was thinking of spending less time and energy (and even thinking of slowly cutting my ties) with some of my closest friends who aren't really bad people but I don't feel that we are on the same wavelength (in terms of interests and values).
What did you feel about the situation/event?	Sad and guilty.
How did it make you feel – physically/how did you express that feeling?	Made me feel a little worried because they might judge me for doing that and they may not understand what I am going through.
What did you use to manage the emotion?	**Honour your feelings.** I acknowledged the feeling of guilt. They've been really good friends to me as well. **Reflect.** I deeply reflect on my WHY for cutting my ties with old friends and on WHY am I feeling guilty. **Do what makes you happy.** When I have recognized that my WHY for doing it is reasonable to me with the help of the Social Category materials in *Lifebook*, I just carry on with what I want and what makes me happy but leaving the negative feelings (guilt) behind. I have to accept that this is part of my transformation and my journey towards a more intentional and meaningful life. **Tell them.** I sent one of them a message and told her I will have limited availability for them as I'm going through this phase of my life. I received a good response in return. **Choose to see the good in people.** I still and will forever choose to see the goodness in them despite the few qualities they have that I'm not looking for a friend. However, for me it doesn't necessarily mean that I have to associate myself with them as we have to be deliberate with our circle of friends and surround ourselves with like-minded people who make us feel good, who are supportive and who help us move forward towards our Life vision.

GUILT RECIPE CARD - Joana Loren Felisarta

Ingredients

- SOMETHING YOU DID OR DIDN'T DO
- SOMETHING YOU THINK YOU DID/DIDN'T DO
- DIDN'T DO ENOUGH TO HELP PERSON/PEOPLE
- CONSIDERED BY OTHERS TO BE DOING BETTER THAN THEM/SOMEONE ELSE

Directions

- HONOUR YOUR FEELINGS
- REFLECT
  - ACCEPT THE FACT THAT THE PAST CANNOT BE CHANGED
  - FORGIVE YOURSELF FOR ANY SHORTCOMINGS OR FOR ANYTHING WRONG YOU MAY HAVE DONE
- DO WHAT MAKES YOU HAPPY
- TELL THEM
- CHOOSE TO SEE THE GOOD IN PEOPLE

SHOPPING LIST

ANGER

ANXIETY

DEPRESSION

EMPTINESS

ENVY

GUILT

LONELINESS

RAGE

REGRET

REMORSE

SADNESS

SHAME

Journal Note

I want to have a fantastic and extraordinary friendship, one that energizes, inspires, supports, trusts, respects, and move each other and help each other learn and grow. I have no time for relationships that do not make sense for me, one that is toxic and draining and lacks honesty. I set my own boundaries and will have the courage to politely tell someone if they ever cross them.

Jordan River - Desire

Jordan River has a story of Temptation which is fuelled by the emotion/feeling of Desire, which is shown in his recipe card on the following page.

Name (& title if applicable)	Jordan River
Country/Location	Chicago, Illinois, USA
What emotion did you feel today?	Temptation
What prompted the emotion?	The sight of unhealthy food at a social gathering
What did you feel about the situation/event?	Everyone is having one, I should indulge
How did it make you feel – physically/how did you express that feeling?	Mouth-watering, taste buds calling out, limbic system engaged
What did you use to manage the emotion?	Take a slow, **deep breath** to break the physiological limbic reaction Close your eyes for **visualization** Connect with your imaginary future self, after you have indulged, and connect with the way you will feel if you break your discipline. Connect with the feeling of regret and feel the "loss." Open your eyes and take **another deep breath** to regain discipline

DESIRE RECIPE CARD - Jordan River

Ingredients

- STRONG FEELING OF;
  - WANTING TO HAVE SOMETHING
  - WISHING FOR SOMETHING TO HAPPEN
- LONGING OR HOPING FOR OR WANT (SOMETHING)
  - PERSON
  - OBJECT
  - OUTCOME
- EXCITING HOPE OR DESIRE
- HAVE OR DO SOMETHING YOU KNOW YOU SHOULD AVOID
- SOMETHING THAT SEDUCES OR HAS THE QUALITY TO SEDUCE
- MISS/REGRET SOMETHING

Directions

- VISUALISATION TECHNIQUES
  - TAKE A DEEP BREATH
  - CLOSE YOUR EYES FOR VISUALIZATION
  - CONNECT WITH YOUR IMAGINARY FUTURE SELF
    - AFTER YOU HAVE INDULGED
  - CONNECT WITH THE WAY YOU WILL FEEL IF YOU BREAK YOUR DISCIPLINE.
    - FEELING OF REGRET
    - FEEL THE "LOSS"
  - OPEN YOUR EYES
  - TAKE A DEEP BREATH TO REGAIN DISCIPLINE

Journal Note

The sight of unhealthy food at a social gathering created temptation as everyone else was having some and I wanted to indulge. I visualised how I would feel after I had indulged, and connected with the way I would feel if I broke my discipline. I took a deep breath and regained my composure.

SHOPPING LIST

APPEAL

ATTRACTION

ALLURE

ENTICEMENT

SEDUCTION

COVET

EAGERNESS

FANCY

HANKERING

CRAVING

LONGING

LUSTING

WANTING

YEARNING

HUNGER

NEED

TEMPTATION

DESIRE

URGE

IMPULSE

INCLINATION

WISH

JW – Sadness, Frustration

JW's story below is showing the emotion of Sadness, but their story also relates to Frustration. You will see their recipe cards on the following 2 pages:

JW could create a single recipe card that covers both of these, but is showing them separately to show their differences.

Name (& title if applicable)	**JW**
Country/Location	**USA/California**
What emotion did you feel today?	**Sadness**
What prompted the emotion?	A quality of misunderstanding, criticism, and disconnection with our grown kids; not of my doing, something each of them are going through
What did you feel about the situation/event?	Sad, annoyed, frustrated, a little helpless
How did it make you feel – physically/how did you express that feeling?	Heavy, weighed down, lethargic in my body, tired; a little stuck in that there is no action that I can take to make things better between us right now
What did you use to manage the emotion?	Facing and accepting the emotions and the situation (**Honour your feelings, Mindfulness, Reflect**) understanding where each of them are coming from (**Choose to see the good in people, Forgiveness**), then redirecting my focus and taking action around things I can have an effect on (**Negative emotion – don't wallow**) – physical exercise (**Exercise, Tune into your mind/body**), creative work, tangible action in other areas (**Do what makes you happy, Know you are in control**)

SADNESS RECIPE CARD - JW

Ingredients

- FEELING OF LOSS
- DISADVANTAGE
- MAY LEAD TO DEPRESSION
- QUIET
- LESS ENERGETIC
- WITHDRAWN TO ONESELF
- SLOPING BODY
- STUCK OUT LIPS
- DOWNCAST APPEARANCE OF THE HEAD

Directions

- HONOUR YOUR FEELINGS
- MINDFULNESS
- REFLECT
- CHOOSE TO SEE THE GOOD IN PEOPLE
- FORGIVENESS
- NEGATIVE EMOTION – DON'T WALLOW
- EXERCISE
- TUNE INTO YOUR MIND/BODY
- DO WHAT MAKES YOU HAPPY
- KNOW YOU ARE IN CONTROL

Journal Note

I experienced a quality of misunderstanding, criticism, and disconnection with our grown kids. It's something each of them are going through, but it left me feeling sad, annoyed, frustrated and a little helpless. I felt a little stuck in that there is no action that I can take to make things better between us right now.

I faced and accepted the emotions, and the situation, understanding where each of them are coming from. Then I redirected my focus and took action around things I can have an effect on;

- physical exercise
- creative work & tangible action in other areas

SHOPPING LIST

SUFFERING

AGONY

HURT

ANGUISH

DISAPPOINTMENT

DISMAY

DISPLEASURE

SHAME

GUILT

REMORSE

REGRET

NEGLECT

INSECURITY

ALIENATION

HOMESICKNESS

EMBARRASSMENT

HUMILIATION

SYMPATHY

PITY

FRUSTRATION RECIPE CARD - JW

Ingredients

- UNABLE TO CHANGE OR ACHIEVE SOMETHING
- PREVENTION OF THE PROGRESS, SUCCESS, OR FULFILMENT
- FEELINGS OF UNCERTAINTY AND INSECURITY
- NEEDS ARE CONSTANTLY IGNORED OR UNSATISFIED

Directions

- HONOUR YOUR FEELINGS
- MINDFULNESS
- REFLECT
- CHOOSE TO SEE THE GOOD IN PEOPLE
- FORGIVENESS
- NEGATIVE EMOTION – DON'T WALLOW
- EXERCISE
- TUNE INTO YOUR MIND/BODY
- DO WHAT MAKES YOU HAPPY
- KNOW YOU ARE IN CONTROL

Journal Note

I experienced a quality of misunderstanding, criticism, and disconnection with our grown kids. It's something each of them are going through, but it left me feeling sad, annoyed, frustrated and a little helpless. I felt a little stuck in that there is no action that I can take to make things better between us right now.

I faced and accepted the emotions, and the situation, understanding where each of them are coming from. Then I redirected my focus and took action around things I can have an effect on;

- physical exercise
- creative work & tangible action in other areas

SHOPPING LIST

ANGER

BITTERNESS

    RESENTMENT

DEFEAT

    BLOCK

    COLLAPSE

    COUNTER

DISAPPOINTMENT

    DEPRESSION

    DISSATISFACTION

DISCOURAGEMENT

DISCONTENT

FAILURE

IRRITATION

    AGGRAVATION

    ANNOYANCE

    EXASPERATION

OBSTRUCTION

    HAMPERING

    HINDERING

    SCUPPERING

QUASHING

    CRIPPLING

    CRUSHING

VEXATION

Kathryn Cartwright - Anger

Kathryn Cartwright has a story that reflects Anger which is shown in her recipe card on the following page.

Name (& title if applicable)	Kathryn Cartwright
Country/Location	United States
What emotion did you feel today?	Anger
What prompted the emotion?	Being upset with something completely out of my control in relation to my ex-husband's lack of helping my children. I realized that I help my children do the right things and model the right things, such as support them in an effort to celebrate their father's birthday and Christmas and Father's Day, while if it weren't for the teachers at school, the kids' babysitter, and one of my closest friends, there would be no supportive effort on his part for my birthday or Mother's Day.
What did you feel about the situation/event?	I felt it was completely unfair and wrong, and I was mad and frustrated and sad to be reminded of one of the many reasons we had relationship issues. It was always his needs and no one else's.
How did it make you feel – physically/how did you express that feeling?	I was moody and short when I was talking to my children. Tense. Wanted to cry, but didn't.
What did you use to manage the emotion?	**90 second rule** **Breathe** **Honoured my feelings** **Mindfulness**

ANGER RECIPE CARD – Kathryn Cartwright

Ingredients

- INJUSTICE
- CONFLICT
- HUMILIATION
- NEGLIGENCE
- BETRAYAL
- VERBAL OR PHYSICAL ATTACK
- SILENT SULKING
- TENSION
- HOSTILITY
- EMPATHISING WITH ANOTHER

Directions

- 90 SECOND RULE
- BREATHE
- HONOURED MY FEELINGS
- MINDFULNESS

Journal Note

My children's father lacks helping my children. It really upset me, as he puts in minimal effort while I'm trying to do the right thing for them. I ended up being moody and short with them even though it wasn't their fault.

SHOPPING LIST

DISGUST
CONTEMPT
   INDIGNATION
   LOATHING
   REVULSION
ENVY
   JEALOUSY
EXASPERATION
FRUSTRATION
IRRITATION
   AGITATION
   AGGRAVATION
   ANNOYANCE
   GROUCHINESS
   GRUMPINESS
RAGE
   BITTERNESS
   DISLIKE
   FEROCITY
   FURY
   HATRED
   HOSTILITY
   LOATHING
   OUTRAGE
   RESENTMENT
   SCORN
   SPITE
   VENGEFULNESS
   WRATH
TORMENT

Maddy – Anger, Frustration, Guilt

Maddy has a story of Anger, which encompasses frustration and guilt, which are shown in her recipe cards on the following 3 pages.

Name (& title if applicable)	Maddy Turning Anger
Country/Location	New Zealand
What emotion did you feel today?	Anger
What prompted the emotion?	I made a comment regarding the length of a DVD we had just watched. My partner questioned me and was getting frustrated at my lack of clarity in my answer. Instead of saying "I don't know" I just confused him more. I wanted to drop it but he stomped off to get his glasses to read the back of the dvd himself. We were shouting at each other over nothing and instead of throwing my tea at him (which occured to me) I took myself away, with the tea and stomped off up to bed.
What did you feel about the situation/event?	angry; guilty; frustrated
How did it make you feel – physically/how did you express that feeling?	I felt all churned up and full of fury; also lost in the frustration of how something so minor could explode into a full-scale argument
What did you use to manage the emotion?	**Take a break to regain composure** **Tell them**

ANGER RECIPE CARD - Maddy

Ingredients

- INJUSTICE
- CONFLICT
- HUMILIATION
- NEGLIGENCE
- BETRAYAL
- VERBAL OR PHYSICAL ATTACK
- SILENT SULKING
- TENSION
- HOSTILITY
- EMPATHISING WITH ANOTHER

Directions

- TAKE A BREAK TO REGAIN COMPOSURE
- TELL THEM

Journal Note

Stupid argument; cooled down and apologised with no 'buts'. Being first to apologise works again and perfect response from Gregg – I love us.

SHOPPING LIST

DISGUST
  CONTEMPT
  INDIGNATION
  LOATHING
  REVULSION
ENVY
  JEALOUSY
EXASPERATION
FRUSTRATION
IRRITATION
  AGITATION
  AGGRAVATION
  ANNOYANCE
  GROUCHINESS
  GRUMPINESS
RAGE
  BITTERNESS
  DISLIKE
  FEROCITY
  FURY
  HATRED
  HOSTILITY
  LOATHING
  OUTRAGE
  RESENTMENT
  SCORN
  SPITE
  VENGEFULNESS
  WRATH
TORMENT

FRUSTRATION RECIPE CARD - Maddy

Ingredients

- UNABLE TO CHANGE OR ACHIEVE SOMETHING
- PREVENTION OF THE PROGRESS, SUCCESS, OR FULFILMENT
- FEELINGS OF UNCERTAINTY AND INSECURITY
- NEEDS ARE CONSTANTLY IGNORED OR UNSATISFIED

Directions

- TAKE A BREAK TO REGAIN COMPOSURE
- TELL THEM

Journal Note

I made a comment regarding the length of a DVD we had just watched. My partner questioned me and was getting frustrated at my lack of clarity in my answer. Instead of saying "I don't know" I just confused him more. I felt lost in the frustration of how something so minor could explode into a full-scale argument. Cooled down and apologised with no 'buts'.

SHOPPING LIST

ANGER

BITTERNESS

RESENTMENT

DEFEAT

BLOCK

COLLAPSE

COUNTER

DISAPPOINTMENT

DEPRESSION

DISSATISFACTION

DISCOURAGEMENT

DISCONTENT

FAILURE

IRRITATION

AGGRAVATION

ANNOYANCE

EXASPERATION

OBSTRUCTION

HAMPERING

HINDERING

SCUPPERING

QUASHING

CRIPPLING

CRUSHING

VEXATION

GUILT RECIPE CARD - Maddy

Ingredients

- SOMETHING YOU DID OR DIDN'T DO
- SOMETHING YOU THINK YOU DID/DIDN'T DO
- DIDN'T DO ENOUGH TO HELP PERSON/PEOPLE
- CONSIDERED BY OTHERS TO BE DOING BETTER THAN THEM/SOMEONE ELSE

Directions

- TAKE A BREAK TO REGAIN COMPOSURE
- TELL THEM

SHOPPING LIST

ANGER

ANXIETY

DEPRESSION

EMPTINESS

ENVY

GUILT

LONELINESS

RAGE

REGRET

REMORSE

SADNESS

SHAME

Journal Note

Stupid argument; cooled down and apologised with no 'buts'. Being first to apologise works again and perfect response from Gregg - I love us.

Mary grace - Anger

Mary grace has shown the emotion of Anger-frustration. This could be represented by one or two recipes. You will see a single recipe card has been created on the following page.

Name (& title if applicable)	Mary grace
Country/Location	Pasay, philippines
What emotion did you feel today?	Anger- frustration
What prompted the emotion?	I have been working to be physically, mentally, spiritually and emotionally healthy and it has been tough for me. I really felt emotionally drained and instead of understanding and encouragement from my own family members, they just criticized what I've been doing and never appreciated the improvements in my life.
What did you feel about the situation/event?	The first thing that came to my mind was "why do I even have them as my family members? Maybe I'm better being an orphan or having another set of supportive family"
How did it make you feel – physically/how did you express that feeling?	I felt like something below my navel was boiling and wanting to reach my head and just pop out with my brain. I clenched my 2 fists
What did you use to manage the emotion?	**Allow yourself to feel your feelings** **Breathe/ breathing relaxation technique** **Know you are in control**

ANGER RECIPE CARD – Mary grace

Ingredients

- INJUSTICE
- CONFLICT
- HUMILIATION
- NEGLIGENCE
- BETRAYAL
- VERBAL OR PHYSICAL ATTACK
- SILENT SULKING
- TENSION
- HOSTILITY

Directions

- ALLOW YOURSELF TO FEEL YOUR FEELINGS
- BREATHE/BREATHING RELAXATION TECHNIQUE
- KNOW YOU ARE IN CONTROL

Journal Note

I have been working to be physically, mentally, spiritually and emotionally healthy and it has been tough for me. I really felt emotionally drained and instead of understanding and encouragement from my own family members, they just criticized what I've been doing and never appreciated the improvements in my life. The first thing that came to my mind was "why do I even have them as my family members? Maybe I'm better being an orphan or having another set of supportive family".

SHOPPING LIST

DISGUST
  CONTEMPT
  INDIGNATION
  LOATHING
  REVULSION
ENVY
  JEALOUSY
EXASPERATION
FRUSTRATION
IRRITATION
  AGITATION
  AGGRAVATION
  ANNOYANCE
  GROUCHINESS
  GRUMPINESS
RAGE
  BITTERNESS
  DISLIKE
  FEROCITY
  FURY
  HATRED
  HOSTILITY
  LOATHING
  OUTRAGE
  RESENTMENT
  SCORN
  SPITE
  VENGEFULNESS
  WRATH
TORMENT

Nora – Anger, Resentment

Nora has a story of Resentment and Anger which are shown in 2 recipe cards on the following 2 pages.

Name (& title if applicable)	Nora
Country/Location	Austria
What emotion did you feel today?	Resentment and Anger
What prompted the emotion?	My boss gave me an additional workload that I had repeatedly communicated I could not handle working part time
What did you feel about the situation/event?	I felt unheard, underappreciated, helpless and overwhelmed
How did it make you feel – physically/how did you express that feeling?	Flushed, shaky with constricted breath
What did you use to manage the emotion?	**I calmed my breath** I **analysed what emotions I was feeling** (in this case anger and resentment) and voiced these emotions and why I was feeling them. I then added the **positive statement** that I love and accept myself. Using this statement, I **applied EFT Tapping** on my meridian points for as long as it was necessary for the emotion to dissolve and for me to **feel calm and in control of my feelings**.

ANGER RECIPE CARD - Nora

Ingredients

- INJUSTICE
- CONFLICT
- HUMILIATION
- NEGLIGENCE
- BETRAYAL
- VERBAL OR PHYSICAL ATTACK
- SILENT SULKING
- TENSION
- HOSTILITY

Directions

- BREATH/BREATHING TECHNIQUE
- PAUSE AND CONSIDER HOW YOU FEEL
- REFLECT
- COACH YOURSELF, IF ITS DIFFICULT
- FOCUS ON POSITIVE ENERGY/BE POSITIVE IN YOUR THINKING
- EMOTIONAL FREEDOM TECHNIQUE (EFT)

Journal Note

My boss gave me an additional workload that I had repeatedly communicated I could not handle working part time. I felt unheard, underappreciated, helpless and overwhelmed. I calmed myself, then analysed my emotions and voiced them to myself, and why I was feeling them. I gave myself a positive statement that I love and accept myself. I applied EFT Tapping on my Meridian points until the emotion had dissolved and I felt calm and in control of my feelings.

SHOPPING LIST

DISGUST
CONTEMPT
   INDIGNATION
   LOATHING
   REVULSION
ENVY
   JEALOUSY
EXASPERATION
FRUSTRATION
IRRITATION
   AGITATION
   AGGRAVATION
   ANNOYANCE
   GROUCHINESS
   GRUMPINESS
RAGE
   BITTERNESS
   DISLIKE
   FEROCITY
   FURY
   HATRED
   HOSTILITY
   LOATHING
   OUTRAGE
   RESENTMENT
   SCORN
   SPITE
   VENGEFULNESS
   WRATH
TORMENT

RESENTMENT RECIPE CARD - Nora

Ingredients

- SENSE OF INJUSTICE OR WRONGDOING
  - NEGATIVE TREATMENT BY OTHERS
  - FEEL LIKE OBJECT OF DISCRIMINATION OR PREJUDICE
  - FEELING USED OR TAKEN ADVANTAGE OF HAVING ACHIEVEMENTS GO UNRECOGNISED
  - REJECTION OR DENIAL BY ANOTHER
  - BEING PUT DOWN OR EMBARRASSED BY OTHERS

Directions

- BREATH/BREATHING TECHNIQUE
- PAUSE AND CONSIDER HOW YOU FEEL
- REFLECT
- COACH YOURSELF, IF ITS DIFFICULT
- EMOTIONAL FREEDOM TECHNIQUE (EFT)

Journal Note

My boss gave me an additional workload that I had repeatedly communicated I could not handle working part time. I felt unheard and underappreciated. I resented him not listening to me.
I calmed myself, then analysed my emotions and voiced them to myself, and why I was feeling them. I gave myself a positive statement that I love and accept myself. I applied EFT Tapping on my Meridian points until the emotion had dissolved and I felt calm and in control of my feelings.

SHOPPING LIST

ANGER

DISPLEASURE

FURY

INDIGNATION

IRE

IRRITATION

MALICE

PIQUE

RAGE

VEXATION

WRATH

BITTERNESS

GRUDGE

RANCOUR

UMBRAGE

GALL

HUFF

HURT

ILL WILL

ANIMOSITY

Patricia – Joy & Happiness

Patricia has a story of Joy & Happiness, which is shown in her recipe card on the following page.

Name (& title if applicable)	Patricia Guest
Country/Location	Canada
What emotion did you feel today?	Joy and Happiness
What prompted the emotion?	Completing my *Lifebook*
What did you feel about the situation/event?	Pride, elation, completion, Like coming home and really grounded in myself
How did it make you feel – physically/how did you express that feeling?	I was giddy with self love, It is the single most loving thing that I have ever done for myself.
What did you use to manage the emotion?	**Do what makes you Happy** **Embody positive & empowering feelings** **Exercise** **Meditation** I went for a walk at a beautiful trail by a stream and thought about my life and my *Lifebook* and integrated that feeling into being me. Later I went to yoga and set my intention to live my *Lifebook*.

JOY & HAPPINESS RECIPE CARD – Patricia

Ingredients

- ENJOYMENT

- SATISFACTION

- PLEASURE

Directions

- DO WHAT MAKES YOU HAPPY

- EMBODY POSITIVE & EMPOWERING FEELINGS

- MEDITATION

- EXERCISE

Journal Note

I completed my Lifebook. I have complete feelings of pride, elation and completion, like coming home and being really grounded in myself. I was giddy with self-love. It is the single most loving thing that I have ever done for myself.

I went for a walk at a beautiful trail by a stream and thought about my life and my Lifebook and integrated that feeling into being me. Later I went to yoga and set my intention to live my Lifebook.

SHOPPING LIST

CHEERFULNESS

    AMUSEMENT

    ECSTASY

    GAIETY

    EUPHORIA

    BLISS

    ELATION

    DELIGHT

    HAPPINESS

    JUBILATION

ZEST

    ENTHUIASM

    EXCITEMENT

    EXHILIRATION

    THRILL

CONTENTMENT

RELIEF

OPTIMISM

PRIDE

ENTHRALLMENT

Santa - Anger

Santa has a story that reflects Anger which is shown in her recipe card on the following page.

Name (& title if applicable)	Santa
Country/Location	Aalborg, Denmark
What emotion did you feel today?	Anger
What prompted the emotion?	My husband got furious at me about something that I think was a very minor problem.
What did you feel about the situation/event?	I felt it was not fair that he was allowed to scream at me, when In similar situations I would be put in place.
How did it make you feel – physically/how did you express that feeling?	I really physically felt like my blood-pressure went up and made me nauseous.
What did you use to manage the emotion?	Took a slow breath, then let it go I did not try to hide my feelings Reflection- It sort of always comes naturally that I would have a discussion in my head on ´what could I have done/ said´ differently. Simple cleaning of house: I have realised through years that the best form of meditation, particularly after a fight with my husband, is cleaning the house. This helps me reflect on situation and calms me down.

ANGER RECIPE CARD - Santa

Ingredients

- INJUSTICE
- CONFLICT
- HUMILIATION
- NEGLIGENCE
- BETRAYAL
- VERBAL OR PHYSICAL ATTACK
- SILENT SULKING
- TENSION
- HOSTILITY
- EMPATHISING WITH ANOTHER

Directions

- 90 SECOND RULE
- ALLOW YOURSELF TO FEEL YOUR FEELINGS
- REFLECTION
- MEDITATE (Simple cleaning of house)

Journal Note

My husband got furious at me about something that I think was a very minor problem. I felt it was not fair that he was allowed to scream at me, when in similar situations I would be put in place. I reflected on the situation and meditated by doing some house cleaning.

SHOPPING LIST

DISGUST
  CONTEMPT
  INDIGNATION
  LOATHING
  REVULSION
ENVY
  JEALOUSY
EXASPERATION
FRUSTRATION
IRRITATION
  AGITATION
  AGGRAVATION
  ANNOYANCE
  GROUCHINESS
  GRUMPINESS
RAGE
  BITTERNESS
  DISLIKE
  FEROCITY
  FURY
  HATRED
  HOSTILITY
  LOATHING
  OUTRAGE
  RESENTMENT
  SCORN
  SPITE
  VENGEFULNESS
  WRATH
TORMENT

Santa - Frustration

Santa has a story that reflects Frustration which is shown in her recipe card on the following page.

Name (& title if applicable)	Santa
Country/Location	Aalborg, Denmark
What emotion did you feel today?	Frustration
What prompted the emotion?	I got frustrated when my son would not get to his school homework after me reminding it several times.
What did you feel about the situation/event?	I felt desperate, I felt as not disciplined enough of a parent, I kept on thinking what is it I am doing wrong that this keep happening again and again.
How did it make you feel – physically/how did you express that feeling?	My voice was getting louder and louder every time I had to remind it to him again. I was sighing and felt like giving up.
What did you use to manage the emotion?	**I did not try to hide my feelings** **Reflection**- It sort of always comes naturally that I would have a discussion in my head on ´what could I have done/ said´ differently. In this case it was not as a reflection after the ´conflict´ that frustrated me, but rather along the way. After asking him to get to homework and starting to get frustrated with him, I began thinking what could I do different since this is not working. I think I sort of also began instinctively to **Coach/guide myself** in my head telling and affirming that it will be ok, "just because you are frustrated with your child does not mean you are a bad mother". It was as if I am trying to give myself a psychology session.

FRUSTRATION RECIPE CARD - Santa

Ingredients

- UNABLE TO CHANGE OR ACHIEVE SOMETHING

- PREVENTION OF THE PROGRESS, SUCCESS, OR FULFILMENT

- FEELINGS OF UNCERTAINTY AND INSECURITY

- NEEDS ARE CONSTANTLY IGNORED OR UNSATISFIED

Directions

- ALLOW YOURSELF TO FEEL YOUR FEELINGS

- REFLECTION

- COACH YOURSELF, IF IT'S DIFFICULT

SHOPPING LIST

ANGER

BITTERNESS

RESENTMENT

DEFEAT

BLOCK

COLLAPSE

COUNTER

DISAPPOINTMENT

DEPRESSION

DISSATISFACTION

DISCOURAGEMENT

DISCONTENT

FAILURE

IRRITATION

AGGRAVATION

ANNOYANCE

EXASPERATION

OBSTRUCTION

HAMPERING

HINDERING

SCUPPERING

QUASHING

CRIPPLING

CRUSHING

VEXATION

Journal Note

I got frustrated when my son would not get to his school homework after me reminding it several times. I felt desperate, I felt as not disciplined enough of a parent, I kept on thinking what is it I am doing wrong that this keep happening again and again. After asking him to get to homework and starting to get frustrated with him, I began thinking what could I do different since this is not working. I realised that just because I was frustrated it didn't mean I was a bad mother.

Santa - Overwhelm

Santa has a story that reflects Overwhelm which is shown in her recipe card on the following page.

Name (& title if applicable)	Santa
Country/Location	Aalborg, Denmark
What emotion did you feel today?	Overwhelm
What prompted the emotion?	Monday this week was going to be particularly busy. There were several work meetings at work scheduled, my child had to be picked up early from school, we had to attend some place with him, and I so much wanted to manage to go to my training and other things, house was still a mess. I felt really really overwhelmed and was not sure how I could manage through that day.
What did you feel about the situation/event?	I felt enormous chaos in my head. It felt like virtual post-its were stacking up in mind- reminding myself ´don't forget this, don't forget that´. Felt the ´classic´ of not having enough hours that day.
How did it make you feel – physically/how did you express that feeling?	I felt a slight turbulence in my body, weak knees. I think my family felt my overwhelm, coz even the smallest thing could get me irritated.
What did you use to manage the emotion?	When everybody was out of the house in the morning, I sat down and **meditated**. I had a little half an hour left before leaving for work, I put some slow **mindfulness** music in background and, sort of, combined the **meditation, mindfulness** with **positive thinking** and **breathing for** relaxation. This helped to gather the thoughts and make up a plan for the busy day ahead. Not this particular day, but if more time, then I think there are plenty of great meditation and mindfulness exercises on YouTube. For my morning I used a simple jazz station on my TV radio

EMOTIONAL OVERWHELM RECIPE CARD
- Santa

Ingredients

- BURY OR DROWN BENEATH A HUGE MASS OF SOMETHING

- A STRONG EMOTIONAL EFFECT

Directions

- MEDITATE

- MINDFULNESS

- BE POSITIVE IN YOUR THINKING

- BREATHE/BREATHING

SHOPPING LIST

DEFEAT

OVERCOME

OVERTRHOW

CONQUER

DESTROY

DROWN

SUBMERGE

INUNDATE

WASTE

ASTONISH

PUZZLE

BEWILDER

CONFOUND

Journal Note

Monday this week was going to be particularly busy. There were several work meetings at work scheduled, my child had to be picked up early from school, we had to attend some place with him, and I so much wanted to manage to go to my training and other things, house was still a mess. I felt really really overwhelmed and was not sure how I could manage through that day. I felt enormous chaos in my head. It felt like virtual post-its were stacking up in mind- reminding myself ´don't forget this, don't forget that´. Felt the ´classic´ of not having enough hours that day. I felt a slight turbulence in my body, weak knees. I think my family felt my overwhelm, coz even the smallest thing could get me irritated. When everybody was out of the house in the morning, I sat down and meditated. I had a little half an hour left before leaving for work. I put some slow mindfulness music in background and, sort of, combined the meditation, mindfulness, with positive thinking and breathing for relaxation. This helped to gather the thoughts and make up a plan for the busy day ahead.

Susie Earl – Joy & Happiness

Susie Earl has a story that reflects Joy which is shown in her recipe card on the following page.

Name (& title if applicable)	Susie Earl *Licensed Health Coach*
Country/Location	Washington State USA
What emotion did you feel today?	Joy
What prompted the emotion?	Spent quality time with friend
What did you feel about the situation/event?	Happy and Grateful
How did it make you feel – physically/how did you express that feeling?	Energized Generously
What did you use to manage the emotion?	Brighten Someone's Day Tell Them I bought them lunch and told them how much I appreciate their friendship.

JOY & HAPPINESS RECIPE CARD
- Susie Earl

Ingredients

- ENJOYMENT
- SATISFACTION
- PLEASURE

Directions

- BRIGHTEN SOMEONE'S DAY
- TELL THEM

SHOPPING LIST

CHEERFULNESS

AMUSEMENT

ECSTASY

GAIETY

EUPHORIA

BLISS

ELATION

DELIGHT

HAPPINESS

JUBILATION

ZEST

ENTHUIASM

EXCITEMENT

EXHILIRATION

THRILL

CONTENTMENT

RELIEF

OPTIMISM

PRIDE

ENTHRALLMENT

Journal Note

I spent quality time with friend. I bought them lunch and told them how much I appreciate their friendship.

Susie Earl - Sadness

Susie Earl has a story that reflects Sadness which is shown in her recipe card on the following page.

Name (& title if applicable)	Susie Earl *Licensed Health Coach*
Country/Location	Washington State USA
What emotion did you feel today?	Sadness
What prompted the emotion?	MIL hurt my children's feelings with unkind words
What did you feel about the situation/event?	Betrayal and Disappointment
How did it make you feel – physically/how did you express that feeling?	Nauseated Exhausted
What did you use to manage the emotion?	SME1 Huna & Ho'oponopono The Hawaiian Code of Forgiveness

SADNESS RECIPE CARD – Susie Earl

Ingredients

- FEELING OF LOSS
- DISADVANTAGE
- MAY LEAD TO DEPRESSION
- QUIET
- LESS ENERGETIC
- WITHDRAWN TO ONESELF
- SLOPING BODY
- STUCK OUT LIPS
- DOWNCAST APPEARANCE OF THE HEAD

Directions

- SME1
  - POSITIVE SELF-TALK
  - PERSONAL CARE
- HUNA & HO'OPONOPONO
- FORGIVENESS
  - THE HAWAIIAN CODE OF FORGIVENESS

Journal Note

When I am feeling sad, I take the time to process my emotion. Then I find a way to brighten someone else's day.

SHOPPING LIST

SUFFERING

AGONY

HURT

ANGUISH

DISAPPOINTMENT

DISMAY

DISPLEASURE

SHAME

GUILT

REMORSE

REGRET

NEGLECT

INSECURITY

ALIENATION

HOMESICKNESS

EMBARRASSMENT

HUMILIATION

SYMPATHY

PITY

Tamara Mihályi – Grief, Guilt, Fear

Tamara Mihályi has a story of Grief, Fear, Sadness and Loss. These are shown as:

- **Grief** which relates to Grief - Sadness.
- **Guilt** which relates to Guilt
- **Fear** which relates to Fear/Insecurity

Tamara could create a single recipe card, that covers all of these, but is showing them separately to show their differences.

Name (& title if applicable)	Tamara Mihályi
Country/Location	Hungary (home country)
What emotion did you feel today?	Grief-Sadness, Guilt and Fear/Insecurity (roots: Loss of Loved One, Love loss, Career change & Finance) *Transforming to Gratitude, Centredness and Joy*
What prompted the emotion?	My darling dad passed on the 27th of December 2016. I was shaken "awake" and that time made me think through what I could have done more, what I can do now for my own happiness and fulfilment in Life – as it seemed it can end quickly. My Love relationship of a decade ended around the same time. So that period has been a magnified turning point in my Life. I took action to make positive changes, understand deeply what makes me happy and learn how I can find and fulfil my Purpose. Consciously investing into my personal growth, learning many tools for this in the past 11 months, has been transformative for me and although before my Losses I was quite a positive person and aimed to intelligently walk through Life and help who I can, but I lived my Life more instinctively – and was submerged into a non-functioning Love Relationship while I should/could have focused more on my Family and my dad's health situation (letting go of guilt is part of my process) - and although I discovered some tools to upgrade myself, I did not believe or empower myself to dare step out of the daily routine earlier and become conscious of my patterns and that I stopped daring dream big.

What did you feel about the situation/event?	So I was devastated, felt guilty for my choices, for not being there enough. I felt awful for not seeing the signs while I still could have helped.
	But as my strong positive internal drive tried to course-correct, I tried to find more and more the Appreciation for the memories and all the value I received from my Father who was/is a wonderful role model of a very strong integrity and graceful Character and also for that Love Relationship that shaped me.
	I'm missing the conversations with my dad, but appreciating so much the legacy he left in me and shaping my own Character and strong integrity.
	Sadness and loneliness and a feeling of being a bit lost followed in those coming months – from someone who is "high on her game" in the job at least, and you know… seemingly successful, trying to be a good person every day… and then this "smack"… well, the Universe certainly got my attention and I asked: what is my right focus here?
	Since then I formed a belief that is very deeply anchored in me: I do believe that everything happens for a Reason.
	I may not (yet) understand all of the details, but I really believe in a Friendly Universe. So, gradually Gratitude started to fill me up and make me strong again and stronger from the core than I've been before.
How did it make you feel – physically/how did you express that feeling?	Loads of crying, some arguments with myself and the Love.
	I felt somewhat weak and definitely vulnerable.
	Hurt, because I didn't understand why this had to happen and what I did do wrong.
	And I felt like a fool too, for not listening to my Inner Voice or just not hearing it…all these scenarios. But because I do not like to dwell too much on things I can't change any more, my Mind started to look for resolution tools. That's where my Personal Growth started in earnest.

What did you use to manage the emotion?	These were the main tools I used over the course of the past 9 months consciously with great results: feeling much more centred and balanced today than in January. **Allow myself to feel my feelings and** **Honour your feelings** – learning to understand that our emotions are there to tell us something and the sooner we deal with that message, the sooner the relief and solution can arrive (in my experience) **Brighten someone's day** – contribute to some else's path definitely raised my feeling of being of value **Coach yourself**, if it's difficult and **Clearing limiting beliefs** – for me self-awareness really and being **conscious of thoughts and limiting beliefs** and letting them go was a great positive impact. Understanding how our brain works (Dr. Joe Dispenza, Dr. Bruce Liption, Vishen Lakhiani and Jeffrey Allen courses – and for someone like me who loves to learn, it was very exciting to learn and understand the patterns of how our Mind works and turn it from self-sabotage/limiting beliefs(society/"standard" set-up) mode to empowering present-future mode, is still being a great Adventure. Like a muscle that you are exercising and you see and feel the progress through the weeks and months. **Do what makes you happy** – talking to Friends and Family are wonderful and connecting to the ones who are "still around" and using that precious time we have in this Life with them was one of the healing methods for me. Walking on the sea shore and marvelling at how beautiful this world is – what a great Painter the Universe is and being right there right then in the moment. Amazing to feel the presence of Now. **Embody positive & empowering feelings** and **Mindfulness** – here for me Gratitude helped a lot and still does just being there in the moment too. "YET" works for me too great! **Meditation – and energy exercises** : Meditation and energy exercises can be another tool to uncover the patterns of our behaviour and limiting beliefs and how to replace them with empowering thoughts. Listening to positive affirmations during the day or during sleep in another tool **Smile, It's Magical**. The Power of Smiling – staying amused as learnt in energy exercises with Jeffrey Allen **Subconscious Programming:** I find that the knowledge and understanding about how our Mind works can be very useful when you are about to uncover limiting beliefs in your life. To even just know about the current neuroscience statement that our Subconscious runs about 95% of our life is pretty powerful. From the things we recorded as children to media messages and negative communication that are reaching our Mind every day, and all these forming into potential limiting beliefs, to reach a level of awareness to identify and eliminate these, is a great exercise.

GRIEF RECIPE CARD – Tamara Mihályi

Ingredients

- LOSS OF SOMEONE OR SOMETHING IMPORTANT TO YOU, TO WHICH A BOND OR AFFECTION WAS FORMED
  - PARTNER
  - FAMILY MEMBER

Directions

- ALLOW YOURSELF TO FEEL YOUR FEELINGS
- HONOUR YOUR FEELINGS
- BRIGHTEN SOMEONE'S DAY
- COACH YOURSELF, IF ITS DIFFICULT
- NEGATIVE BELIEF CLEARING
- DO WHAT MAKES YOU HAPPY
- EMBODY POSITIVE & EMPOWERING FEELINGS
- MINDFULNESS
- MEDITATION
- CONSCIOUSNESS/SUBCONSCIOUS PROGRAMMING
- SMILE, IT'S MAGICAL

Journal Note

My darling Dad passed on, on 27th December, 2016. I felt I wasn't there enough and felt awful for not seeing the signs while I still could have helped. In order to reframe my mind, I tried to focus more on the appreciation for the memories and the value my Dad gave me. He was a wonderful role model, of a very strong integrity and graceful character. Gratitude has filled me up and made me stronger from the core than I've ever been.

SHOPPING LIST

AFFLICTION
ANGUISH
  AGONY
  ANGST
  DISTRESS
  HEARTBREAK
  PAIN
  SUFFERING
  TORMENT
BEREAVEMENT
  LOSS
DEJECTION
  DESPONDENCY
MORTIFICATION
MOURNING
  GRIEF
  LAMENT
  SORROW
PINING
REGRET
REMORSE
SADNESS
  BLUES
  DESOLATION
  DESPAIR
  DESPONDENCY
  GRIEF
  HEARTACHE
  MISERY
  SORROW
  WOE

GUILT RECIPE CARD – Tamara Mihályi

Ingredients

- SOMETHING YOU DID OR DIDN'T DO
- SOMETHING YOU THINK YOU DID/DIDN'T DO
- DIDN'T DO ENOUGH TO HELP PERSON/PEOPLE

Directions

- ALLOW YOURSELF TO FEEL YOUR FEELINGS
- HONOUR YOUR FEELINGS
- BRIGHTEN SOMEONE'S DAY
- COACH YOURSELF, IF ITS DIFFICULT
- NEGATIVE BELIEF CLEARING
- DO WHAT MAKES YOU HAPPY
- EMBODY POSITIVE & EMPOWERING FEELINGS
- MINDFULNESS
- MEDITATION
- CONSCIOUSNESS/SUBCONSCIOUS PROGRAMMING
- SMILE, IT'S MAGICAL

Journal Note

I felt guilty for my choices, for not being there enough. I should have seen the signs while I still could have helped. I cried a lot and felt foolish for not listening to my Inner Voice, or just not hearing it…. I do not like to dwell too much on the things I can't change anymore, so I started working on my personal growth in earnest.

SHOPPING LIST

ANGER

ANXIETY

DEPRESSION

EMPTINESS

ENVY

GUILT

LONELINESS

RAGE

REGRET

REMORSE

SADNESS

SHAME

FEAR RECIPE CARD – Tamara Mihályi

Ingredients

- IMPENDING DANGER
- SURVIVAL MECHANISM
- REACTION TO NEGATIVE STIMULUS
- MILD CAUTION OR EXTREME PHOBIA
- TRIVIAL OR SERIOUS

Directions

- ALLOW YOURSELF TO FEEL YOUR FEELINGS
- HONOUR YOUR FEELINGS
- BRIGHTEN SOMEONE'S DAY
- COACH YOURSELF, IF ITS DIFFICULT
- NEGATIVE BELIEF CLEARING
- DO WHAT MAKES YOU HAPPY
- EMBODY POSITIVE & EMPOWERING FEELINGS
- MINDFULNESS
- MEDITATION
- CONSCIOUSNESS/SUBCONSCIOUS PROGRAMMING
- SMILE, IT'S MAGICAL

Journal Note

I felt vulnerable when my Dad passed on and I chose a career change with some financial insecurity at first.

I did not believe or empower myself before I dare to step out of the daily routine and become conscious of my patterns and I realized I had stopped daring to dream big. My belief that everything happens for a reason helped me through that. I feel much more centred and balanced now.

SHOPPING LIST

NERVOUSNESS

ANXIETY

APPREHENSION

DISTRESS

DREAD

EDGINESS

JUMPINESS

TENSENESS

UNEASINESS

WORRY

HORROR

ALARM

FRIGHT

HYSTERICAL

MORTIFICATION

OVERWHELMED

PANIC

SHOCK

TERROR

Y Sim - Hurt

Y Sim has a story of Hurt which you will see in her recipe card on the following page.

Name (& title if applicable)	Y Sim
Country/Location	Dublin, Ireland
What emotion did you feel today?	Hurt
What prompted the emotion?	Someone who I thought was a true friend told someone something that was untrue about me and ruined a career opportunity
What did you feel about the situation/event?	Betrayed
How did it make you feel – physically/how did you express that feeling?	Physically sick to my stomach
What did you use to manage the emotion?	**Journaling**

HURT RECIPE CARD – Y SIM

Ingredients

- PAIN CAUSED BY SOMEONE WE INTERACT WITH;
  - INSULT
  - REJECTION
  - JUDGEMENT
  - IGNORED BY
  - DIFFERING VIEWS
- BELIEF IN WHAT OTHERS SAY AND THINK

Directions

- JOURNALING
  - **W** HAT TOPIC?
  - **R** EVIEW/REFLECT
  - **I** NVESTIGATE
  - **T** IME YOURSELF
  - **E** XIT SMART

Journal Note

I cannot believe that X said that about me, I'm literally in shock. I called her on it straight away and she had nothing to say for herself. I am beyond hurt, she knows me inside and out for years. Why would she even think that let alone go and say it? What does that say about me? What does it say about how I've felt this friendship meant? Am I someone who goes into a role and just wipes out the competition? Am I ruthless in work or just competent? I always want to go above and beyond. I don't see the point in slacking. I love the end of a project, seeing the final result. Knowing you've done an amazing job. Is that so wrong? Secretly does X dislike that trait in my personality? Have I misread the friendship all along? Where do we go from here? Can I ever feel the same again about this relationship? Should I cut ties and walk away? I need to take time out away from this toxicity and reflect. I'm not ready to forgive or if I ever can.

SHOPPING LIST

AFFLICTION

    MISFORTUNE

    TROUBLE

ANGUISH

    DISTRESS

    PAIN

    TORMENT

    UPSET

    WOE

DETRIMENT

    DAMAGE

    DISADVANTAGE

    HARM

    INJURY

    TRAUMA

DISBELIEF

GRIEF

    MISERY

    SADNESS

    SORROW

    SUFFERING

    WRETCHEDNESS

IMPAIR

    MAIM

    WOUND

MALTREAT

    ABUSE

    TORTURE

Yvette Ryan - Overwhelmed

Yvette Ryan has a story of being overwhelmed which you will see in her recipe card on the following page.

Name (& title if applicable)	Yvette Ryan
Country/Location	Ireland
What emotion did you feel today?	Overwhelmed
What prompted the emotion?	Lots to be done today
What did you feel about the situation/event?	Stressed & pressure
How did it make you feel – physically/how did you express that feeling?	I felt tense, tight physically & emotionally drained
What did you use to manage the emotion?	**90 second rule**: I took a deep breath & breathe in & out slowly **Allow yourself to feel your feelings**: Didn't resist tension, let it be & it dissipated **Do what makes you happy**: Looked over my list of appreciation for my favourite things in my life & remembered how they felt. This changed my emotional state **Mindfulness** I meditated to further calm my mind. Took back control of my mind by observing thoughts rather than assessing situation with mind chatter. Let my mind be as it is. Going forward I would like to **exercise** to relieve tension before it builds up Continue to meditate & appreciate my favourite moments in life.

EMOTIONAL OVERWHELM RECIPE CARD
- Yvette Ryan

Ingredients

- BURY OR DROWN BENEATH A HUGE MASS OF SOMETHING

- A STRONG EMOTIONAL EFFECT

Directions

- 90 SECOND RULE

- ALLOW YOURSELF TO FEEL YOUR FEELINGS

- DO WHAT MAKES YOU HAPPY

  - APPRECIATE MY FAVOURITE THINGS

- MINDFULNESS

- MEDITATE

SHOPPING LIST

DEFEAT

OVERCOME

OVERTRHOW

CONQUER

DESTROY

DROWN

SUBMERGE

INUNDATE

WASTE

ASTONISH

PUZZLE

BEWILDER

CONFOUND

Journal Note

There was a lot to be done today and I felt stressed and pressured. I felt tense, tight physically & emotionally drained. I took a deep breath & breathe in & out slowly. I didn't resist the tension, I let it be & it dissipated. I looked over my list of appreciation for my favourite things in my life & remembered how they felt. This changed my emotional state. I meditated to further calm my mind. I took back control of my mind by observing thoughts rather than assessing the situation with mind chatter. I let my mind be as it is.

Going forward I would like to exercise to relieve tension before it builds up, and continue to meditate & appreciate my favourite moments in life.

LAST BUT NOT LEAST...THANK YOU'S AND RESOURCES

Thank you!

I couldn't end this without thanking:

My husband, my friend, my lover; Paul Tyler, the man that has stayed with me, through the rough and the smooth and has been my rock. The person I can depend on, no matter what. You are the love of my life and I cannot think of anyone else I would want to spend the rest of my life with. We have our Life Vision to step forward into together.

To my beautiful daughter, and my best friend Sammy, who she says I've inspired, but who inspires me every day with her talent, strength, determination and most importantly her love. You've overcome so much and grown, despite it all. I have learnt more from you than you will ever know.

Vishen Lakhiani for his amazing vision of '*Mindvalley.com*' which he created, and enabled the beginning of my learning journey.

Jim Kwik – Superbrain. The man with the broken brain. The tools and techniques you taught were incredible. They were fun and inspiring. They started me on my journey of exponential growth. I am eternally thankful. I'm still getting the hang of some of them, but '*practice makes progress*'.

Donna Eden - Energy Medicine. There aren't enough words to describe how thankful I am for having found you. Your Energy methods have transformed my health. I know I can cure myself. I've made such dramatic progress thanks to you and your beautiful family. I'm doing things now I could never have imagined when I first started. I was sceptical, but no more. I'm so looking forward to meeting you all in April 2021, with Paul of course.

Lion Goodman - Belief Clearing. When I listened to your podcast I had absolutely no expectation of feeling anything, let alone removing an extremely old and deep-rooted belief. I thought I was just going to listen and that be it. I didn't just listen. I immersed myself into every word you spoke. My mind created every element of the mental image I was to create. Every cell in my body stood to attention and became absorbed into what was happening. I cried and sobbed like my life depended on it, and then I was free. Thank you from the bottom of my heart.

Lifebook Online, Lifebook Mastery & Membership (Jon & Missy Butcher) You spurred my quest for learning and gave me the tools to drive myself forward. Your whole approach to personal development is genius. I now have a group of friends around the world who share the same passion for learning. The fabulous love of my life who has shown me such amazing support for both my learning and the creation of this book. We've grown so strong as a partnership, and we are more in love now than we were over 30 years ago when we first met. I am truly living a 12-category smart life, with an assessment score of over 140! I am already living a completely different life now, each and every day.

My habits have changed, I push to achieve my goals and even though I sometimes slip, I know my Life Vision is on its way. That's mind blowing.

To my friends, around the world, who've contributed to this book with their own challenges. You are all truly amazing people who are moving toward your own life vision. I can't wait to see your updates and progress.

To my friends, around the world, who were unable to contribute to this book, but wanted to. Stay focussed on your own Life Vision and know the Universe has your back, and me too.

To my Editor, Kathryn Cartwright, for being so kind, generous and loving. You are beautiful.

To Dani Glaeser, for her poetry, breathing fresh air into how we think about and work through our emotions.

To the raft of people who I have learnt so many insights from, that continue to keep my brain conscious with an absolute desire to learn more. I know that I can heal my own body, that my energy systems contain the history of my life, and I have the ability to manifest what I want for my future.

To everyone I have ever met and had an interaction with, whether it be positive or negative. You helped me become the person I am today. Thank you.

To Mum,

On the leaflet I created and handed out at your cremation, my final words were 'until we meet again'. I put them because they fitted with your beliefs, not mine. All these years later, I now know we will meet again one day. Until then, I love you.

To Dad,

You were so hard to know or get close to. You'd never been loved and didn't know how to show it, other than in your usual way of buying something. I learnt that from you, but it doesn't mean or show love. Your dad did love you. I've read letters, since you passed away, that your dad sent to your Grandmother. The woman who raised you because your mother had died just 2 weeks after you were born. Your dad did want you, he even asked when he could come and get you. I do hope you've come across his energy wherever you both are now. I love you and I know you loved me. So, 'until we meet again'.

To you, the reader, for purchasing my book and taking the first step toward managing your emotions in a positive way. Thank you. I wish you all the Joy & Happiness and Love in the world. I would love to hear how using the emotion recipes helps you, so do keep in touch via my website www.amixtureoffeelings.com

Resources

All of the resources shown in this section are listed based on the benefits gained by the author and/or book contributors, all of whom are working on their own personal development journey. There are, of course, a raft of other fantastic resources, so looking for and finding what works for you is absolutely key.

✳ ✳ ✳

Books

Title	Author	ISBN Number
Belong	Radha Agrawal	ISBN-10: 1523502053 ISBN-13: 978-1523502059
Beside Every Good Man: Loving Myself While Standing by Him*	Serita Ann Jakes	ISBN-10: 0446531308 ISBN-13: 978-0446531306
Between Parent and Child	Hiam Ginott	ISBN-10: 9780609809884 ISBN-13: 978-0609809884
Book of Joy	Dalai Lama & Desmond Tutu	ISBN-10: 178633044X ISBN-13: 978-1786330444
Conversations with God, Book 1 – An Uncommon Dialogue	Neale Donald Walsch	ISBN-10: 0340693258 ISBN-13: 978-0340693254
Energy Medicine: How to use your body's energies for optimum health and vitality	Donna Eden, John Feinstein	ISBN-10: 0749929669 ISBN-13: 978-0749929664
Heal Your Wounds and Find Your True Self	Lise Bourbeau	ISBN-10: 2920932217 ISBN-13: 978-2920932210
In an Unspoken Voice: How the Body Releases Trauma and Restores Goodness	Peter Levine	ISBN-10: 1556439431 ISBN-13: 978-1556439438
Integrate the Shadow, Master Your Path	Dr. Matt James	ISBN-978-1-4524-8446-1
Language of Letting Go Journal, The (Hazelden Meditations)	Melody Beattie	ISBN-10: 1568389841 ISBN-13: 978-1568389844
Learned Optimism: How to Change Your Mind and Your Life	Martin Seligman	ISBN-10: 9781473684317 ISBN-13: 978-1473684317
Love 2.0: Finding Happiness and Health in Moments of Connection	Barbara Fredrickson	ISBN-10: 9780142180471 ISBN-13: 978-0142180471

Title	Author	ISBN Number
The Four Agreements: Practical Guide to Personal Freedom**	Don Miguel	ISBN-10: 9781878424310 ISBN-13: 978-1878424310 ASIN: 1878424319
The Magic of Forgiveness – Emotional Freedom and Transformation at Midlife, A Book for Women	Tian Dayton, Ph.D.	ISBN-10: 0757300863 ISBN-13: 978-0757300868
The Positive Discipline**	Jane Nelson, Ed.D	ISBN-10: 0345487672 ISBN-13: 978-0345487674
The Secret	Rhonda Byrne	ISBN-10: 1847370292 ISBN-13: 978-1847370297
The Science of Self-Discipline: The Willpower, Mental Toughness and Self-Control to Resist Temptation and Achieve your Goals	Peter Holins	ISBN-10: 197905116X ISBN-13: 978-1979051163
The Tapping Solution	Nick Ortner	ISBN-10: 1781806195 ISBN-13: 978-1781806197
What the EMF?: How to Protect Your Home from EMF Exposure, Improve Sleep, Reduce Anxiety, and Live a Happier, Healthier Life!	Risa Suzuki	ISBN-10: 1950043002 ISBN-13: 978-1950043002

* Specifically, helpful for anger caused by a partner

** Pedagogical ideas on child raising

Websites

A Mixture of Feelings www.amixtureoffeelings.com

Belief Clearing https://liongoodman.com/

Beyond Diet https://www.beyonddiet.com/

Eden Energy Medicine https://edenenergymedicine.com/

Happiness & Good Habits https://gretchenrubin.com

Journal Therapy https://journaltherapy.com/journal-cafe-3/journal-course/

Leadership Training https://jockopodcast.com/jockopodcast-books/ (various)

Lifebook https://www.jonandmissy.com/

Mastering Happiness www.drjoelwade.com

Personal Development www.mindvalley.com and https://www.dailyom.com/

The Tapping Solution https://www.thetappingsolution.com/nick-ortner/

Wildfit https://getwildfit.com/

✳ ✳ ✳

Courses

Mindvalley Quests; www.mindvalley.com

- *Energy Medicine*, Donna Eden
- *Lifebook*, Jon & Missy Butcher
- *Superbrain*, Jim Kwik
- *Duality* (meditation, clearing limiting beliefs) – Jeffrey Allen
- *Becoming Limitless*, Vishen Lakhiani
- *Bending Reality* – Vishen Lakhiani

Introduction to Meditation course   https://learn.dandapani.org/

Paid course has 2 parts;

1) Foundation of the Mind – understanding how the mind works, how to control it and how to direct it to create the life that you want.

2) Introduction to Meditation – building the habit of meditation.

Social Media

Meditation

6 Phase meditation with binaural beats – Vishen Lakhiani

Chopracentermeditation.com – Deepak Chopra

Dr Joe Dispenza Meditation (various)

Energy Medicine

Donna Eden – Daily Energy Routine (DER)

Donna Eden – Energy Medicine

Emotions

Control your Emotions   Dr Joe Dispenza

Health/Healing

Esoteric Healing   The Lune Innate

Yoga   Brett Larkin (You Tube)

Various

Ralph Smart (YouTube)

Jai Madaan (You Tube, Instagram, Facebook)

Reiki Healing sessions

Pranic Healing Sessions

Other

Quantum Model of Reality   Dr Joe Dispenza

Other

Noble Science Retreat (like vipassana)

Neuro Linguistic Programming

Exercise to relieve tension

Meditate and appreciate favourite moments in life

✳ ✳ ✳

Feedback

If you have any feedback or recipes you would like to be considered for the website, or the next book, please notify me via the

website: www.amixtureoffeelings.com or my

email: heidi@amixtureoffeelings.com

If by chance you find any typos or errors in my book, do please take the time to let me know using my email: heidi@amixtureoffeelings.com

✳ ✳ ✳

Printed in Great Britain
by Amazon